Kashmir Problem
and
India - Pakistan

A Study of Post Abolishing of Article 370 and 35 A

Kashmir Problem and India - Pakistan

A Study of Post Abolishing of Article 370 and 35 A

Dr. Sanjay Kumar
Associate Professor
Department of Defence Studies
Meerut College, Meerut (UP)

Dr. Neelam Kumari
Associate Professor
Department of Chemistry
Meerut College, Meerut (UP)

Ankit Publications
Delhi - 110009

Kashmir Problem and India - Pakistan : A Study of Post Abolishing of Article 370 and 35 A

First Published in 2021

₹ 895

ISBN 978-81-950132-3-4

The responsibility for the facts or opinions expressed is entirely of the Author and not of the Publishers.

Published by : **Ankit Publications**
R-69, 3rd Foor, Model Town-3,
Delhi-110009
Tel. : 9891553405
E-Mail: ankitpublications@gmail.com

Laser Typesetting : Aarati Computers, Delhi-110 009

Printed at : Balaji Offset, Delhi

Contents

Preface

The present book has made a descriptive analysis on 'Kashmir Problem and India Pakistan: A study of Post Abolishing of Article 370 and 35 A' India desires peaceful and cooperative relations with Pakistan, but lack of positive response from the Pakistan side has delayed the process. The issue of terrorism and Kashmir factor heavily on the bilateral engagement between the two sides. Indian want Pakistan to come to the agreement that all the issues can be resolved through dialogue. But, since there is no sign of reduction in Islamabad involvement in cross border terrorist violence in our country and in particular to the state of Jammu and Kashmir, India has made it clear that terror and talks cannot go together.

The topsy-turvy character of the relationship between India and Pakistan has existed over the last more than seven decades. This has seriously undermined the significance of the bilateral relationship between the two powerful nuclear capable states of South Asia. The relations between India and Pakistan have seen great uncertainty and ambiguity as both the countries have adopted divergent approach for their respective national interests. India and Pakistan are the two largest countries in South Asia wherein there exists a very low level of engagements. The two South Asian regional powers remain strategic rivals competing for regional influence and engage in contradictory and counterproductive acts. There exists a serious politico-security conflict between the two South Asian rivals which pose a hindrance to maintaining close relation for the mutual benefit.

The prolonged dispute over the Kashmir has deeply affected the security and development scenario on both sides of the borders. Over the Kashmir issue, both sides have fought three wars, the latest being the Kargil conflict of 1999. Pakistan has in the past made unsuccessful attempts to directly or indirectly extract J&K from India. Future attempt by the Pakistan Army in coordination with the terrorist groups operating in the country cannot be ruled out. Because, Pakistan Army in particular has not completely erased its aggressive Kashmir policy.

We express our gratitude to the *Indian Council for Social Science Research (ICSSR), New Delhi* for providing the grant for the research project for one years. Without financial support from the ICSSR, this report would not have seen the light of day. The completion of this research project was made possible through the support of people whom we would like to acknowledge. We would like to acknowledge the unwavering support of Prof. Rajendra Prasad, Vice-Chancellor of Allahabad State University, Prof. Prashant Agarwal, Allahabad University, Dr. Mohammad Samir Hussain, Meerut College, Meerut for their insightful suggestions in the initial stage of the research project.

Nevertheless, we also extend our heartiest thankful to the members and staff of the Library of United Service Institution, Institute of Defence and Strategic Analysis, Jawaharlal Nehru University, India International Centre, Observer Research Foundation and Teen Murti library for extending the much-needed support while collecting the research material.

The study was taken in a systematic manner and all relevant aspects were researched and analysed. Once the research was complete it was organised in a logical manner as under :-

(a) Fundamental Issues between India and Pakistan which need resolution.

(b) The centrality of Kashmir emerged most prominent and same is discussed thread bear.

(c) The role of external forces particularly of China was analysed in depth and measures suggested.

(d) The other contentious issues which are less important but causing irritation were also researched in detail.

(e) Based on the research about major issues an attempt has been made to suggest measures to resolve the problem between the two neighbours.

Dr. Sanjay Kumar
Dr. Neelam Kumari

1

Introduction

India and Pakistan enjoy not only the status of core states of South Asia, but are historically, culturally, linguistically and geographically closed to each other. Despite sharing a lot of commonalities, the relations between the two neighbours has never been cordial. One of the key reason being the Kashmir issue which deepen the mutual misunderstanding between the two sides. There are several areas where the interests of the two sides diverge - ranging from the issue of territorial disputes to demarcation of land and maritime boundaries, radicalisation, trade, water sharing, illegal immigration to limited or large-scale wars and fears of hegemony towards the peripheral states.[1] The relations between India and Pakistan will have a significant bearing on the international security in general and South Asian security in particular. That's the reason why the relation between the two has always been a subject of great international interest.

Owing to complicated border between India and Pakistan, the relations between the two sides has been historically disputed. Refuting India's claim over the whole of Jammu and Kashmir, Pakistan has made several unsuccessful attempts to directly and indirectly wrest Jammu and Kashmir from India.[2] India and Pakistan have had a history of conflict with each other ever since the independence of the Indian subcontinent, and its partition into India and Pakistan in 1947. Kashmir has always remained a bone of contention between the two South Asian rivals, India and Pakistan. The origin of Kashmir issue dates back to Britain's withdrawal from South Asia in 1947 as a colonial power. Since then, India and Pakistan have so far fought four wars in 1947, 1965, 1971 and 1999 but still there is no hope of resolving it. Several efforts have been made in the past to resolve the issue but without any significant results due to the divergent stand over the dispute by both sides. Also, it was the Pakistan involvement in proxy war to destabilize India which has only hardened New Delhi's position on Kashmir issue. With both sides not in a position to come to the terms on Kashmir issue and the possibility of issue escalating into a nuclear war has made Kashmir as the "world's most dangerous place."[3]

Barry Buzan, a renowned academician and social scientist has made a sound argument that,"Their historical, geographic and cultural ties do not allow them to ignore each other...but their organization principles pose a permanent threat to each other." The very foundation of India and Pakistan were done on two different ideologies. India on the one side emerged as a secular state, whereby religion has no role to play. Whereas, Pakistan was founded as a Muslim state.[4]

A large portion of the territory of Jammu and Kashmir is under the control of India, while the remaining portion is occupied by Pakistan and China. India and Pakistan claims jurisdiction over the whole of the territory.[5] As both countries consider it strategically necessary to control the state in order to secure defensible borders. From the Pakistan's perspective, as pointed out by Mohammed Akbar Khan, general in charge of the tribal invasion into Kashmir in

1947, "... Pakistan's military security would be seriously jeopardized if Indian troops came to be stationed along Kashmir's western borders. ...We would remain permanently exposed to a threat of such magnitude that our independence would never be a reality."[6] This had influenced Pakistan since 1947 to make rigorous efforts to gain Kashmir at any cost from a much stronger neighbour, India. Both countries are involved in a prolonged arms race leading to feeling of insecurity among each other. The prolonged rivalry revolved around three long standing issues - Kashmir, religion and military rivalry. India and Pakistan are both nuclear weapon and missile capabilities having the potential to destroy each other. Pakistan has for long been feared the Indian hegemonic design and have raised voice against it.[7] Former Pakistan President Pervez Musharraf has noted that, "We are like two elephants in South Asia, trampling the grass in our fight... Look where it has taken us. South Asia is one of the poorest regions and our economy refuses to take off because of our preoccupation with this dispute."[8] The statement highlight the way on how the strategic rivalry has diluted the prospect of prospective cooperation between the two sides.

Pakistani leaders, statesmen and even scholars have from time to time tried to project India as the only threat to Pakistan's existence. According to I.H. Qureshi, a renowned Pakistani scholar, 'Pakistan believes that Indian hostility poses a far greater problem to them than Chinese expansion or Soviet threats, neither country having a dispute with Pakistan.'[9] India and Pakistan have shared a feeling of "mutual distrust" ever since the partition of India and the eventual creation of Pakistan as an independent state. This distrust was an outcome of the colonial legacy of 'divide and rule.' Throughout this enduring rivalry the two nations have experienced four major wars, punctuated by an array of intermittent crises - culminating in the present spectre of nuclear conflagration. The conflict between these two nations is simultaneously over disputed territory, competing national identities, and relative power position in the region. However, at the heart of Indo-Pakistani hostility lays a contentious dispute over ownership of a relatively small border region known as Kashmir - the unfinished business of partition politics. One of the key arguments is that conflict in Kashmir, in its present form, has the potential to spark off future armed confrontations leading to war between India and Pakistan especially given the kind of animosity that the two countries share. There is no hope for resolution of the Kashmir issue in the distant future due to divergent stand taken by both sides.[10] The paper argues that the Kashmir issue has been and continues to remain the main area of irritant between the two South Asian rivals but resolving the Kashmir issue will not ensure lasting peace, security and prosperity in the region.

Pakistan claim to Kashmir is deeply rooted in the two nation theory. It invalidate the provisions of the Indian Independence Act and the Instruments of Accession signed between maharaja of Jammu and Kashmir and Indian government. It also questions the decision taken by Sheikh Abdullah to make Jammu and Kashmir a part of India.[11]

Map 1.1

Geo-Strategic Location of Jammu and Kashmir

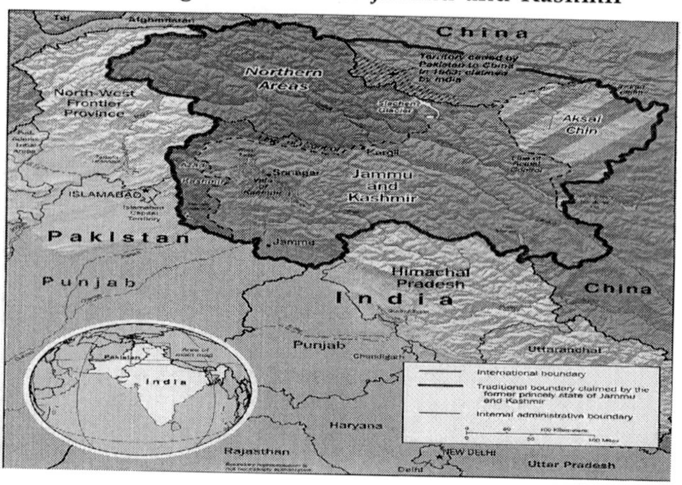

Kashmir is a landlocked region in South Asia, sandwiched between India, Pakistan, Afghanistan and China. It is spread across an area of 86,000 square miles, an area bigger than 87 sovereign countries. Though mostly Muslim, the state also has significant Hindu, Buddhist and Sikh population. Cradled by the mighty Himalayas and fed by rivers like the Satluj and Indus, Kashmir, has often been described as a 'Paradise on Earth'. However, terrorism and a border dispute between India and Pakistan have given this very paradise the name 'Hell on Earth'.

Over the last many decades, strategic rivalry have been a constant feature of India-Pakistan relations. To reduce mutual distrust and strategic rivalry, India and Pakistan have entered into a number of agreements at the political, military, cultural, economic and trade level. The prominent among them are the Lahore Declaration, the Simla Agreement, the Tashkent Agreement; each of them seek to promote peaceful bilateral relations. Besides, they have signed some very specific agreements to prevent awkward incidents from taking place such as reducing the risk of nuclear accidents, pre-notification of ballistic missile tests, military exercises and prohibition of attack on nuclear installations.[12]

Statement of Problem

Tensions between India and Pakistan have persisted since their independence from British rule in 1947. Several decades of armed conflict, bilateral talks and gradually rising trust deficit have become distinctive features of mutual Indo-Pakistani relations. Even though they share linguistic, cultural, geographic, and economic links their relationship has been plagued by hostility and suspicion. The two states have fought four wars during this time, the most recent in 2001, after each had become a nuclear power. The almost constant presence of either full war or tense relations between India and Pakistan produces deep insecurity for the states themselves, and for the rest of the international community, which fears the outbreak of nuclear war in the region.

There witnessed a fundamental transformation underway with regard to the conflict in and on Kashmir. Geo-strategically and geo-economically, the Kashmir valley is of utmost significance. The geographical location of Kashmir is such that it is surrounded by a number of foreign countries such as Tibet in its east and Pakistan, Afghanistan, China and Commonwealth of Independent States (CIS) in its West and North. The southern part is bordered by Punjab and Himachal Pradesh. Such a geostrategic location makes the Kashmir valley very important from strategic angle for both India and Pakistan. The strategic importance of controlling Kashmir from the Indian point of view can be reflected from the statement of Indian's first Prime Minister Jawaharlal Nehru when he asserted that "India without Kashmir would cease to occupy a pivotal position on the political map of Central Asia. Its northern frontiers... are connected with three important countries, Afghanistan, the USSR and China. Thus, strategically, Kashmir is vital to the security of India~ it has been so since the dawn of history."

While from the Pakistan point of view, the occupation of Kashmir is of security significance. As Liaquat Ali Khan, the Pakistani Prime Minister, claimed that "Kashmir is very important, it is vital to Pakistan's security. Kashmir, as you will see from the map, is like a cap on the head of Pakistan. If I allow India to have this cap on our head, then I am always at the mercy of India...The very position, the strategic position of Kashmir, is such that without it Pakistan cannot defend herself against an unscrupulous government that might come in India."

There are factors within and outside between India and Pakistan which still impact their relations, for instance, border, terrorism, water, Afghanistan and China issues. These bilateral issues will not only effect on their present relations but is most likely to have a negative impact on their future relations as well. Besides, it will also affect the process of their rise and the peace and stability in and outside the region.

India has time and again accused Pakistan for large scale terrorist attacks in Jammu and Kashmir and in other parts of the country. For instance, India cannot forget the memories of the well planned terrorist attack on the Jammu and Kashmir Assembly complex on 01 October 2001, Indian Parliament attack on 13 December 2001. This was followed by Pak sponsored terrorist attack in Mumbai on 26 Nov 2008, bomb explosion in Mumbai in July 2011 and a similar explosion near the New Delhi High Court in September 2011. The recent incidents of Pathankot Air Force Base attack and Uri incident have further deteriorated the situation.

The other key issue is that of water dispute. India and Pakistan have both faced challenges in water management and proper river basin management. The consequence of this has been a severe water crisis, which has a bearing on both ground and surface water. The gifting of the river waters of the Indian part of the region to Pakistan by treaty has hampered development in India which as resulted into popular grievance - a situation compounded by a Pakistan-abetted Islamist insurrection. There have been repeated calls in the elected legislature of Indian Jammu and Kashmir for revision or abrogation of the Indus treaty.

Another issue which is closely related to the continued animosity between India and Pakistan in Article 370. Article 370, makes temporary provisions with respect to the state of Jammu and Kashmir, and therefore confers upon it, the special status. Article 370 of Indian Constitution grants special status to Jammu and Kashmir within the India Union and therefore Jammu and Kashmir's constitutional position and its relation with the Central Government differs from rest of the other states. The autonomy of state is higher than the Union. Under Article 370, Jammu and Kashmir has the power to limit the applicability of Constitution of India. It also confers powers to Jammu and Kashmir, with respect to many matters that are generally not provided to any State Government. Owing to certain relaxation, it is being argued that the Article 370 has become the major stumbling block in the emotional integration of Kashmir with the rest of the country.

Kashmir and Its Geo-Strategic Significance

Geo-strategically and geo-economically, the Kashmir valley is of paramount significance. Geographically, Kashmir is located at the intersecting point between South Asia and Central Asia, and is India's northern most state, often seen as the starting point of the great Himalayan mountain range. This is a disputed territory between India and Pakistan. The history of Kashmir over the past fifty years is the history of two territories with different patterns of development, but the populations of both areas continuing to dispute the division.[13] The geographical location of Kashmir is such that it is surrounded by a number of foreign countries such as Tibet in its east and Pakistan, Afghanistan, China and Commonwealth of Independent States (CIS) in its north and west. The southern part is bordered by Punjab and Himachal Pradesh. Such a geostrategic location makes the Kashmir valley very important from strategic angle for both India and Pakistan. This has made India and Pakistan to believe that the control of Kashmir is so important, thereby making it difficult for both sides to come to the terms on resolving the issue which has cost thousands of lives. Both sides are never ready to bargain on the issue at any cost. They perceive the place key to their national security.

Even now both sides are desperate to acquire Kashmir to strengthen their respective visions of nationhood. Pakistan has never accepted India's control of Kashmir as it still believes today that Kashmir should be part of Pakistan. Kashmir is not merely a territorial dispute but is deeply intertwined in the domestic politics and ideologies of India and Pakistan. The strategic importance of controlling Kashmir from the Indian point of view can be reflected from the statement of India's first Prime Minister Jawaharlal Nehru when he asserted that "India without Kashmir would cease to occupy a pivotal position on the political map of Central Asia. Its northern frontiers...are connected with three important countries, Afghanistan, the USSR and China. Thus, strategically, Kashmir is vital to the security of India~ it has been so since the dawn of history."

While from the Pakistan point of view, the occupation of Kashmir is of economic, political, security and strategic significance. As Liaquat Ali Khan, the former Pakistani Prime Minister has noted that,

> "Kashmir is very important, it is vital to Pakistan's security. Kashmir, as you will see from the map, is like a cap on the head of Pakistan. If I allow India to have this cap on our head, then I am always at the mercy of India...The very position, the strategic position of Kashmir, is such that without it Pakistan cannot defend herself against an unscrupulous government that might come in India."[14]

References

1. Mussarat Jabeen, "SAARC and Indo-Pakistan Relationship", Journal of Political Studies, Vol. 1, No, 2, p. 132.

2. Happymon Jacob, "China, India, Pakistan and a Stable Regional Order", in Francois Godement (ed.), What Does India Think (London: European Council on Foreign Relations, 2015), p. 91.

3. Sumit Ganguly, Conflict Unending: India - Pakistan Tensions since 1947 (New Delhi: Oxford University Press, 2002).

4. Sanjeet Kumar, "Indo-Pak Relations in the Twenty First Century", Ph. D Thesis Submitted to the Department of Political Science, Central University of Haryana,

Mahendergarh, Haryana, August 2014, pp. 10-11.

5. Navnita Chadha Behera, Demstifying Kashmir (Washington, D.C: Brookings Institution Press, 2006), p. 1.
6. Ibid., p. 22.
7. Umbreen Javaid and Marium Kamal, "Security Dilemma in South Asia", Journal of Political Studies, Vol. 22, No. 1, 2015, pp. 122-23.
8. Ibid., p. 122.
9. O. P. Gulia, "History of India-Pakistan Relations Through Chinese Prism", in Sanjay Kumar et al. (eds.), India-Pakistan Relations: Past, Present and Future (New Delhi: G B Books Publishers and Distributors, 2018).
10. Mohammad Samir Hussain, "India-Pakistan Unending Rivalry: Kashmir as a Factor" Suraksha Chintan, Vol. 6, No. 6, January 2013.
11. Ashu Pasricha, "India-Pakistan Relations", in Sanjay Kumar et al. (eds.), India-Pakistan Relations: Past, Present and Future (New Delhi: G B Books Publishers and Distributors, 2018).
12. Dilip Sinha, "International Dispute Settlement Mechanism and India-Pakistan Disputes", Indian Foreign Affairs Journal, Vol. 12, No. 3, July-September 2017, p. 210.

13 Ellis and Khan in I. Talbot and G. Singh, (eds.), Region and Partition: Bengal, Punjab and the Partition of the Subcontinent (Oxford: Oxford University Press, 1999), p. 270.

14. A.Z. Hilali, "Historical Developments of the Kashmir Problem and Pakistan Policy after September 11", Perceptions, Journal of International Affairs, Vol. 9, June-August 2004.

2

Kashmir Problem: A Study of Post Abolishing of Article 370 and 35A

This chapter discusses in length the Kashmir dispute, which has over the last seven decades remained the bone of contention between India and Pakistan. India and Pakistan obtained freedom from the British rule in 1947. Prior to 14 August 1947 both these complicated nations were part of Indian sub-continent. The partition of India and Pakistan laid the foundation for a bitter rivalry between the newly emerged nations on many fronts. With the origin of these new states, there unearthed a fresh rivalry on the war front, for the advantage of territorial dominance. Both nations accused each other for violating LOC 'line of control' which has been demarcated to solve the cross border terrorism and forcible infiltration. With mutual hostility of religion and nationalism both these have confronted globally on all fronts.

Kashmir issue continues to serve as the main cause of rivalry between India and Pakistan over the last more than seven decades. Both sides have so far been unsuccessful to come to a bilateral negotiated settlement over Kashmir dispute. Stephen P. Cohen, an expert who closely watches the development and change in the relations between India and Pakistan is of the perception that, 'Kashmir is the most important single conflict in the subcontinent, not just because its territory and its population are contested, but because larger issues of national identity and regional power balances are imbedded in it.[1] This has opened the scope for interference by other states in finding a lasting solution to the dispute. Several attempts have been made in the recent past, but failed to borne fruit. The UN in particular has been actively involved by way of appointment of a special representatives or mediators in finding a diplomatic solution to the dispute. Lack of positive response on the part of the conflicting parties have been a problem.[2]

According to Wesis, 'The Kashmir conflict represents a self-determination movement for Kashmiris; an irredentist movement for Pakistan and Pakistan-controlled Kashmir; and a civil insurgency for India.'[3] However, from the point of view of Lt. Gen. S.K. Sinha, former Governor of J&K, the ongoing low intensity conflict in J & K is a vicious mix of insurgency, terrorism and proxy war.[4] There is a common understanding in Pakistan that P, K and S stand for Punjab, Kashmir and Sindh. Pakistan considers the partition process incomplete as long as Kashmir became a part of India. To them the popular slogan is 'Hans ke lia hai Pakistan, Larkar lenge Hindustan.'[5]

Kashmir figures prominently in Pakistan's foreign policy approach towards India. Kashmir factor influenced Pakistan to wage a war in 1947-48. Pakistan tried to annex Kashmir by force through 'Operation Gibraltar' in 1965 and then in 1971 but failed miserably. Failure to acquire the land of Kashmir by forceful means, Pakistan have entered into a number of agreements with India such as the Tashkent Declaration of 1966 and Shimla Agreement of 1972 to resolve the misunderstanding by peaceful means.[6]

Kashmir dispute will not only effect on their present relations but is most likely to have a negative impact on their future relations as well. Besides, it will also affect the process of their rise and the peace and stability in and outside the region. Kashmir has been and continues to remain the main cause of friction between India and Pakistan. That is why many have termed it as a 'nuclear flashpoint'. Kashmir issue has gained both regional and global significance. The geo-strategic and geo-economic significance of the Kashmir has made India and Pakistan to believe that the control of Kashmir is so important, thereby making it difficult for both sides to come to the terms on resolving the issue which has cost thousands of lives. It is surrounded by a number of foreign countries such as Tibet in its east and Pakistan, China and Commonwealth of Independent States (CIS) in its west. The southern part is bordered by Punjab and Himachal Pradesh. Such a geostrategic location makes the Kashmir valley very important from strategic angle for both India and Pakistan. Having fought three wars over the Kashmir issue in 1947, 1965, and 1999, still there is no hope of resolving it in the near future.

India and Pakistan have been unsuccessful in the past and present attempt made to alter the status quo in Kashmir. For which, both sides have adopted different political and military strategies seeking to serve their national interests. Till January 2004, over the Kashmir issue, the leaders of the two sides have met on more than thirty-five occasions. Besides, at the highest level, there were at least twelve rounds of talks between 1989 and 1998 before the Lahore and Agra Summits. Neither the meetings at the Heads of State level nor at the Foreign Secretary level could bring any fruitful results.[7]

Efforts have been made in the past to resolve the key issue but without any significant results due to the divergent stand adopted over the dispute by both sides. Also, it was the Pakistan involvement in proxy war to destabilize India which has only hardened New Delhi's position on Kashmir issue.

With both sides not in a position to come to the terms on Kashmir issue and the possibility of issue escalating into a nuclear war has made Kashmir as the "world's most dangerous place."

The present chapter traces the historical background to the Kashmir conflict between India and Pakistan. It also discusses the geo-political and geo-strategic significance of Kashmir for the competing countries. Then, it assesses the clash of interests between the two countries over the Kashmir issue. Later, it gives an account of the Pakistan's Kashmir policies and strategies. Last, but not the least, it highlights the Pervez Musharraf four step proposal on Kashmir dispute.

Background of the Kashmir Dispute

Kashmir dispute has its roots in the developments leading to and following the partition of the Indian subcontinent. The nature of Kashmir problem has undergone a change in keeping with the developments in South Asia, on the one hand, and the changing international scenario, on the other. This was clearly manifested during the cold war period and now in the post-cold war period too. Kashmir is an issue clearly linked to the partition of the Indian subcontinent in August 1947. At the time of India's independence, the "princely" state of Jammu and Kashmir had the option of acceding to either India or Pakistan like any of the other princely states at that time. Maharaja Hari Singh, ruler of Kashmir at that time, contemplated keeping off both. Hence, he decided to enter into "Standstill Agreements" with both India and Pakistan. In the process, his ambition of an independent Kashmir was kept alive. To this, Mohammed Ali Jinnah retaliated by imposing a total economic and trade blockade of Jammu and Kashmir. Pakistan also incited an invasion of Kashmir by Army Regulars in the guise of tribals in late 1947. When invaders closed in on Srinagar, the capital of Kashmir, Maharaja Hari Singh appealed to India for help and acceded to India by signing the

Instrument of Accession.[8] Given Kashmir's geographical, economic, and socio-cultural links with contending neighbours, the Maharaja of the princely state of Jammu and Kashmir was in dilemma over choosing one between the two. What complicates further is that the Maharaja's political future was at stake.[9] However, Pakistan's coercive tactics compelled the maharaja to move into India's arms.[10]

Not able to digest the whole issue of the accession of Jammu and Kashmir to India, Pakistan's Prime Minister, Liaquat Ali Khan, described the accession of Jammu and Kashmir 'fraudulent' and even said 'Pakistan's very existence is the chief casus belli so far as India is concerned.'[11] In his enthusiasm to get the Pakistanis out of Kashmir, India's first Prime Minister, Jawahar Lal Nehru, took the matter to the United Nations (UN) in good faith. *"What perhaps went wrong was to ask the Security Council to take action under Chapter VI and not Chapter VII of the UN Charter."*[12] The UN Security Council ordered cease fire on 24th January 1948 and voted on the holding of a plebiscite in Kashmir. The resolution envisaged the complete withdrawal of Pakistani troops from Pakistan occupied Kashmir (POK) as a precondition to the holding of plebiscite. The Security Council could not get the Pakistani troops out of POK which further complicated the matters in spite of Nehru's best intentions.

When the relations between the two sides was not going well, the leaders of the two sides met whereby they issued a joint statement that noted,

> 'Both the Prime Ministers were actuated by a firm resolve to settle these problems as early as possible peacefully and cooperatively to the mutual advantage of both countries... The most feasible method of ascertaining the wishes of the people was by a fair and impartial plebiscite... the next step would be the appointment of a Plebiscite Administrator by the end of April 1954.'[13]

Pakistan has not shown any sincerity in resolving the Kashmir dispute. Pakistan has rejected any settlement of the dispute along the Line of Control. Instead, she continued to claim the whole of Kashmir Valley and all the Muslim majority areas including the districts of Poonch, Rajouri, Doda and Kargil.[14]

The most significant event in India-Pakistan relations was the second Indo-Pakistan war in Sep 1965. Pakistan's military junta decided to take India by surprise and attacked Kashmir in the hope of conquering the part of Kashmir still in Indian hands. But this was not to be and ended with the Tashkent Agreement and arms embargo to both India and Pakistan. This was followed by the third round in 1971 which resulted in dismemberment of Pakistan. The Shimla Agreement was signed between the two countries, in which India did not look for punitive peace but hoped to initiate a new policy towards Pakistan, based upon a more relaxed and understanding approach. By the Shimla Agreement, Islamabad sought to gain time in order to make strategic asymmetry between India and Pakistan less worrying than it in fact was.[15]

Hence it is clear from the above that the state of Jammu and Kashmir which acceded to India in 1947 did so only after the Pakistani raiders were knocking at the doors of Srinagar and this continues to be an area of conflict between India and Pakistan. Defence, Diplomacy and Democracy seems to have failed leading to a sort of 'Proxy War' being waged between the two countries in the state. Terrorism as a means to destabilise the law of the land is being extensively sponsored by Pakistan. The people of the state have been reduced to a pitiable condition with murder, rape and extortion rampant. The economy is in ruins with people barely being able to eke out a living. In the words of Andrea Benvenuti,

"Since the first Indo-Pak war, Kashmir has been the 'apple of discord' between India and Pakistan. Not only were strategic issues involved, but more so an ideological one. In fact, for India (a state created upon the principle of laicism and multi-ethnicity), Kashmir, a region with Muslim majority, meant a testing bench of its capability of ruling over different communities. On the contrary, Pakistan, founded as a homeland of the Muslims of the Subcontinent, could not accept the fact that a region with a Muslim majority and territorially contiguous, formed part of Hindu dominated India."

Kashmir - Location and Its Geo-Political and Geo-Strategic Importance

A close look at the map of Jammu and Kashmir would highlight the geo-strategic importance of the State. Geo-strategically located at the confluence of three major historical empires namely, India, Central Asia and China, the region provides the land bridge between them. It was a natural bulwark against China to the North-East as also a land-link to China as well as the Central Asian States of the former Soviet Union.[16] It was thus natural that both India and the State-to-be Pakistan would vie for this pristine land. Furthermore, the demography of the State was such that the decision facing the Maharaja would not be easy. Whereas the bulk of the population, nearly 75 percent, was in the Valley and mostly Muslim, one could not forget that the majority in Jammu, which accounted for over 20 percent of the state's population, was Hindu. The rest of the population in Ladakh, Gilgit and Hunza was again Muslim except in Ladakh which had a Buddhist majority. However population was very sparse in these areas.

Table 2.1 : Area and Population of the Three Region

Region	Area (Sq. Miles)	Population (2011 Census)
Kashmir Valley	8639	5,350,811
Jammu Region	12,378	6,907,623
Ladakh Region	33,554	290,492
Total	**54,571**	**12,548,926**

Source: Government of India, Ministry of Home Affairs.

Table 2.2

Religious Demography in Jammu and Kashmir - Census 2011

Division	Population			
	Muslim	Hindu	Sikh	Buddhist
Kashmir	97.16%	1.84%	0.88%	0.11%
Jammu	30.69%	65.23%	3.57%	0.51%
Ladakh	47.40%	6.22%	-	45.87%
Jammu and Kashmir	66.97%	29.63%	2.03%	1.36%

Source: Election Commission of India, 2014

Kashmir is strategically located in the northern part of our country. From a geographical point of view, Kashmir occupies a very small portion of the larger state of Jammu and Kashmir. It accounts for 6.98 per cent of the total land mass of undivided Jammu and Kashmir. Of a total area of 222,236 square kms for the state of undivided Jammu and Kashmir, Kashmir accounts for 15,520.3 square kms.[17] Being a landlocked territory, it is surrounded on northeast by the Uygur Autonomous Region of Sinkiang and Tibet (both parts of the Peoples Republic of China), on the South by the Indian state of Himachel Pradesh and Punjab; on the northwest by Afghanistan and on the west by Pakistan.[18] It is surrounded by great Himalayas and origin point of many rivers.[19]

Geo-strategically and geo-economically, the Kashmir valley is of paramount significance for both India and Pakistan. The geographical location of Kashmir is such that it is surrounded by a number of foreign countries such as Tibet in its east and Pakistan, China and Commonwealth of Independent States (CIS) in its west. While, the southern part is bordered by Punjab and Himachal Pradesh. Such a geostrategic location makes the Kashmir valley very important from strategic angle for both India and Pakistan.

This has made India and Pakistan to believe that the control of Kashmir is so important, thereby making it difficult for both sides to come to the terms on resolving the issue which has cost thousands of lives. Both sides are never ready to bargain on the issue at any cost. They perceive the place key to their national security.

Even now both sides are desperate to acquire Kashmir to strengthen their respective visions of nationhood. Pakistan has never accepted India's control of Kashmir as it still believes today that Kashmir should be part of Pakistan. Kashmir is not merely a territorial dispute but is deeply intertwined in the domestic politics and ideologies of India and Pakistan.

India's first Prime Minister, Pandit Jawaharlal Nehru while highlighting the strategic importance of Kashmir has underlined that,

> "Kashmir's northern frontiers ... runs in common with those of three countries: Afghanistan, the USSR and China. Security of Kashmir which much depend upon its internal tranquillity ... is vital to security of India, especially since part of Southern boundary of Kashmir and India are common".[20]

India's former Prime Minister Atal Bihari Vajpayee had in his Independence Day address in 2002 has pointed out that,

> 'Kashmir is not a piece of land; it is a test case of .... secularism. India has always stood the test of a secular nation. Jammu and Kashmir is a living example of this. And this itself is Kashmiriyat.'[21]

India-Pakistan Clash of Interests in Kashmir

The leaders of the two South Asian neighbours are locked in a mindless competition over tactical advantage and scoring diplomatic points in Kashmir.[22] This has led both sides to adopt contradictory strategies and position over the issue. Both have totally different perception about the Kashmir issue. Pakistan's own understanding is that since Kashmir being a Muslim majority state, it should be merged with Pakistan. Pakistan claims Kashmir on the basis of two nation theory, not on law of any kind, as opposed to India which has perfectly valid legal claim in international law. In fact, Islamabad at present is engaged in proxy wars, promoted subversion, and sabotage not only in Jammu and Kashmir but in other parts of our country. The options of solving the Kashmir problem on the basis of status quo has been available to Pakistan since a long time but it wants to incorporate all the Muslim areas of the state.[23] From the Pakistan perspective, Kashmir issue is more of an ideological rather than a territorial dispute, whereas India perceives Kashmir as a symbol of its secularism and composite nationalism.[24] The implications Kashmir had on the ideological foundations of each state really influenced both sides to take a hard stand, which left very little or negligible scope to compromise on the dispute.[25]

Once the State of Jammu and Kashmir had legally acceded to India, the geo-strategic importance of the State became an important aspect influencing Indian policy on Kashmir. Unlike in the past, Kashmir gained strategic value in the post 1947 era. The strategic relevance of Kashmir for both South Asian rivals rests in its utility for each state's defense attitude. From New Delhi's point of view, control over the Kashmir Valley is really significant for the protection of remote Ladakh located next to the Chinese borderland. In any sort of conflict with Pakistan, India could be vulnerable to a fast penetration of Kashmir by Pakistani armour and tactical airpower aiming to sever the territory off from India proper.[26]

Time and again New Delhi has made it clear that Kashmir is an integral part of India. Prime Minister P.V. Narasimha Rao, while speaking at Harvard University in 1995 underscored that, 'Kashmir was, is and will remain an integral part of India and not a millimetre of its land will be given away.' He further added that, 'no compromise would be made on Kashmir and supported his stand by stating the fact that no country in the world could afford to lose its territory.' He further clarified that the only unfinished task in Kashmir was the restoration of the portion of Kashmir illegally occupied by Pakistan to India.[27] Indian leaders, analysts and policy makers have consistently argued that the decision to accede to the Indian Union is final and legal and it cannot be disputed. As regards the UN Resolutions that calls for the will of the people to be ascertained are no longer acceptable because Pakistan has to first withdraw from the territory it occupied through coercive action.[28]

While from the Pakistan point of view, the occupation of Kashmir holds political, economic and strategic significance. It remains in the heart of every Pakistani that accession of Kashmir to India is a threat to the security of Pakistan.[29] Given the ideological connection with Kashmir, Pakistan's official stance is that Kashmir is the main crux of hostility with India. Pakistan's claim over Kashmir is based upon the principle of 'Two-nation Theory'.[30] Since the annexation of Kashmir to India goes against the interests of Pakistan. As a result of which Pakistan calls the accession of Jammu and Kashmir to India unlawful and considers it as a disputed territory. In sympathy towards Kashmiris, Pakistan call upon the UN-sponsored plebiscite. Pakistan strongly believes that the annexation of Kashmir as the logical culmination of the triumph of the '*two nation theory*' and the basis of the birth of Pakistan that stipulated that Hindus and Muslims of the subcontinent were two nations."[31]

There is a common understanding among the Pakistan leaders that without any doubts Kashmir would have come to them. The events that followed partition created a deep scar in their psyche. Pakistan's entire objective became the humiliation of India and the merger of Kashmir to Pakistan. A study of any move the Pakistani Government makes will prove that it will do all in its power to pull Kashmir away from India. In fact, Pakistan views taking over of Kashmir as pivotal to their very existence. To this end Pakistan has made the so-called 'liberation' of Kashmir the cornerstone of their domestic and foreign policies. Thus, they have gone all out to create and ferment trouble in the Valley. Former Pakistan Prime Minister, Liaquat Ali Khan has noted that,

> "Kashmir is very important, it is vital to Pakistan's security... the very position, the strategic position of Kashmir, is such that without it Pakistan cannot defend herself against an unscrupulous government that might come in India."[32]

The prolonged Kashmir issue that has not shown any fruitful prospect for resolution has only sent a wrong message to the international community that resolution is the key to progress in bilateral ties between the two South Asian powers. This is not true in real sense because Pakistan on its part has not shown any eagerness to improve ties with India through discussion and instead they were engaged in illegal activities of proxy war that seriously threatens India's security.[33] The resolution of the Kashmir issue would require both sides to make certain changes to their policies of the past. They need to adopt a positive approach in lieu to the changing scenario to the resolution of the Kashmir dispute. Their rigid stand and not showing any flexibility in their respective stand has only worsened the possibility of bringing fruitful solution.

The resolution of the Kashmir issue would require understanding and reduction of mistrust between the two countries. To ensure understanding, normalization of the conflictual situation has to be erased from their minds. Both sides must engage in economic and other cooperation that would no doubt bring close understanding between the two counties. Peace must be restored between the two countries. For which Pakistan on its side must abandon its support for militancy, ensure that it is not engaged in any kind of proxy war against India that has a serious consequences in the border region. India on its part must ensure that there is good governance in the state of Jammu and Kashmir that listens to the grievances of the citizens and work for the prosperity of the state. Lack of good governance has given way to agitation of the local people.

Pakistan in particular has not shown any political commitment in the past; instead they have promoted separatism and encourage militancy in the Indian State of Jammu and Kashmir. The militancy supported by Pakistan has led to increased violence in Kashmir. It seeks to resolve the issue by force and through outside support rather than dialogue, while India on the other hand seeks to resolve bilaterally through consensus. Whenever India agreed to enter into a fruitful dialogue, it was the Pakistan double standards stand that circumscribed the possibility of any success. For instance, the summit meeting between former Prime Minister of India and Pakistan, Mr. Atal Bihari Vajpayee and Mr. Nawaz Sharif respectively at Lahore in February 1999 was not able to bring out fruitful result due to alleged invasion by the Pakistan military into the Indian Territory. This was followed by the attack on the Indian Parliament in December 2001 that comes just after General Pervez Musharraf's visit to India for the Agra summit in 2001. These events did not allow the climate to be created for the successful solution of the dispute.[34]

Also, Pakistan military leadership obsession with the Kashmir dispute has also been one of the main determinants to creating a climate suitable for resolution. Too much of military influence and the resulting weakness in political leadership has not allowed for the Pakistan government to assert its political will for peace with India. Start from General Zia-ul-Haq to General Musharraf and even today there has been no change in their stand on Kashmir problem. It was General Zia-ul-Haq who began to call Kashmir as the core dispute and all other relations with India would be dependent on the solution of the core dispute. This was followed by what former Pakistan General Pervez Musharraf has said that 'even if the Kashmir issue is resolved, Kargils would happen.[35] Pakistan Prime Minister Mr. Shaukat Aziz during his visit to Hongkong has declared that until the Kashmir issue is resolved, economic relations with India could not fully restored. Such stand precludes the possibility of any resolution. For the sake of Kashmir, Pakistan wants to normalize the relations with India and nothing else.[36] Therefore the paper argues that resolving the Kashmir issue will not bring peace, security and prosperity in the region. Also it sends a wrong message to the international community that Pakistan is not concerned about stability and security in the region.

Former Pakistan President, General Musharraf had during his visit to Muzaffarabad on December 27, 1999 stated that "Pakistan is Kashmir and Kashmir is Pakistan." He further added that, "I want to reiterate that there is a change in the policy towards India. Earlier we used to say that we will negotiate all issues, including Kashmir. But now we will discuss the Kashmir issue first." He is of the perception that Kashmir is the core issue and "there is no negotiations with India unless the Kashmir issue is discussed".[37]

Pakistan's Kashmir Policy and Strategy: Mixed Response

Pakistan has over the last seven decades maintained its Kashmir policy of Kashmir's accession to Pakistan. In support of this policy, it has continuously argued that Kashmir is indivisible and Kashmir's right to self-determination should be fulfilled in accordance with the 1948 United Nations Security Resolutions.[38] Since 1947, Pakistan has laid down the ideological nature of its claim over Kashmir, with a sharp rejection of any proposed solution that called for the division of Kashmir.[39] Against the consistent demand by the people of Kashmir since 1947, the right of self-determination has been denied through the forceful control of the state.[40] Pakistan had adopted a no-compromise Kashmir policy.

Pakistani as well as Kashmiri leaders refuted India's claim of Kashmir as an integral part of India. Instead they declared the accession of Kashmir as the biggest fraud of 20th century. In support of what Pakistani leaders have been claiming over last many decades, Alaster Lamb, a well known political analysts, went on to say that the instrument of accession had not been signed between India and Kashmir.[41]

Unlike strategy, Pakistan's Kashmir policy has remained static since the partition of the Indian subcontinent. It is unlikely to change in the distant future because it is inextricably connected to Pakistan's struggle with its national identity, and the prolonged strategic rivalry with India. Pakistan's strategy is flexible and has shifted from conventional war to diplomacy and then to proxy war owing to different circumstances. The strategy adopted is influenced by a combination of internal and external factors.[42]

Given Kashmir's territorial connectivity and its economic and political ties with Pakistan, Pakistan leaders held a firm belief that the Muslim majority should be part of Pakistan. Pakistan has often argued that Kashmir's accession to India was an attempt to weaken and eventually eliminate Pakistan.[43]

When bilateral dialogue and over 14 years of diplomacy failed to provide the countries national interests, Pakistan took a decision to launch a military attack against a much stronger Indian side in 1965. Later, Pakistan initiated a strategy of proxy war against India in Kashmir.[44] Since then successive leaders of Pakistan have made it very clear that it would not abandon its Kashmir policy at any cost. Taking advantage of the situation within the state of Jammu and Kashmir, growing militancy in the state, Pakistan have adopted a need based strategy of support Kashmir insurgency and the cross border terrorism. When Pakistan saw New

Delhi's reluctance to sincerely negotiate, it sought to apply a military solution to the Kashmir dispute.[45]

Under the so called proxy war strategy, Pakistan started to provide weapons, training, and assistance to insurgents infiltrating across Indian side of Kashmir. While doing so, Islamabad seeks to attract international attention to Kashmir issue. The idea is to keep Pakistan's claims to Kashmir intact thereby putting a pressure on India. In addition, the proxy war strategy had the added advantage that it provided Pakistan with plausible deniability and made the possibility of Indian retaliation against Pakistan more problematic.[46]

India have time and again raised the issue of Pakistan supporting cross border terrorism in the state of Jammu and Kashmir at the bilateral and international level. To put pressure on India, Pakistan seek to attract the international attention by revealing the worst human rights violations in the state of Jammu and Kashmir in the name of fight against terrorism. Pakistan believes that for the sake of right to self determination, the people of Jammu and Kashmir have made a lot of sacrifice over last many decades. Pakistan as usual will continue to provide the much needed support to the Kashmiris cause without any hesitation. As expected, Pakistan raised the issue at the regional and global as a stakeholder.[47]

From the Pakistan point of view, any solution to the Kashmir problem has to take place according to UN resolutions. Pakistan stands tall in support for the Kashmir people and is very much eager to engage in a fruitful dialogue with India. However India has a firm stand on its commitment that Kashmir is the integral part of India. However, at the same time India wants to enter into the meaningful dialogue on Kashmir problem on the condition that Pakistan must stop cross border terrorism.[48] Highlighting the failed approach of Pakistan towards the resolution of the Kashmir dispute, Aqil Shah of the Department of International and Area Studies at the University of Oklahoma, put forth an argument that although Pakistan has repeatedly asked for a plebiscite in Kashmir, in reality, Islamabad has not been serious in honoring its legal commitments concerning a plebiscite or any other resolution. As opposed to the UN resolutions of 1948-49, Pakistan has obstructed the process by refusing to meet its obligation to demilitarize the area unless India simultaneously withdrew its troops.[49]

In his address to the people of the nation, Pakistan President had on 12 January 2002, reiterated that,

> 'Kashmir runs in our blood. No Pakistani can afford to sever links with Kashmir. We will continue to extend our moral, political and diplomatic support to Kashmiris. We will never budge an inch from our principle stand on Kashmir... No organization will be allowed to indulge in terrorism in the name of Kashmir... Let there be no attempt of crossing the border in any sector as it will be met with full force. Do not entertain any illusions on this count.[50]

In response to Pakistan's Kashmir policy and its support for the Kashmiri people, India has made its stand clear to Pakistan and the international community that the real problem in Kashmir is one of cross border terrorism directed by Pakistan. In addition, India has also categorically ruled out any scope for international mediation in Kashmir by moving a unanimous resolution in a joint sitting of the two houses of Parliament which stated that Kashmir is an inalienable part of the Republic of India. Pakistan's diplomatic efforts to win international support for a UN-sponsored plebiscite in Kashmir proved to be unproductive which pose a serious setback for Pakistan's Kashmir policy.[51]

Musharraf Four Step Proposal on Kashmir Dispute

Former Pakistan President Pervez Musharraf put forward a four point proposal for resolving the Kashmir entanglement. The four steps proposal are envisaged as:

(a) Official talks commence.

(b) Centrality of the Jammu and Kashmir dispute is acknowledged.

(c) Any proposal unacceptable to India, Pakistan or Kashmiris is taken off the table.

(d) Best solution acceptable to India, Pakistan and the Kashmiris is taken.

The four-step proposal was discussed in length amongst the officials of both countries during the course of Composite Dialogue Process. In September 2004, General Musharraf and Manmohan Singh met in New York and signed a joint statement indicating their eagerness to look for options on Kashmir and take the peace process forward. On December 2006, Musharraf further refined his ideas and put forward the 'four point formula':

(a) Softening of LoC for trade and free movement of people.

(b) Self governance/ autonomy.

(c) De-militarization from whole of Jammu and Kashmir.

(d) Joint supervision/ management.[52]

Conclusion

Despite being the oldest unresolved border dispute that exists in the present era, there is very little hope for resolution in the near future. Both India and Pakistan claimed Jammu and Kashmir as 'an integral part of Indian union' and 'unfinished business of 1947', respectively. The strategic importance of the dispute for regional and global peace and security has increased over the last many decades. From the view point of Teresita C. Schaffer, a renowned scholar who closely analyses the relations between India and Pakistan that, "The Kashmir problem began as a dispute over territory; what has made it toxic has been incompatible national identities."[53]

The Kashmir problem is a result of the long neglect and the callous attitude of the leaders of both India and Pakistan. Pakistan's fishing in troubled waters and stoking of communal hatred was only to be expected given the long history of animosity. The challenge to the nation involves a firm hand to tackle the militancy and to win the hearts and minds of the populace by constructive involvement in developmental and political activities. Sumit Ganguly has in his book titled, *The Crisis in Kashmir: Portents of War, Hopes of Peace,* raised the argument that,

> "any option that fails to recognise the fundamental territorial integrity of India will not meet the test of political feasibility. No government in India will concede Kashmir, even if it entails continuing losses in blood and treasure..."[54]

Pakistan has so far blamed India for the lack of sincerity to engage in a meaningful dialogue with Pakistan over Kashmir, instead New Delhi insists to discuss on all outstanding issues with Pakistan. Victoria Schofield raises a sound argument that the grievances amongst the Kashmiris, which had been allowed to fester, the steady erosion of the 'special status' promised to the state of Jammu and Kashmir in 1947, the neglect of the people by their leaders, were clearly India's responsibility. Another analysts from India says that Kashmir would not have become an issue 'if the valley had not exploded on its own thanks to Delhi's misguided policies'."[55] These viewpoints raised the lacklustre approach on the part of the successive Indian government towards the Kashmir issue and the demands of the people. The policy adopted by the successive government of our country have failed to win the heart and minds of the people of Kashmir. Very rightly, an analysts has pointed out that the central government appointed Governor Shri Jagmohan's policy pushed the populace to becoming anti-Indian and turned the most apolitical Kashmiris into active supporters of militancy.[56]

The central government handling of the militancy and rising terrorist violence in the state is also disappointing. It gives an opportunity for the leaders of Pakistan and Kashmir to raise an issue at the international level. The Amnesty International report of 1992 highlighted the widespread violations of human rights in the state in a way that,

> "Widespread human rights violations in the state since January 1990 have been attributed to the Indian army, and the paramilitary Border Security Force (BSF) and Central Reserve Police Force (CRPF)... Torture is reported to be routinely used during these combing operations as well as in army camps, interrogation centers, police stations and prisons. Indiscriminate beatings are common and rape in particular appears to be routine... In Jammu and Kashmir, rape is practiced as part of a systematic attempt to humiliate and intimidate the local population during counterinsurgency operations."[57]

Both India and Pakistan till now are playing a blame game over the resolution of the prolonged Kashmir conflict. Several proposals have been put forth by various stake holders to resolve the ongoing conflict in Kashmir but very little success could be seen. There was an occasion in which both sides came very close to reaching an agreement over the issue. Both sides have to be blamed for the lack of sincerity because none of them are ready to give up the rigid stand taken up by them in the recent past. It is highly imperative that both sides develop a political understanding which would create a platform for conducting a bilateral composite dialogue over the Kashmir and other related issues.

First came the abrogation of Articles 370 and 35-A of the Indian constitution through a dubious amendment described by some scholars of jurisprudence as a constitutional heist. The Indian Occupied Jammu and Kashmir lost its special status on the basis of which some Kashmiris had agreed to remain under Indian sovereignty.

The proclamation of Jammu and Kashmir as a Union territory was accompanied by the induction of hundreds of thousands of additional troops in the Valley to enforce a lockdown unprecedented in its scope and severity. The outraged human rights community has denounced these actions in unambiguous terms.

The Commissioner of Human Rights, the principal officer of the United Nations system entrusted with the promotion and protection of human rights, has issued two scathing reports on the situation in the Valley. As expected, reactions from governments, including those which are traditionally on the forefront of human rights advocacy, were muted.

Considerations of national interest derived from India's growing economic importance and strategic relevance clearly accounted for this silence which was but sporadically punctured by a few mild and innocuous statements. Reactions inside India ranged between grudging endorsement and resounding support.

Dissenting voices were muffled and scattered. In the parliament, the amendments had sailed through with a consensus. Even the diehard proponents of secularism and constitutional propriety had gone along. The horror story in Kashmir continues to this day largely unnoticed and un-mourned by the world.

On February 25, South Asia woke up to an unexpected and, in the context of the harsh bitterness that had characterised relations between the two countries since Modi's ascension to power, a radical development. The directors general of military operations for India and Pakistan issued a joint declaration committing their militaries to re-establishing the ceasefire agreement of 2003 and pledging to address each other's 'core issues and concerns' in the interest of achieving mutually beneficial and sustainable peace along the borders.

The ceasefire, whose merit was deemed questionable in some quarters, was in fact suggestive of the dawn of rationality on both sides. Conflict for its own sake without any dividends, immediate or anticipated, is not supported by any military doctrine. Daily exchanges of fire, including heavy artillery were causing unnecessary waste of men and material without accruing any tangible gain, tactical or strategic to either side.

One would be hard pressed to find a similar example anywhere else in the world where two adversaries routinely target each other's posts without a clear cut military or political objective. The Indian claim that violations were initiated by us in order to facilitate the movement of militants across the LoC is as spurious as it is self-serving primarily because limited inductions would have had no impact whatsoever on the situation in the Valley.

Such activity on our part would also have invited negative international attention which we just cannot afford with the FATF sword hanging over our head. By all counts, restoration of the ceasefire agreement represents a display of maturity by the two sides as both stand to benefit from it in concrete terms. Despite Indian military's tall claims of its ability to successfully wage a two-front war the hammering it received in Laddakh must have opened its eyes to the hallucinatory character of its strategy.

For Pakistan, the stakes were even higher. With its economy in severe distress compounded by serious issues of governance combined with the very real apprehensions of instability on its western border following the impending US withdrawal from Afghanistan, a ceasefire was both desirable and necessary. It is now incumbent on the two sides to ensure that the guns remain silent across the LoC and the Working Boundary.

The fact that the ceasefire agreement was not an isolated event divorced from the overall context of Indo-Pakistan relations has been reinforced by recent developments. Several reports from various quarters suggest that representatives from the two countries have been conducting clandestine interlocutions in various locations around the world. This needs to be welcomed and encouraged.

History tells us that major diplomatic breakthroughs were made possible in conditions of strict confidence and away from the glare of the media. Henry Kissinger's landmark visit to China, Paris negotiations between him and his Vietnamese counterpart, the Oslo Accords, back channel diplomacy on Kashmir during the Musharraf era, the nuclear deal with Iran, come readily to mind.

Confidentiality is integral to forward movement on complex diplomatic issues. As a citizen one wonders what these backchannel interactions are intended to achieve. These could possibly include preservation and consolidation of the ceasefire, amelioration of the plight of the Kashmiris, Siachin and Sir Creek, cooperation for promoting stability and durable peace in Afghanistan without prejudice to the legitimate interests of either side, particularly Pakistan's given our special concerns arising from the reality of a long shared border, mutually beneficial confidence building measures, mitigation of the devastating effects of climate change on South Asian economies, overall regional cooperation, amongst others.

A formidable agenda indeed, but progress in one or more of these areas would have a stabilising effect on a perennially volatile region while expediting our transition from a geo-strategic to a geo-economic matrix. During these conversations, however, we need to be mindful of one fundamental point. Following our listless response to the seminal events of August 5, 2019, when the Kashmiris needed us most, we are no longer in a position to appropriate to ourselves the right to negotiate and decide on their behalf.

We should scrupulously avoid giving any undertakings to the Indians on the future of Kashmir as that right today belongs exclusively to the Kashmiris. They have earned it through their heroic struggle against unbelievable odds and the sheer magnitude of their sacrifice. Let them now decide their destiny, through whatever means available to them, unencumbered by our disabilities both internal and external.

Ours should be a supporting role. In a more just world this should not have been the denouement of a 73-year old saga during which we stood shoulder to shoulder with our Kashmiri brethren, even during the most trying and testing times. The iron grip of circumstance, occasioned in large part by our own fragilities with which we can barely cope, has largely reduced our role to that of a sympathetic bystander. The least we can do is to use our diplomatic capital to try to alleviate their suffering without compromising our time-honoured position that lasting peace will continue to elude this troubled region till the Kashmir dispute is resolved in consonance with the aspirations of the Kashmiri people.

It's important to begin by making one thing very clear-Article 370 of the Indian Constitution has not been revoked. Rather, the President of India has made modifications to it, which is allowed by certain provisions in the article itself. On August 5, Union Home Minister Amit Shah announced in the Rajya Sabha that the Government had scrapped the special status granted to the state of Jammu and Kashmir (J&K) by modifying Article 370 of the Constitution. (The same day, the Rajya Sabha also passed the Jammu and Kashmir Reorganisation Bill, which proposes the bifurcation of the state into two union territories-Ladakh and Jammu-Kashmir.)

What did Article 370 mean for Jammu and Kashmir?

Included in the Indian Constitution on October 17,

1949, Article 370 is a 'temporary provision', which exempts Jammu and Kashmir from the Indian Constitution, permitting it to draft its own Constitution and restricting the Indian Parliament's legislative powers in the state. In short, it accorded special status to the state, giving the J&K legislature free rein to draft its own laws, except in the areas of communications, defence, finance and foreign affairs. As a result, Jammu and Kashmir had its own constitution, flag, and penal code.

Can Article 370 be repealed?

The Constituent Assembly of Jammu and Kashmir was empowered to recommend which articles of the Indian Constitution should apply to the state, or to recommend the abolition of Article 370 altogether. However, the J&K Constituent Assembly was dissolved after it drafted the state's constitution, and during its existence, did not comment on the abrogation of Article 370. However, Clause 3 of the article gives the President of India the power to amend its provisions and scope. The Narendra Modi-led government has sought to take advantage of this clause, and has brought in a Presidential Order that extends all provisions of the Indian Constitution to Jammu and Kashmir.

But there may still be a legal hurdle. Though Clause 3 allows the President of India to declare that Article 370 has ceased to be operative or that it remains operative with exceptions, such a decision must be recommended by the Constituent Assembly of the state. Since J&K's Constituent Assembly was dissolved on January 26, 1957, one legal opinion is that Article 370 can never be repealed. The presidential order, issued on August 5, says that "the expression "Constituent Assembly of the State referred to in Clause (2)" shall read "Legislative Assembly of the State". As the Assembly is in suspension, the president recognises the concurrence of the Governor as the concurrence of the legislative assembly of Jammu and Kashmir.

The Union government, in a written reply on the topic to Parliament in 2018, had said there was no proposal to remove Article 370. In 2017, Delhi High Court rejected a petition demanding the repeal of Article 370. In April 2018, the Supreme Court had ruled that despite the head-note of Article 370 using the word 'temporary', that it was not temporary. The Supreme Court had also set an earlier precedent on the matter in a case in 1969, making the same determination. At the time, it had said: "Article 370 has never ceased to be operative."

Constitutional experts are divided over the legal validity of the Presidential Order limiting the scope of Article 370. "It is utterly and palpably unconstitutional," said constitutional expert A.G. Noorani. "After the dissolution of the [J&K] Constituent Assembly in 1957, the power [to abrogate] Article 370 vanished." Congress spokesperson and Rajya Sabha MP Abhishek Manu Singhvi has called the resolution legally flawed and indefensible. However, Supreme Court advocate Rakesh Dwivedi believes that any plea against the government's decision will not be successful. A former secretary general of the Lok Sabha, Subhash Kashyap, agrees with Dwivedi, saying, "As [J&K] is under the Centre's rule, Parliament can be interpreted as the legislature of Jammu and Kashmir. So, no concurrence is required from the state government to make changes."

What is Article 35 (A)?

Article 35(A) stems from Article 370, and was introduced through a Presidential Order in 1954, on the recommendation of the J&K Constituent Assembly. This article empowered the state legislature to define who the state's 'permanent residents' were, along with their special rights and privileges. For instance, no one, except those defined as 'permanent residents of J&K' are entitled to property rights in the state, employment in state government, or to scholarships and other social benefits provided by the state. Initially, under this provision, if a Kashmiri woman were to marry a citizen from another Indian state, she would lose her Kashmiri citizenship and property rights. However, this provision was struck down by the Jammu and Kashmir High Court in October 2002, with the court ruling that the daughter of a permanent resident of J&K would not lose her permanent resident status as a result of such a marriage. However, the children of such a union would not get succession rights. Though the constitutional validity of Article 35 (A) has been challenged in the Supreme Court, the apex court has rejected three appeals.

So what happens now?

Though the Presidential Order may face legal scrutiny, as matters currently stand, Jammu and Kashmir will witness historic political and geographic changes. It is to be divided into two union territories-Ladakh and Jammu and Kashmir. Ladakh will not have a legislature, while Jammu and Kashmir will have a legislative assembly with 107 members-however, this assembly will not have the authority to pass laws relating to 'public order and the police'. The single largest party in the assembly will form the government, headed by a chief minister, and the assembly will have a five-year term, not six, as was the earlier case. A Lieutenant Governor will govern both Union territories. Of the six Lok Sabha seats currently with the state of Jammu and Kashmir, five will remain with the union territory of Jammu and Kashmir, while one will go to Ladakh.

However, the biggest fallout for the state will stem from the abolition of its special status under Article 370. These are the likely major changes:

- Jammu and Kashmir will no longer have separate constitution, flag or anthem. The citizens of Jammu and Kashmir will not have dual citizenship-they will be citizens of India alone.

- As the new union territory of Jammu and Kashmir will be subject to the Indian Constitution, its citizens will now have the Fundamental Rights enshrined in that document-until now, this was not the case. Article 360, which can be used to declare a Financial Emergency, will now also be applicable.
- All laws passed by Parliament will be applicable in Jammu and Kashmir, including the Right to Information Act and the Right to Education Act.
- The Indian Penal Code will replace the Ranbir Penal Code of Jammu and Kashmir
- As the government has modified the Article 370, diluting special status to Jammu and Kashmir, Article 35 (A), which originates from the provisions of Article 370 stands null and void. Any Indian citizen from any part of the country can now buy property in Jammu and Kashmir, take a state government job and enjoy scholarships and other government benefits. Children of a woman marrying outside Jammu and Kashmir will not lose property rights.

References

1. Stephen P. Cohen was quoted in Sachinkumar Manikrao, "Areas of Contestation and Debate between India and Pakistan: A Critical Study", Ph. D Thesis Submitted to the Department of Political Science, Sahyadri Arts College, Kuvempu University, Karnataka, 2014, p. 107.
2. Najmudheen T. and Farhana Kousar, "Significance of Indo-Pak Cordial Relations in South Asia", International Journal of South Asian Studies, Vol. 5, No. 1, Jan-June 2012, p. 146.
3. Rehana Saeed Hashmi and Aila Sajid, "Kashmir Conflict: The Nationalistic Perspective (A Pre-Partition Phenomenon)", South Asian Studies, Vol. 32, No. 1, January-June 2017, p. 229.

4. S.K. Sinha, "The Kashmir Imbroglio", in Arun Dalvi (ed.), India's Security and Defence - Swatantryaveer Sawarkar Memorial Lectures (Pune: University of Pune Press, 2006),p. 125.

5. Ibid., p. 127.

6. Sumita Kumar, "Trends in Indo-Pakistan Relations", Strategic Analysis, Vol. 24, No. 2, May, 2000, p. 224.

7. Sachinkumar Manikrao, "Areas of Contestation and Debate between India and Pakistan: A Critical Study", Ph. D Thesis Submitted to the Department of Political Science, Sahyadri Arts College, Kuvempu University, Karnataka, 2014, pp. 107-08.

8. The Instrument of Accession signed between the Maharaja and India was fully ratified in the Kashmir Assembly by the Government of Sheikh Mohammed Abdullah. A copy of the Instrument of Accession is attached in the Appendix.

9. Navnita Chadha Behera, Demstifying Kashmir (Washington, D.C: Brookings Institution Press, 2006), p. 25.

10. Ibid., p. 27.

11. Ibid., p. 28.

12. M J Vinod, "Kashmir and India-Pakistan Relations", Strategic Analysis, November 1995, p. 1142.

13. Sisir Gupta, Kashmir: A Study in India-Pakistan Relations (New York: Asia Publishing House, 1966), p. 270.

14. K. V. Krishna Rao, "Kashmir: Past, Present and the Future", Gautam Sen (ed.), National Security - Gen. B. C. Joshi Memorial Lectures (Pune: University of Pune Press, 2006), p. 51.

15. Andrea Benvenuti, USI Journal, July-September 95, Vol. CXXV, No. 521, p. 339.

16. Jasjit Singh, Pakistan Occupied Kashmir under the Jackboot (New Delhi: Siddhi Books, 1995).

17. Claws Research Team, "Jammu and Kashmir Realities Revisited", Scholar Warrior, autumn 2011, p. 25.

18. Syed Rifaat Hussain, "Resolving the Kashmir Dispute: Blending Realism with Justice", The Pakistan Development Review, Vol. 48, No. 4, Winter 2009, p. 1007.

19. Syed Waqas Haider Bukhari and Tahira Parveen, "China's Approach Towards Kashmir Conflict: A Viable Solution", Journal of Professional Research in Social Sciences, Vol. 1, No. 1, July 2014, p. 14.

20. Ted Svensson, Production of Postcolonial India and Pakistan: Meanings of Pakistan (London and New York: Routledge, 2013).

21. See, Prime Minister Shri Atal Bihari Vajpayee's Independence Day Address, New Delhi, 15 August 2002, available at *<https://archivepmo.nic.in/abv/speech-details.php?nodeid= 9040>*.

22. Stephen P Cohen, "Kashmir : The Roads Ahead", A Note presented for the Study of Foreign Affairs; Foreign Service Institute, U.S. Department of State; Washington, May 28, 2002.

23. A K Verma, "India's problems with Pakistan", South Asia Analysis Group, Paper No. 185.

24. Veena Kukraja, "India-Pakistan Relations: The Contemporary Phase", in Mohammed Badrul Alam (ed.), Contours of India's Foreign Policy: Changes and Challenges (New Delhi: Reference Press, 2014), p. 253.

25. Matthew P. Taylor, "Pakistan's Kashmir Policy and Strategy Since 1947", Master Thesis Submitted to the Naval Post-graduate College, Monterey, California, March 2004, p. 1.

26. Mahnaz Z. Ispahani, Roads and Rivals: The Politics of Access in the Borderlands of Asia (London: I.B. Tauris & Co. Ltd., 1989), p. 184.

27. Rakesh Kumar, "Kashmir Issue in Indo-Pak Relations", Journal of Global Research and Analysis, Vol. 3, No. 2, December 2014, p. 8.

28 Syed Rifaat Hussain, op cit., p. 1009.

29. Sadia Fayaz, "Kashmir Dispute between Pakistan and India: The Way Out", The Dialogue, Vol. XI, No. 1, p. 65-6.

30. Rehana Saeed Hashmi and Aila Sajid, n. 3, p. 227.

31. Sumaira Shafiq, "Pakistan's Policy towards Kashmir Dispute (2001-2014)", Margalla Papers, 2015, p. 135-36.

32. A.Z. Hilali, "Historical Developments of the Kashmir Problem and Pakistan Policy after September 11", Perceptions, Journal of International Affairs, Vol. 9, June-August 2004.

33. Milind Thakar, "Coping with Insecurity: The Pakistani Variable in Indo-US Relations", in Gary K. Bertsch, et. al., (eds.), Engaging India-U.S. Strategic Relations with the World's Largest Democracy (New York: Routledge, 1999), p. 227.

34. See, "India/Pak Relations and Kashmir: Steps Toward Peace", International Crisis Group Asia, Report No. 79, 24 June 2004, pp. 2-3.

35. Kalim Bahadur, "India-Pakistan Relations", in V.D. Chopra (ed.), India's Foreign Policy in the 21st Century (New Delhi: Kalpaz Publications, 2006), pp. 147-49.

36. Ibid., p. 152.

37. Ajay Pratap Singh, "Indo-Pak Relations Since 1990", Ph. D Thesis Submitted to the Department of Defence and Strategic Studies, T. D. P. G. College, V. B. S Purvanchal University, Jaunpur, 2001, p. 15.

38. Matthew P. Taylor, n. 22, p. 4.

39. Ibid., p. 17.

40. Amjad Abbas Khan, Sardar Sajid Mehmood and Mehbood Alam, "Kashmir and Global Powers", South Asian Studies, Vol. 33,No. 1, Jan-June 2018, p. 148.

41. Ibid., p. 148.

42. Matthew P. Taylor, op cit., p. 3.

43. Ibid., p. 6.
44. Ibid., p. 9.
45. Ibid., p. 11.
46. Ibid., p. 69.
47. Khursheed Ahmad, "What Should be the Kashmir Policy of Pakistan", The News, 21 August 2016, available at < *https://www.thenews.com.pk/print/144022-What-should-be-the-Kashmir-Policy-of-Pakistan*>.
48. Sadia Fayaz, n. 26, p. 68-9.
49. Umair Jamal, "Pakistan's Failed Kashmir Policy", The Diplomat, 27 July 2016, available at <*https://thediplomat.com/2016/07/pakistans-failed-kashmir-policy/*>.
50. See, "Text of President Musharraf's Address to the Nation", 12 January 2002.
51. Rajat Ganguly, "India, Pakistan and the Kashmir Dispute", Asian Studies Institute, Victoria University of Wellington.
52. Sachinkumar Manikrao, n. 5, pp. 108-09.
53. Asma Yaqoob, "India-Pakistan Confrontation: What Has Changed About Indian - Held Kashmir Since 1947", Regional Studies, Vol. XXXIV, No. 2, Spring 2016, p. 4.
54. Sumit Ganguly, The Crisis in Kashmir: Portents of War, Hopes of Peace (Harvard: Cambridge University Press, 1997), p. 145.
55. Sumit Ganguly, The Kashmir Question: Retrospect and Prospect (London: Routledge, 2004), p. 46.
56. Asma Yaqoob, op cit., p. 14.
57. See, 'India—Torture, Rape and Deaths in Custody', Report Prepared by Amnesty International, New York, 1992.

3

India-Pakistan Relations : Current Situation

The present chapter attempts to put in perspective the political, economic and security dimensions of the bilateral relations between India and Pakistan. It would also discuss the issues and challenges that prevent both countries from reaching their full potential of bilateral engagement which definitely would have both regional and global significance. India enjoys strong cultural, linguistic and ethnic connections with the neighbouring countries of South Asia. Among the South Asia countries, India is the largest which accounts for 70 per cent of population, nearly 80 per cent of the gross domestic product (GDP) and about 75 per cent of the regional economic output. India shares boundary with all the South Asian neighbours. The changing environment also demands India to maintain stability in its relations with its neighbours.[1] From the geo-strategic and geo-political point of view, India's relations with the South Asian neighbours have been guided by – first, its desire to protect the sub-continent from the adverse external forces that might destabilise India's security environment and secondly, its desire to ensure that geographically proximity and ethno-religious affinities do not lead to instability on or near its border, particularly as they inevitably may affect its domestic, ethnic, religious and political relationships.[2]

India's relations with Pakistan have been aptly described by former India's Prime Minister, Inder Kumar Gujral as 'tormented one'. Pakistan has been one of the major concerns for India's foreign policy for many decades.[3] The relations between India and Pakistan have seen great uncertainty and ambiguity as both the countries have adopted divergent approach for their respective national interests. India and Pakistan are the two largest countries in South Asia wherein there exists a very low level of engagements. The two South Asian regional powers remain strategic rivals competing for regional influence and engage in contradictory and counterproductive acts. There exists a serious politico-security conflict between the two South Asian rivals which pose a hindrance to maintaining close relation for the mutual benefit.

Since their independence, India and Pakistan have failed to come out of mutual suspicion and discord of each other. It has its implications on the decision making process and policy formulation of both countries. It has also promoted the image of each other as an enemy with minimal hope for constructive politico, strategic and economic engagement.[4] In the post 1947, both countries have witnessed enduring divergences over a range of issues resulting in adoption of divergent approach to serving its interests. Both India and Pakistan have so far failed to develop cordial relationship from the long-term perspective with each other due to various issues which includes border dispute, cross border terrorism, clash of interests over Afghanistan, etc. The relationship between the two sides has been marked by suspicion, hatred and distrust. Tense and hostile situation which existed since 1947 has resulted in three wars and various crises between them. They have made significant effort in the past to resolve some of the key issues by holding peace talks and even by concluding various agreements. But this situation could not last long owing to suspensions in the peace process which had further enhanced suspicion and mistrust on both sides. By adopting antagonistic approach towards each other, both sides have failed to develop consensus on the need to develop the atmosphere of peace and security as key to achieving mutual trust. Misperception developed in the minds of policy makers of both states regarding different issues. The hostile attitude towards each other has severely undermined the prospect of socio-economic development of both countries.[5] It argues that lasting security and other development pursuits of both India and Pakistan would considerably rely upon cordial and mutually cooperative relations between these two neighbours.

Despite successive efforts by the Indian government, Pakistan's attitude of cross border terrorism along the Kashmir border and anti-Indian stance have derailed the prospects of dialogue and resumption of the peace process. The bilateral dialogue process which started in 2004 was stopped following the Mumbai attacks of 2008. It couldn't lasts long as the peace process resumed in 2011, but very little improvement could be seen in bilateral relations.[6]

Historical Analysis of India-Pakistan Relations During the Cold War Era

India and Pakistan have a history of unique relations. The diplomatic relations developed soon after their inception but lacked the character of cordial and friendship engagement. The historical relations between the two sides has been characterised by prolonged conflict and rivalry; discord, mutual distrust and suspicion.[7] The historical animosity that carried over into the post 1947 period, the bloody partition and the accession of Kashmir to India remains a constant cause of political, ideological and military hostility between them.[8]

The Maharaja of Kashmir, Hari Singh was in dilemma on whether to accede to India or to Pakistan. But when the tribal raiders with the support of Pakistani soldiers attacked the state and were about to capture the airfield of Srinagar,[9] the Maharaja asked for help from India. The then Indian Prime Minister Nehru agreed to provide the necessary military support and assistance in return for his acceptance of Kashmir's legal accession to India. Maharaja Hari Singh had no choice but to comply.[10] Finally, Hari Singh took a bold decision to accede to India instead of Pakistan and an Instrument of Accession was signed on 26th October 1947. Upon the accession, the Pakistan Government declared it as fraud and was never ready to accept it. India and Pakistan together made a series of attempts to resolve the bilateral dispute through direct negotiations. The leaders of the two sides were in communication with each other between August 1953 and September 1954. However, the discussion couldn't bring any fruitful results as both adopted a different stand on the issue.[11]

Pakistan instead of engaging in peaceful dialogue, started creating border violations on a large scale along the Indian side of the border on May 1965. India took the issue seriously as it posed a serious threat to the peace and stability in the state, and even complained to the Security Council about heavy concentration of Pakistani troops along the Indian border.[12] In response, India launched operation Meghdoot and captured 80 per cent of Siachen Glacier. Then in 1971, India and Pakistan fought another war leading to the creation of independence of Bangladesh. In 1972 Indian Prime Minister Indira Gandhi and Pakistan Prime Minister ZA Bhutto met in Shimla and signed a agreement for the release of 90,000 prisoners of 1971 war.[13] Under the Simla agreement, both sides have agreed to settle their disputes through peaceful bilateral negotiations or through other means mutually agreed upon between them. The agreement ruled out the possibility of any third party involvement, especially on the disputes which are being negotiated within the rubric of the eight baskets mechanism.[14]

Since 1980s, the relations became more suspicious and soured owing to several factors such as the Siachin Glacier conflict, militancy in Kashmir, cross border terrorism, etc. Pakistan offer of military hardware and training to the militant groups operating in Jammu and Kashmir. Their support hold the key to carrying out terrorist act not confined to just the Kashmir region but also in various sections of our country.[15] In December 1988, Benazir Bhutto and Rajiv Gandhi resumed talks to discuss on different issues not confined to just border issues but also the prospect of bilateral trade between the two sides. The change in leadership brought some hope in the relations between the two neighbours. Both sides also pledged not to attack each other's air space and to notify the other in advance of military exercises.[16]

India's Political Relations with Pakistan

The political understanding between India and Pakistan has witnessed more ups than downs ever since both countries have gained their independence. The political environment between the two neighbouring countries continues to be marred by mutual distrust and suspicion. Despite significant potential, the relationship between the two sides has seen no significant improvement. The relationship between the two sides is perceived to be beneficial in various areas of interests including security, economic, energy and socio-cultural aspects. The two South Asian regional powers, India and Pakistan remain strategic rivals competing for regional influence and engage in contradictory and counterproductive acts. There exists a serious politico-security conflict between the two South Asian rivals which pose a hindrance to maintaining close relation for the mutual benefit.

The change in global politico-strategic environment in the aftermath of Soviet disintegration didn't usher any remarkable change in the relations between the two South Asian neighbours. In fact, the relations between the two sides have seen more low points than high points in the changed scenario. To start the relations on a positive note in the immediate years of the end of Cold War, India and Pakistan hold bilateral talks during the Jakarta Summit of the Non-Aligned Movement on September 1992. On this occasion, Prime Minister. P.V. Narsimha Rao said, "After going into all the details of the setbacks that we came up against, we still feel that we have to continue our efforts, not always expecting immediate or instantaneous success but realising that the effort itself is worth making irrespective of the immediate results." In response, Pakistani Prime Minister said, "We should continue discussing things."[17]

A series of bomb blasts in Mumbai on March 1993, brought a setback to the bilateral talks for the start of healthy relations in the changed post Cold War era. Preliminary investigations make it clear that the blasts were orchestrated by the ISI of Pakistan, in response to events in Ayodhya. To reduce the damage done by the blasts, Islamabad brought up the issue of Kashmir and even refused to hold talks with India unless the "core" issue, Kashmir, was taken up first and resolved.[18]

Several key issues have not allowed the development of close ties between India and Pakistan. The military officers of both sides met in 1996 at Line of Control (LoC) to wind down border tensions. The same year bilateral official diplomatic talks were held to discuss on border issues. In the year 1997, Pakistan proposed to discuss terms for a non-aggression treaty and for restraints on nuclear and missile capabilities. In the early 1999, the leaders of the two sides realised the necessity for holding a composite dialogue for discussion on bilateral issues before they can be peacefully resolved.[19] Their political commitment did bring positive results when the foreign secretary level talks were held in New Delhi in March 1997. However, real breakthrough came in May 1997, when Indian Prime Minister I.K. Gujral met his Pakistani counterpart Nawaz Sharif at Maldives whereby they agreed to release prisoners from each other's countries, enter into hotline agreement, establish working group to address various outstanding issues.[20]

The victory of Nawaz Sharif in Pakistan's elections in February 1997 and the declaration of the Gujral Doctrine was a plus point in the direction of India-Pakistan relations. The doctrine encouraged India to be cooperative in its dealing with the smaller neighbours. Commenting on Gujral Doctrine, I.K. Gujral said in March 1997 that,

> "I am willing to make concessions on anything, except the sovereignty or secular character of our nation. That is non-negotiable. There will not be another partition of India."[21]

During the tenure of the then Prime Minister I.K. Gujral and Nawaz Sharif rounds of foreign secretaries talks were held in Islamabad in March 1997. Both sides agreed to set up a joint working group to discover modalities for bilateral talks and final mechanism to address all the issues in an integrated manner. For the first time both sides agreed to an eight point agenda to resume dialogue including the most contentious one - Kashmir dispute. The other issues were Siachin, Wullur Barrage, Tulbul Navigation Project, Sir Creek, Terrorism and Drug Trafficking. However, as expected, all efforts proved futile as Pakistan insisted on addressing Kashmir agenda first.[22]

The relations suffered a severe blow in the aftermath of the nuclear tests by the two neighbours and sensitized the Kashmir question by linking it with the nuclear tests. However, the seed for improvement was borne out of the meeting between Vajpayee and Nawaz Sharif at New York on September 1998 during the UN General Assembly session. It was agreed that two foreign secretaries would meet in

Islamabad from October 1998 to focus on Kashmir and peace and security, including confidence building measures, etc.[23] As regards the nuclear tests, Prime Minister Atal B. Vajpayee has made a statement to the Lok Sabha on 27 May 1998 that, "India does not intend to use these weapons for aggression or for mounting threats against any country; these are weapons of self defense, to ensure that India is not subjected to nuclear threats or coercion."[24]

Both sides have reached an understanding in New York in September 1998, on the sidelines of the U.N. General Assembly Session to start a bus service between Delhi and Lahore.[25] Prime Minister Vajpayee made a historic visit to Pakistan after a gap of almost a decade. He was accompanied by several cabinet colleagues.[26] The Memorandum of Understanding (MoU) was signed by the Indian Foreign Secretary, K. Raghunath and his counterpart, Shamshad, wherein both sides agreed that they shall periodically review the implementation of existing Confidence Building Measures (CBMs) and where necessary set up appropriate consultative mechanisms to monitor and enhance effective implementation of CBMs. Under the Declaration, both parties were convinced of the importance of mutually agreed confidence building measures for improving the security environment. It also emphasized that peace and cooperation would serve the vital interests of the people on both sides of the border.[27]

The effort made by the leaders of the two sides got shattered by the Kargil conflict initiated by Pakistan conflict and was well responded by India through Operation Vijay. The withdrawal of the Pakistan's forces from Kargil was followed by military coup in the state. It reflects Pakistan Army involvement in Pakistan's politics and its disinterest in finding political solution of the Kashmir problem.[28]

The series of move aimed at improving close ties between India and Pakistan got a massive blow when the terrorist attack the Indian Parliament on 13 December 2001 and the Kaluchak massacre in Jammu on 14 May 2002. After the twin incident, both countries came very close to waging the fifth war with much more devastating potential than the earlier once.[29]

The 2001-02 crises ended in April 2003 with Indian Prime Minister Atal B. Vajpayee offered bilateral talks to his Pakistani counterpart Zafarullah Khan Jamali[30] and the latter announcement of a ceasefire along the Line of Control (LoC). The situation influenced both sides to seriously think of resuming the composite dialogue. Both sides held a series number of talks at the official level and non-official level. Discussion on the bilateral disputes between the two countries improved after the replacement by Mr. Manmohan Singh as the new Prime Minister of India in 2004.

In a bid to resolve the long standing bilateral disputes, both sides reached an agreement on five broad areas- no change in the current division of Kashmir into Pakistan and Indian areas, creation of soft border along the Line of Control that would ensure greater freedom of movement of people and goods, greater autonomy and self-governance for both India and Pakistan administered parts of Kashmir, the establishment of a consultative mechanism across the LoC and lastly, demilitarisation of Kashmir.[31]

Considering the security scenario that prevails in the South Asia in general and India in particular, it was India's Prime Minister Atal Bihari Vajpayee who made peace offer in Srinagar on April 2003. Following which, rail and diplomatic links between the two sides were restored. In addition, decision was also taken to opening up of the bus route between Srinagar and Muzzafarabad and between Manabao and Kokhrapur.[32] Besides, New Delhi took the initiative of 12 point confidence building measures on October 2003.

It ranges from resumption of civil aviation and rail links to sporting links; provision of visa camps in both the countries in various cities, etc.[33]

To take advantage of the developing scenario, both sides agreed to launch the peace process in January 2004. The decision augurs well for a promising trade, improved people to people contact, a ceasefire on both sides of the borders and the implementation of number of confidence-building measures in disputed Kashmir. In addition, it also opens up serious back channel negotiation on the Kashmir dispute.[34] Both sides started the Composite Dialogue Process (CDP), which emphasizes an eight-point agenda such as peace and security, Jammu and Kashmir, Siachen, Sir Creek, Wullar Barrage, terrorism and drug trafficking, economic and commercial cooperation, and the promotion of friendly exchanges in various fields. The CDP without any doubt has opened up the dialogue, leading to more transparency and confidence building measures, but has failed to make a real impact in resolving deep-seated mistrust.[35]

At the New Delhi summit held in April 2005, General Pervez Musharraf in a sharp departure from its past stand recognised that borders cannot be redrawn though the LoC could not become the permanent border between the two countries. Moreover, the joint statement issued at the conclusion of the summit meeting declared that the peace process was not irreversible.[36] Former Indian Prime Minister, Manmohan Singh has in early 2007 reiterated the need to develop close connections between the two countries, "I sincerely believe that the destiny of the people of South Asia is interlinked. It is not just our past that links us, but our future too. India cannot be a prosperous, dynamic economy and a stable polity if our neighborhood as a whole is also not economically prosperous and politically stable. Similarly, our neighbors cannot prosper if India does not do so as well. There are enormous opportunities for promoting mutually beneficial cooperation in South Asia. To exploit these opportunities, the nations of South Asia have to work sincerely to control the scourge of terrorism and extremis ..."[37]

This was the period where both military and non-military Confidence Building Measures (CBMs) improves. For instance Agreement on Advance Notification of Ballistic Missile Tests–brought into effect in 2005, establishment of a Communication Link between Pakistan Maritime Security Agency and Indian Coast Guard–brought into effect in 2005. Both the rail services between Attari and Lahore, and air linkages between the two countries were resumed in 2004. This was followed by the resumption of Samjhauta Express, which runs between Delhi and Lahore in 2005, and the first bus service between Srinagar and Muzaffarbad also started this year. Joint Economic Commissions and Joint Business Councils were reactivated in 2004. Moreover, Foreign Ministers of both countries agreed to a series of Kashmir-specific CBMs to facilitate crossing the LoC in 2008.[38] Nevertheless, the effort did not so far pay-off owing to continuing Pakistan's aggressive attitude toward India and its involvement in Proxy War in J&K and terrorists attacks in rest of India.

The year 2006 witnessed the resumption of peace process when Indian Prime Minister Manmohan Singh met General Musharraf on the sidelines of the Non Aligned summit in Cuba. During the May 2008 foreign ministers and foreign secretaries level talks between India and Pakistan, both sides reviewed the 'composite dialogue' and the 'peace process'. To development closer understanding between the two, they agreed to increase the frequency of movement of people and goods across the border through rail, road and air.[39]

At this critical juncture, the 26/11 Mumbai incidents only aggravated the already not so good relations between India and Pakistan. Since then political understanding between the two countries has come down to a much lower level. Angered by the response of Pakistan, India cancelled any forms of dialogue with Pakistan. This way, the events put a brake to ongoing composite dialogue that is meant for resolving the bilateral problems including the Kashmir issue. This had only strengthened India's position that unless there is a positive response from Pakistan regarding cross border terrorism to India there can be very little hope for a composite dialogue. Pakistan must seriously take the issue and ensure that they are not involved in such activities and that their territory is not used for such illegal activities by the perpetrators. India's positive response to Pakistan demand for peaceful dialogue after the Mumbai events would require Pakistan to take stringent action against those involved in such heinous activities. This would help ensure that India is ready for composite dialogue.[40]

Sensing the need to engage in peaceful dialogue between the two sides, Pakistani Foreign Minister, Shah Mehmood Qureshi has noted that, "We want to...resume dialogue with India because we feel that if we want regional peace, then normal friendly relations between Pakistan and India will play a significant role."[41] The year 2011 provided some breakthrough when the high level meetings between the two sides was held at the level of the secretaries of home, commerce, defence and water resources to sort out the differences. Pakistan responded positively by agreeing to setting up of a judicial commission to visit India for transparent and speedy trial of the 26/11 perpetrators.'[42]

Under pressure from the international community, India-Pakistan peace process has gained momentum since minister-level talks were restarted in early 2011. Since then considerable progress could be seen in India's engagement with Pakistan. In response to New Delhi's decision to export electricity to energy-starved Pakistan, Islamabad had not only allowed Indian officials to visit Pakistan to investigate the 2008 Mumbai terrorist attacks, but also granted most-favoured nation status to India.[43]

Both sides met again on the sideline of 16th NAM summit in Tehran in August 2012 whereby they discussed about the imperative need for CBMs. Pakistani President invited Dr. Singh to visit Pakistan.[44] The political relations between Pakistan and India in the aftermath of 26/11 have been marked with periodic diplomatic efforts along with escalating tensions along the Line of Control (LoC). India's Prime Minister, Narendra Modi invited his Pakistani counterpart Nawaz Sharif at his swearing in ceremony, sending a positive message of the former commitment towards developing cordial relations. Islamabad failed to respond to its successive commitment of putting a brake on terrorist activities along the Kashmir border. To put a pressure to the Pakistan government vis-a-vis cross border terrorism in Kashmir, the present BJP led government has adopted the tough strategy of just not to hold any talks with its counterpart but also isolate Pakistan at regional and global forums. India called off Foreign Secretary level talks with Pakistan in August 2014 which has without any doubt brought a setback to the already patchy relations. Since 2014 to date, the Line of Control (LoC) and Working Boundary have not only remained tense, but also witnessed repeated violations coupled with hostile statements from both sides of the border.[45]

In July 2015, the Prime Minister of both sides met on the sidelines of the Shanghai Cooperation Organisation (SCO) Summit in Ufa. After the meeting, it was announced that both sides would hold bilateral security talks, and also sought their commitment to restart the dialogue process which is the need of hour. The high level talks between India's National Security Advisors Ajit Doval and Sartaj Aziz in August 2015 buckled after the latter invited Kashmiri leaders to consult on the talks. By the end of the year, the National Security Advisors, Doval and Janjua met in Bangkok and the External Affairs Minister Sushma Swaraj met former Prime Minister Nawaz Sharif and Sartaj Aziz. The terrorist attack of Pathankot in January 2016 brought a serious setback to all sort of efforts made earlier for the resumption of the much needed bilateral dialogue. The relationship got further jolt when India blamed Pakistan for its involvement in Uri attack in September 2016.

Diplomatic relations became exacerbated after New Delhi and Islamabad decided to expel diplomatic missions on charges of espionage and declaring persona non grata and asking diplomats to leave within 48 hours.[46]

Given the prolonged conflicts, mutual misunderstanding and suspicion, peace process have suffered setbacks. Effort has been made in the recent past to introduce constructive dialogue process, but couldn't succeed owing to one or the other issue. Thus there is an imperative need for CBMs so that a bridge can be created between them. Experiences of CBMs in other parts of the world reveal that it helped to reduce tensions among states and facilitated the peace processes between them. CBMs are agreements seeking to introduce openness, mutual understanding and communication, designed to reduce the possibility of conflict either through accident, miscalculation or failure of communication; thereby increasing stability in times of crisis.[47]

India-Pakistan Security Relations

Lack of political understanding and the state of the feeling of insecurity among each other has undermined any sort of security relations between the two sides. There are other factors that impinge on security ties are cross-border firing, LoC violations, looming threat of conflict and Pakistan's alleged involvement in cross border terrorism. Besides, the Kashmir dispute, Siachen Glacier issue, Sir Creek and water dispute remain the cause of friction.[48]

India's security relations with Pakistan has over the last many decades been dominated by latter's attempt at seeking to destabilise the security scenario in Kashmir and also in other parts of our country. Despite repeated commitments, the terrorists violence occurs in one way or another in our country. In addition there exists a constant ceasefire violations along the border, have debarred any scope for peaceful security dialogue between the two sides.[49]

Terrorism has been another major issue of concern in

India's bilateral engagement with Pakistan. One of the key challenges India face at present is the one posed by terrorism from beyond its borders. India is seriously challenged by the menace of terrorism in multiple forms for the past many decades. It is facing the most unique, difficult and gruesome faces of terrorism. No other country in the world is so deeply entangled in this problem as India face at present. Eradicating the menace of terrorism poses a serious challenge to international community in general and in particular to India. It has been facing this problem for the last many decades and has lost thousands of innocent lives fighting the menace. Terrorism poses a serious threat not only to peace and security but also hinders economic development of our country.

Pakistan involvement in deteriorating the security scenario in the Kashmir is not new. It offers covert and overt support, backing and giving the direction to the militancy in Jammu and Kashmir. In fact, it is no more secret that the hand of the infamous Inter Services Intelligence (ISI) of Pakistan is behind nearly all the militant and terrorist groups operating in the troubled state of Jammu and Kashmir. The extent of Pakistani involvement is documented by the Task Force on Terrorism and Unconventional Warfare of the House Republican Research Committee, of the United States House of Representatives. In its report dated 1 February 1993, it is mentioned that, "... sponsoring international terrorism and separatist subversion is not new to Pakistan. Since the 1970's, Islamabad has been training Sikh and other Indian separatist movements as part of (former Prime Minister) Z.A. Bhutto's strategy of 'forward strategic depth'." It added that, "Having witnessed the initial impact of the Islamist message in Indian Kashmir, Islamabad began to broaden its horizons and set its sights on bigger goals. Thus in 1986, with growing experience with training, organizing and running the Afghan Mujahedeen and with military supplies available (through the United States, Saudi Arabia and other foreign assistance), Pakistan began expanding its operations to sponsor and promote separatism and terrorism, primarily in Kashmir, as a strategic long term programme."[50] In the Pakistan Frontier Post of 29 May 1991, the noted Pakistani journalist, Mushahid Hussain admits, "The approach which Pakistan has adopted is the 'Afghan Model'; essentially a protracted war, which has made Kashmir a bleeding wound for India."[51] The code name for this operation, christened by Late General Zia-ul-Haque was 'Operation Topac'.[52]

India's main concern has been the terrorist violence which emanates from territory under Pakistan's control. The Ministry of External Affairs in its *Annual Report 1998-1999* has underlined the fact that,

> 'Our concerns regarding Pakistan's continued, and active involvement in instigating and sponsoring terrorism in J&K and other parts of India, were made clear to them on several occasions during the year – and reiterated during the composite dialogue, and conclusive evidence to this effect was also presented. It was emphasised that our resolve to defeat cross-border terrorism and to safeguard our security interests was total. We have advised them that abandonment of this activity, and full respect for their commitments under the Shimla Agreement, including avoidance of provocative acts across the LOC and hostile propaganda, were essential steps.'[53]

India urges Pakistan to act seriously to defeat and stop the alleged extremist infiltrations into Indian territory. While, Pakistan repeatedly denies such charges and holds Indian government itself responsible for its failure to check cross border incursions. Pakistan must seriously take the issue and ensure that they are not involved in such activities and that their territory is not used for such illegal activities by the perpetrators. India has time and again sought a firm and abiding commitment from Pakistan that it will not allow its territory and territory under its control to be used for the aiding and abetting of terrorist activity directed against India and for providing sanctuary to such terrorist groups. India has consistently stressed the need for Pakistan to fulfill its oft-repeated assurances, given to us at the highest level, that territory under its control would not be allowed to be used for anti-India activities in any manner that would seriously threaten our country's national security. It is critical for the security of the region that Pakistan undertakes determined action to dismantle the terrorist networks, organizations and infrastructure within its own territory.[54]

India has time and again accused Pakistan for large scale terrorist attacks in Jammu and Kashmir and in other parts of our country. For instance, India cannot forget the memories of the well planned terrorist attack on the Jammu and Kashmir Assembly complex on 1 October 2001, Indian Parliament attack on 13 December 2001. This was followed by bomb explosion in Mumbai in July 2011 and a similar explosion near the New Delhi High Court in September 2011.[55]

The first meeting of the Indo-Pak joint mechanism to combat terrorism was held in Islamabad on March 2007. But, the significant breakthrough came when Prime Minister Manmohan Singh met Pakistani President Pervez Musharraf in Havana on the sidelines of the NAM summit in September 2006 whereby they agreed to convey information that will help prevent violence and terrorist acts on either side of the border. After years of discussion, Pakistan finally accepted the Indian argument that prevention of terrorists acts alone will not bring any suitable results unless those involved in such acts are punished heavily.[56]

India-Pakistan Relations: Economic Dimension

India and Pakistan are the two largest economies in South Asia which account for 90 per cent of the gross domestic product (GDP) and 85 per cent of the population of the region. Despite the fact, India-Pakistan economic and trade relations has remained so far very limited with neither country falling in the category of top trading partners of each other. This can be reflected from the very fact that as of 2007/8, the share of total trade in goods between the two sides was less than 0.5 percent of their combined trade with the rest of the world. The reasons for the extremely low level of bilateral trade between the two can be attributed to border disputes and political tensions, but also of inward-looking import-substitution growth strategies.[57] The antagonistic relationship between India and Pakistan, have resulted in lack of constructive economic engagement. Despite sharing the 11th longest international border in the world miniscule bilateral trade between India and Pakistan has remained as low as US$ 2.6 billion in 2013. The longest international border share is between the United States and Canada, accounting for 8893 km. The bilateral trade between them is US$ 632 billion (for more details refer to Table 3.1).

Table 3.1

Trade Volume between Neighbouring Countries of the World

Rank	Countries	Border Length (in km)	Trade as of 2013 (in US$ billions)
1	US-Canada	8893	632
2	Russia-Kazakhstan	6846	28.5
5	India-Bangladesh	4096	6.6
6	China-Russia	3645	88
9	China-India	3380	65.8
10	US-Mexico	3141	506.7
11	India-Pakistan	2900	2.6

Source: Chandrani Sarma, "Indo-Pak Trade and Political Balance", *ISAS Insights*, National University of Singapore, No. 271, 21 November 2014, p. 2.

Going by the past and present state of trade exchange between the two sides, it can be observed that both sides have failed to extract the benefit of their constructive economic engagement. With the improvement of bilateral trade, it can be expected that the cross border terrorism and violence would decrease. Since increased trade relations is in the mutual economic benefit of the two. Both sides may have differences over a number of issues but better trade activities can transform their aspect of political relations. Bilateral trade has the potential to not only removing misperceptions but also open up more avenues for cooperation in the long run. To further promote the present level of trade ties, both sides will need to open more trade routes because the current trade volume is much below the desired one.[58]

The performance of trade exchange between India and Pakistan was quite satisfactory in the immediate years after independence. The exports and imports to and from Pakistan was much better than the present scenario. In 1948-49, 56 per cent of Pakistan exports of goods and items went to India which declined to a much low of just 4 per cent in 1958. In 1948-49, 50 per- cent of India's exports of goods and items went to West Pakistan and 80 per- cent to East Pakistan. However, in 2010 it was just one per cent of the total trade of India and little above one per cent for Pakistan. Despite the fact that both countries are bestowed with rich natural resources, raw materials, and possess the same industrial or agricultural basis and are at the same stage of industrialization. One reason for unsatisfactory trade relations can be attributed to the absence of trade agreements between India and Pakistan, the joint ventures. To create a conducive climate for better trade relations, India has extended MFN status to Pakistan way back in 1996, but lack of positive response from Pakistan side has only derailed the prospects. The economic dialogue between the two sides has failed to deliver the much needed results since the 2008 Mumbai terror attack.[59] Despite repeated commitment, Pakistan so far has not granted the MFN status to India which is a serious violation of the SAFTA.[60]

The two-way merchandise trade between India and Pakistan had witnessed a leap from paltry US$250.86 million in 2000-01 to US$2666.13 million in 2010-11 (Refer to Table 3.2). Although, the bilateral trade is yet to reach the actual potential, but the trade volume has increased by more than nine times during the period between the 2000 and 2011. Total trade between the two countries was US$ 1.97 billion in 2011, of which India's exports to Pakistan were US$ 1.66 billion and imports US$ 313 million. Between 2009 to 2012, the average annual rate of growth of imports from Pakistan has been 23 per cent while that of exports has been just nine per cent. In the year 2011, India's top three items of exports to Pakistan are chemicals, textiles and vegetable products accounting for 68 per cent of total exports to Pakistan. While, India's top three items of imports from Pakistan include mineral products, vegetable products and textiles accounting for 59 per cent of total imports.[61]

The main items of export from India to Pakistan are cotton, organic chemicals, food products including prepared animal fodder, vegetables, plastic articles, man-made filament, coffee, tea and spices, dyes, oil seeds, etc. While the main items of import by India from Pakistan comprises of copper and copper articles, fruits and nuts, cotton, salt, sulphur and earths and stones, organic chemicals, mineral fuels, rubber plastic products, wool, etc.

India's share of total Pakistan export has been less than one per cent during the last one decade since the turn of twenty first century. While Pakistan share of India's total export has also remained the same except during the financial year 2006-07 and 2007-08, it was a little over one per cent. The result of such a paltry trade volume is a result of Pakistan government insistence that expanded economic and trade ties would be conditional upon the resolution of the issues over the Kashmir. The current trade volume is almost nothing when the combined population of India and

Pakistan is even more than that of China. This is something both sides should seriously look at and closer cooperation would be mutually beneficial to both countries.

According to a study carried out by Peterson Institute for International Economics (PIIE) using gravity model, the potential of formal trade between India and Pakistan is roughly 20 times larger than what has been recorded at present. This means that at 2008 trade levels total trade (exports plus imports) between India and Pakistan could expand from its current level of a little above US $2 billion to as much US$42 billion if the 'normal' relations estimated by the PIIE gravity model for trading partners were to hold for the two countries. However, achieving a formidable trade volume would require increase political understanding and also there is a need for both to discuss on trade barriers such as high tariff and nontariff barriers, inadequate infrastructure and transportation facility. Once the political understanding and the trade barriers are erased, there are huge scope for economic and trade progress.[62]

The share of top five export items from India to Pakistan accounted for 70 per cent of the total exports (as shown in Table 3.3 and 3.5). While, the share of top five import items from Pakistan to India accounted for 65 per cent of the total exports (as shown in Table 3.4 and 3.6).

The actual potential of bilateral trade between India and Pakistan is yet to materialize. This would require concerted efforts on the part of both countries. From the Pakistan side, it is yet to declare the most favoured nation (MFN) status for India. From the Indian side, it will need to reduce tariff and non-tariff barriers which pose a serious roadblock to the trade exchange. Besides, there are other reasons such as the inadequate transportation facility equipped with patchy railway and road connections and bureaucratic regulations and restrictions. The bilateral trade as the percentage of India's total trade has been decelerated significantly during the recent years.[63]

During the period between 2001-2002 and 2010-2011, the total share of Pakistan in India's total exports has increased from 0.33 per cent to 0.99 per cent. In case of total imports of India, Pakistan's share has marginally declined from 0.13 percent in 2001-2002 to 0.09 percent by 2010-2011. However, when looked at from the SAARC point of view, India's trade with Pakistan has remained far below than other economies of the region.[64]

Table 3.2

India-Pakistan Merchandise Trade From 2000-01 to 2018-19 (Apr-Oct) (in US$ millions)

Year	India's Exports to Pakistan	Growth Rate (%)	India's Imports from Pakistan	Growth Rate (%)	Trade Turnover	Balance
2000-01	186.83	101.01	64.03	-6.14	250.86	122.8
2001-02	144.01	-22.92	64.76	1.14	208.77	79.25
2002-03	206.16	43.16	44.85	-30.74	251.01	161.31
2003-04	286.94	39.18	57.65	28.54	344.59	229.29
2004-05	521.05	81.59	94.97	64.75	616.02	426.08
2005-06	689.23	32.28	179.56	89.06	868.79	509.67
2006-07	1,350.09	95.88	323.62	80.23	1,673.71	1,026.47
2007-08	1,950.53	44.47	287.97	-11.02	2238.5	1,662.56
2008-09	1,439.88	-26.18	370.17	28.54	1,810.05	1,069.71
2009-10	1,573.32	09.27	275.94	-25.45	1,849.26	1,297.38
2010-11	2,039.53	29.63	332.51	20.50	2,666.13	2,081.11
2011-12	1,541.56	-24.42	397.66	19.59		
2012-13	2,064.79	33.94	541.87	36.26		
2013-14	2,274.26	10.15	426.88	-21.22		
2014-15	1,857.18	-18.34	497.31	16.50		
2015-16	2,171.17	16.91	441.03	-11.32		
2016-17	1,821.87	-16.09	454.49	03.05		
2017-18	1,924.28	05.62	488.56	07.50		
2018-19 (Apr-Oct)	1,179.91		338.65			

Source: Export-Import Databank, Directorate General of Foreign Trade, Ministry of Commerce and Industry, Government of India.

India and Pakistan still use tariff and nontariff barriers to protect their domestic producers even after reforms have led to overall economic liberalization. The other trade barriers are related to poor trade logistics and inadequate infrastructure. Besides, there persists a problem of restrictive visa regime.[65] The Pakistan government has time and again expressed unhappiness over the fact that their businessmen face nontariff barriers in reaching to the Indian market. Both sides have in the past expressed readiness to address the perceived barriers as well. During the discussion, it was found that the issue of tariff barriers is a result of a general lack of awareness amongst Pakistani businessmen on the regulatory regimes in India. To further ease the way for better trade exchange, both sides arranged interactive sessions between the Indian regulators and Pakistani businessmen in New Delhi. Followed by another session in Pakistan in January 2012.[66]

Another area where both sides need to focus is on trade diversification. So far the trade relations between the two has been accused for the less diversified export base of Pakistan. This can be reflected from the very fact that almost 60 per cent of its exports are accounted for two products - agricultural and textile items. The same is the case for India's exports too.[67]

Scholars and industry experts from both sides have put forth several recommendations to ease trade. They include travel/visa issues should be made simpler, regulatory framework should be put in place to facilitate investments across the countries etc. In addition, there is also a need for both countries to open more points of trade through the land route.[68] Close economic engagement would benefit both sides. Pakistan in particular would benefit significantly as India offer a lucrative market for Pakistan products. This has been pointed out time and again by various experts and officials from Pakistan. Pakistani Foreign Minister, Hina Rabbani Khar stated in a speech at the Lahore University of Management Sciences (LUMS) that more trade with India would enhance Pakistan's prospects for peace and prosperity, and "put in place the conditions that will enable Pakistan to better pursue its principled positions" on territorial issues.[69]

The South Asia Free Trade Agreement (SAFTA) since July 2006 has opened up the avenues for free trade of goods and services among the South Asian countries, The prolonged politico-security conflict has undermined the development of closer economic ties between New Delhi and Islamabad. Pakistan has refused to extend the negotiated tariff concessions to items beyond the positive list to India, thereby restricting exports only to items on the positive list. Despite the initiation of trade via road on October 2008, the progress of trade is still far behind the satisfactory level. In addition to Srinagar-Muzafarabad and Poonch Ralwalkot routes, triple entry permits for LoC crossings were introduced, with effect from 1 October 2008.[70]

Figure 2 : India's Trade with SAARC Countries

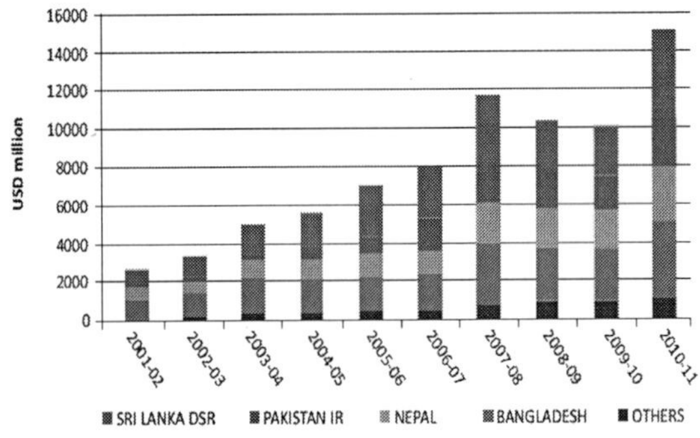

Note: Others include Afghanistan, Bhutan and Maldives.

Source: Loknath Acharya and Ashima Marwaha, "Status Paper on India-Pakistan Economic Relations", prepared by FICCI, February 2012, p. 10.

There was a constant fear among the policy makers of Pakistan that granting the MFN status to India would lead to the flooding of Pakistani markets with Indian goods. In fact, the availability of a large number of Indian goods in Pakistan and vice-versa will increase the competition on both sides of the border and serve the mutual interests of India and Pakistan. India granted MFN status to Pakistan in 1996, but Islamabad was taking time to make a decision on it. To appease Pakistani businesses, India has send a clear message that it will not allow any non-tariff barrier to come in the way of bilateral trade.[71] It was unanimously decided that the two countries will enjoy mutual MFN treatment from January 2013, but failed to materialise owing to political conflict. It is expected that the current government of Pakistan will soon fulfill its promise to grant MFN status given the pressure from business community within the country and international donor agencies.[72]

Between 2004 and 2007, four rounds of trade talks were held between the two countries seeking to strengthen economic ties. In 2008, both sides have agreed to liberalize their visa regime that would facilitate people-to-people contacts. The bilateral trade have benefited out of the composite dialogue. Exchange of goods via bus and train between the two countries have become more routine. Bilateral relations of both countries appeared to be on the course towards normalization. However, the Mumbai Attacks brought the economic engagement to the backburner.[73]

Table 3.3 : Top Five Export Items from India to Pakistan (in US $ millions)

SL. No.	HS Code	Commodity	2012-13	2013-14
1	52	Cotton	471.93	467.30
2	23	Residues And Waste From the Food Industries; Prepared Animal Foder.	293.52	311.78
3	29	Organic Chemicals	273.07	271.55
4	7	Edible Vegetables, Certain Roots and Tubers	144.51	218.68
5	39	Plastic And Articles Thereof	110.73	163.90

Source: Export-Import Databank, Directorate General of Foreign Trade, Ministry of Commerce and Industry, Government of India.

Table 3.4

Top Five Import Items from Pakistan to India (in US $ millions)

SL. No.	HS Code	Commodity	2012-13	2013-14
1	74	Copper And Articles Thereof.	149.53	6.09
2	8	Edible Fruit And Nuts; Peel Or Citrus Fruit Or Melons.	92.55	100.15
3	52	Cotton	60.38	44.03
4	25	Salt; Sulphur; Earths And Stone; Plastering Materials, Lime And Cement	53.54	44.27
5	29	Organic Chemicals	38.90	26.88

Source: Export-Import Databank, Directorate General of Foreign Trade, Ministry of Commerce and Industry, Government of India.

Table 3.5

Top Five Export Items from India to Pakistan (in US $ millions)

SL. No.	HS Code	Commodity	2016-17	2017-18
1	07020000	Tomatoes Fresh or Chilled	55.01	0.05
2	07132000	*Chickpeas (Garbanzos) Dried and Shld	21.68	21.70
3	09024020	Tea Black, Leaf in Bulk	13.68	14.39
4	04021010	Skimmed Milk	11.92	3.79
5	09083110	Large (Amomum)	7.16	4.00

Note: * ITC HS Code of the Commodity is either dropped or re-allocated from April 2018

Source: Export-Import Databank, Directorate General of Foreign Trade, Ministry of Commerce and Industry, Government of India.

Table 3.6

Top Five Import Items from Pakistan to India (in US $ millions)

SL. No.	HS Code	Commodity	2016-17	2017-18
1	08041030	Dry Dates Hard (Chhohara or Kharek)	125.80	111.30
2	28362020	Disodium Carbonate Light	8.04	4.67
3	09109914	Ajwan Seed (Bishop Seed)	5.25	2.63
4	52094200	Denim	4.31	3.42
5	22072000	Ethyl Alchl And Othr Spirits Denaturd of Anystrungth	3.47	2.46

Source: Export-Import Databank, Directorate General of Foreign Trade, Ministry of Commerce and Industry, Government of India.

Economic Engagement in the Post 26/11 Mumbai Attack

Without any doubt, the Mumbai Attacks brought a serious setback to the already not so good economic engagement between the two sides. It further deepen the political misunderstanding which cast a shadow on the economic relations between the two. The confidence building measures and other initiatives for bring a permanent peace prior to 26/11 went in vain. The Indian government took the issue seriously and reacted severely to the incident. It terminated the secretary level talks on important issues related to security, commerce, etc. Relations in the immediate years after the Mumbai attacks, came to the lowest point but after the lapse of three years diplomatic ties in early 2011 were re-established. However, the revival of the bilateral dialogue eased the way for improved trade relations in March 2011. Initiatives were taken by business communities at both sides to restart the trade ties.[74]

Despite efforts to improve the trade ties between the two sides, the series of security events one after another destroyed the prospects of improvement. The Kargil events of 1999 not only slowed down the trade ties but also brought the relations to a historic low between India and Pakistan. Following which the attack on Indian Parliament by the militants supported by Pakistan in December 2001 further widen the gap between them. Besides, the terrorist attack in Mumbai in November 2008 has brought the trade relations to a standstill. Then after a gap of three years, India and Pakistan decided to resume trade by opening an Integrated Check Post at Attari-Wagah border.[75]

India's share of export to Pakistan in India's total exports has been declined to 0.73% during the period 2010-12 from 1.01% during the period 2007-09. While, the share of India's imports from Pakistan in India's total imports has been declined to 0.09% during the financial year 2010-12 from 0.14% during the period 2007-09.[76]

In the aftermath of Mumbai terrorists attack trade exchange has significantly declined owing to political tension. According to Indian Chamber of Commerce and Industry, bilateral trade has decreased by almost 60%. Economic dialogue have been terminated and also that the Businessmen in both countries refuse to travel to each other.[77]

The commerce secretaries of the two countries met in the mid of November 2011 in New Delhi to find the way out to the trade normalization which would ease the trade exchange between the two sides. Both sides have finally agreed to phase out the negative list step by step by the end of 2012.[78] Before doing so, both sides have a Joint Working Group meeting on "Economic and Commercial Cooperation and Trade Promotion" on August 2011 in New Delhi. Followed by a Commerce Minister level talks in September 2011 in New Delhi.

The Pakistan's Commerce Minister visited India after a gap of 35 years between September and October 2011 signifying the political will and commitment to improve economic and commercial relations. The Commerce Ministers express desire to move beyond just normalization of trade to a preferential trading arrangement, under the framework of South Asian Free Trade Agreement (SAFTA). The Ministers agreed to work closely to increase trade from current level of USD 2.7 billion to USD 6 billion. In a very unequivocal message the ministers agreed that "the bilateral trade liberalization process should be uninterruptible and irreversible". The visit was a memorable one as the Pakistan side express their commitment to improve intra-regional connectivity via road, rail, shipping and air.[79]

Both sides will need to understand the very fact that expanding trade relations will be beneficiary to them. In addition to making effort at the bilateral level, both sides must consider using the platform of SAARC to enrich potential benefits of trade and impediments in economic cooperation.[80]

Underlying Key Issues Constraining India-Pakistan Relations

This section of the chapter would discuss the key issues that prevent Pakistan and India from reaching their full potential of bilateral engagement which definitely would have both regional and global significance. There are factors within and outside between India and Pakistan which still impacts their relations, for instance, border issue, terrorism issue, Afghanistan issues, etc. These bilateral issues will not only effect on their present relations but is most likely to have a negative impact on their future relations as well. Besides, it will also affect the process of their rise and the peace and stability in and outside the region.[81]

Afghanistan Issue

Indian interests clash with Pakistan over Afghanistan. India and Pakistan have been vying for strategic influence in Afghanistan. Pakistan is seriously concerned about India all-out effort to expand its strategic influence in Afghanistan post 9/11. India's long-term strategic interests entail the re-establishment of a peaceful, stable and friendly Afghanistan. Taking account of the ground realities, India has effectively pursued proactive diplomacy and has to a large extent been successful to create pro Indian lobbies in Afghanistan. India firmly believes that an unstable and fragile Afghanistan would pose a serious threat to India national security. Pakistan expresses apprehension over the growing Indian involvement in Afghanistan in the socio-economic development and military build-up. This has resulted in close political understanding between New Delhi and Kabul.

Afghanistan is central to India's closer economic and security engagement with Central Asian Republics and Persian Gulf. India is closely working with the international community to bring lasting socio-economic and security stability in Afghanistan which continue to face lots of domestic problems. India seeks to build indigenous Afghan capacity and institutions covering multi-dimensional sectors. Reconstruction work and development programmes have been designed to support the priorities of Afghan government and people. India has made significant investment in mineral, industrial, agricultural and other sectors of Afghanistan to help build sustainable economy.

Pakistan's only ambition in Afghanistan is achieving its long cherished goal of strategic depth, which is in sharp contrast to India's interests of ensuring lasting stable security in Afghanistan. Pakistan wants to see puppet regime such as the Taliban regime in Afghanistan that would work according to their interests. Pakistan believes that if India continues to expand its influence in Afghanistan then it would derail its prospects of gaining strategic depth in Afghanistan. Strategic depth in Afghanistan would give Pakistan an edge to deter India from two fronts. Also, it would seek to use the state of Afghanistan as a launching and training pad for terrorism.

Instead of working sincerely with the NATO forces to restore lasting peace in Afghanistan, Pakistan seeks a strong Taliban in Afghanistan to offset the rising Indian influence there. Pakistan is involved in back door support to Taliban which hold the key to the survival and sustenance of the latter. Pakistan military and Inter Service Intelligence (ISI) believes that their support to Taliban and its associates is central to achieving gaining influence in Afghanistan.[82]

Pakistan has not given up the hope of creating anti-Indian, pro-Pakistan government in Afghanistan for their interests. From the security perspective, Pakistan strongly believes that a strong and Pakistan-friendly government in Afghanistan will result in a secure western border. If there is no friendly government in Afghanistan then it would pose a security threat to Pakistan.[83] Therefore, Pakistan does not want to see India expanding its influence in Afghanistan, which according to Islamabad would help the Kashmir issue to turn in their favour. This is the missing link between the United States and Pakistan that has only favoured Pakistan and a setback for India. It was during the visit to Islamabad by the U.S. Director of Intelligence, Mike McConnel in 2008, a Pakistani General has told that "we must support the Taliban so that there is a government friendly to Pakistan in Kabul. Otherwise India will reign." With such stand it is less likely that Pakistan would take steps sincerely to dismantle Taliban in Afghanistan and Pakistan and al-Qaeda. On the basis of this, Pakistan has criticised India for over involvement in Afghanistan.[84] If Pakistan continues to remain intact with the past stand taken in Afghanistan then it would pose a serious roadblock to restoring peace in the Kabul.

To deceive the international community about its covert intentions, Islamabad has blamed New Delhi's positive intentions in Kabul of trying to destabilize their country and to undermine Pak-Afghan relations. Islamabad strongly believes that long-term Indian presence in Afghanistan would be detrimental to Pakistan's multi-dimensional interests.

Instead what India is doing is good for Pakistan because a stable Afghanistan that does not pose a threat to it would help Pakistan a secure western border. Whatever may be the apprehension raised by Pakistan, the Afghan Government led by Karzai has welcomed India's hard effort in the reconstruction of Afghanistan.[85] Against the interests of Pakistan, the Afghan officials have blamed Pakistan's intelligence agency ISI involvement in aiding and abetting of extremists and terrorists. When Indian embassy in Kabul was attacked on 14 July 2008 Karzai, without wasting time, accused the ISI of being behind the terrorist attacks which rocked Afghanistan and caused heavy casualties and destruction.[86]

Conclusion

India and Pakistan will need to realize the need to reduce the trust deficit that continues to serve as the key roadblock to constructive bilateral engagement. From the geo-strategic, political, economic point of view, it is imperative for both the countries to have close and cordial relations. Establishing cordial relations between these two can contribute a lot in making this strategically important region prosperous.[87] However, it is very difficult to make a prediction of how the relations between India and Pakistan would look alike in the coming years or so. But one thing is sure, for bilateral relations between any two countries to improve, it becomes imperative for a positive response from them. India and Pakistan will need to first change the perception about each other as strategic rival. In doing so, Pakistan has to change track on its 'Kashmir first' policy and shifting gear to a process of building co–operation and confidence in other areas. Similarly, India too, has to show a big brotherly attitude and offer some liberal concessions to the Pakistan without compromising any security needs. Such a positive attitude will reduce tension and ease the way for cordial relationship between the two countries. Ayesha Siddiqa, a well-known scholar from Pakistan has very rightly pointed out two factors which hinder the prospect for peace between India and Pakistan – first, outstanding political/territorial disputes between the two countries; and second, historical perceptions of each other, especially Pakistan's perception of India.[88]

The two countries have maintained a patchy ceasefire over the LoC in Kashmir since 2003. Current spate of ceasefire violations began in January, 2013; by the close of year such incident could be around 200, far exceeding last year's total of 117. Things came to a crisis situation is September, 2013 when, just short of high-profile talks between Nawaz Sharif and Manmohan Singh on the sidelines of 68th UNGA session, militants of unknown identity killed eight Indian security personnel and a civilian. The attack was deliberately timed, and follows a pattern of attempts by vested interests to frustrate the bilateral peace process. Dr. Singh, despite domestic electoral compulsions, could not be provoked to the level of calling off the talks. However, the bilateral was grossly de-scaled…from a breakfast meeting to a display of glass of water. Narendra Modi, the BJP's prime ministerial candidate, had advised Dr. Singh to skip his meeting with Nawaz Sharif.[89] Pakistan and India are neighbouring countries whose future is entwined and dependent upon each other. It is up to the two countries to find a way that leads to peace and prosperity of not only the two countries but also of the region.

It can also be observed that trade relations between the two sides are largely influenced by political, security and strategic factors. The trade volumes between them would largely depend on erasing barriers to trade such as tariffs and non tariffs barriers and the quality and quantity of trade-related infrastructure.[90]

References

1. K.S. Sidhu, "Sino-Indian Relations in the Context of South

Asia", in Sanjay Kumar and Dhirendra Dwivedi (eds.), India-China: Conflict or Cooperation (New Delhi: Pentagon Press, 2015), p. 131.

2. Amitabh Mattoo, "Shadow of the Dragon: Indo-US Relations and China", in Garry K. Bertsch, et. al., (eds.), Engaging India: US Strategic Relations with the World's Largest Democracies (New York: Routledge, 1999), pp. 219-20.

3. Inder Gujral statement on India-Pakistan relations has been quoted from David Scott, "India's Relations with Pakistan", in David Scott (ed.), Handbook of India's International Relations (London and New York: Routledge, 2011), p. 59.

4. Veena Kukraja, "India-Pakistan Relations: The Contemporary Phase", in Mohammed Badrul Alam (ed.), Contours of India's Foreign Policy: Changes and Challenges (New Delhi: Reference Press, 2014), pp. 253-54.

5. Gulshan Majeed, "South Asian Security Compulsions: A Historical Analysis of India-Pakistan Relations", Journal of Political Studies (Lahore), Vol. 20, No. 1, 2013, pp. 219-21.

6. Aymen Ijaz, "Pakistan-India Relations Under Prime Minister Modi's Government (2014-2016)", Journal of Current Affairs, Islamabad, Vol. 2, No. 1, 2017, p. 75.

7. Sanjeet Kumar, "Indo-Pak Relations in the Twenty First Century", Ph. D Thesis Submitted to the Department of Political Science, Central University of Haryana, Mahendergarh, Haryana, August 2014, p. 4.

8. Ibid., p. 10.

9. Sachinkumar Manikrao, "Areas of Contestation and Debate between India and Pakistan: A Critical Study", Ph. D Thesis Submitted to the Department of Political Science, Sahyadri Arts College, Kuvempu University, Karnataka, 2014, pp. 42.

10. Ibid., p. 79.

11. Ibid., p. 45.

12. Ibid., pp. 48-9.
13. Asif Ahmed, "An Analysis of India-Pakistan Relations From Past to Present - Strategic Implications for India", Suraksha Chintan, Vol. 3, No. 3, July 2011, pp. 91-2.
14. Sanjeet Kumar, n. 7, p. 9.
15. N. P. Singh and R. S. Rawat, "Future of Indo-Pakistan Relations", Suraksha Chintan, Vol. 3, No. 3, July 2011, p. 26.
16. Asif Ahmed, n. 13, pp. 92-3.
17. Ram Kumar, "Indo-Pak Relations in the Post Cold War Era", Ph. D Thesis Submitted to the Department of Political Science, Himachal Pradesh University, Shimla, 2012, p. 139.
18. Ibid., p. 140.
19. Asif Ahmed, op cit., pp. 93-4.
20. Sanjeet Kumar, op cit., p. 45.
21. Ram Kumar, op cit., p. 141.
22. Sachinkumar Manikrao, op cit, p. 4
23. Sanjeet Kumar, op cit., pp. 45-6.
24. Ram Kumar, op cit., pp. 144-45.
25. Ibid., p. 147.
26. Ibid., pp. 147-48.
27. Sachinkumar Manikrao, n. 9, pp. 4-5.
28. Ibid., pp. 149-50.
29. Ibid., p. 6.
30. Ashutosh Misra, "India-Pakistan Peace Process: Gathering Momentum", in S.D. Muni, (ed.), IDSA Asian Strategic Review 2007 (New Delhi: Academic Foundation, 2008), p. 79.
31. Hilary Synnott, Transforming Pakistan: Ways Out of Instability (London: Routledge, 2009), pp. 143-44.
32. Sachinkumar Manikrao, op cit., p. 7.

33. Ram Kumar, op cit., p. 159.
34. Sanjeet Kumar, op cit., p. 6.
35. Zareen F. Naqvi, "Pakistan-India Trade Potential and Issues", The Lahore Journal of Economics, September 2009, pp. 184-85.
36. Kalim Bahadur, "India-Pakistan Relations", in V.D. Chopra (ed.), India's Foreign Policy in the 21st Century (New Delhi: Kalpaz Publications, 2006), p. 151.

37 Sanjeet Kumar, op cit., pp. 6-7.

38. Samarjit Ghosh, "Two Decades of Indo-Pak CBMs: A Critique from India", IPCS Issue Brief 132, September 2009, pp. 1-2.
39. Sanjeet Kumar, op cit., p. 56.
40. Hilary Synnott, n. 31, pp. 139-41.
41. This statement was found quoted in Mushtaq A. Kaw, " Border Politics in South Asia: A Case Study of India, Pakistan and Afghanistan", Eurasia Border Review Part II, p. 55
42. Ram Kumar, op cit., p. 183.
43. Michael Kugelman, "The Long and Rocky Road to India-Pakistan Rapprochement", NOREF Expert Analysis, Norwegian Peacebuilding Resource Centre, October 2012.
44. Sanjeet Kumar, op cit., p. 58.
45. Aymen Ijaz, n. 6, p. 84.
46. Ibid., pp. 85-6.
47. Surender Singh, "India-Pakistan Peace Process: Problems and Prospects of Confidence Building Measures (CBMs)", Ph. D Thesis Submitted to the Department of Political Science, Kurukshetra University, Kurukshetra, 2015, pp. 2-3.
48. Aymen Ijaz, op cit., p. 86.
49. Happymon Jacob, "China, India, Pakistan and a Stable Regional Order", in Francois Godement (ed.), What Does

India Think (London: European Council on Foreign Relations, 2015), p. 91.

50. Salman Khurshid, Beyond Terrorism: New Hope for Kashmir (New Delhi: UBS Publishers, 1994).

51. Ibid, p. 69.

52. KK Nanda, Conquering Kashmir - A Pakistani Obsession (New Delhi, Lancer Publications, 1994), p. 300.

53. Annual Report 1998-1999, Ministry of External Affairs, Government of India.

54. Refer to, "India-Pakistan Relations", Ministry of External Affairs, Government of India, April 2014, available at <*http://www.mea.gov.in/Portal/ForeignRelation/Pakistan_April2014.pdf*>.

55. Veena Kukraja, n. 4, pp. 256-57 and 267.

56. Ram Kumar, op cit., pp. 167-68.

57. Zareen F. Naqvi, n. 35, pp. 171-72.

58. Muhammad Ali, et al., "Pakistan-India Relations: Peace through Bilateral Trade", Developing Country Studies, Vol. 5, No. 2, 2015, p. 85.

59. Muhammad Imran Mehsud, "Liberalism in India-Pakistan Relations: A Critique of Realism", Cambridge Journal of China Studies, Vol. 12, No. 1, p. 73.

60. M. Umar Farooq Baloch, "Prospects for Sustained Economic Cooperation between India and Pakistan", Institute for Strategic Studies, Research and Analysis (ISSRA) Papers, National Defence University, Islamabad, 2015, p. 3.

61. Sanjeet Kumar, op cit., p. 114.

62. Mohsin S. Khan, Improving India-Pakistan Relations through Trade", East Asia Forum, available at <*http://www.eastasiaforum.org/2010/04/19/improving-india-pakistan-relations-through-trade/*>.

63. See, 'India-Pakistan Bilateral Trade: Past, Present and

Future", Study conducted by PHD Research Bureau, PHD Chamber of Commerce and Industry, New- Delhi, February 2013, p. 3.

64. Loknath Acharya and Ashima Marwaha, "Status Paper on India-Pakistan Economic Relations", Prepared by FICCI, February 2012, p. 9.
65. Zareen F. Naqvi, op cit., pp. 187-89.
66. Sanjeet Kumar, op cit., p. 129.
67. M. Umar Farooq Baloch, op cit., p. 5.
68. Chandrani Sarma, "Indo-Pak Trade and Political Balance", ISAS Insights, National University of Singapore, No. 271, 21 November 2014, pp. 7-8.
69. This statement has been quoted from Michael Kugelman, "The Pakistan-India Trade Relationship: Prospects, Profits and Pitfalls", in Michael Kugelman and Robert M. Hathaway (eds.), Pakistan-India Trade: What Needs to be Done? What Does it Matter? (Washington, D.C.: Woodrow Wilson International Center for Scholars' Asia Program and the Fellowship Fund for Pakistan, 2013), p. 2.
70. Ram Kumar, op cit., p. 185.
71. Ibid., p. 186.
72. M. Umar Farooq Baloch, op cit., pp. 10-11.
73. Muhammad Ali, n. 58, p. 84.
74. Muhammad Ali, op cit., p. 84.
75. Kishore C. Dash and Robert K. McCleery, "The Political Economy of Trade Relations between India-Pakistan", Journal of Economic and Financial Studies, Vol. 2, No. 2, April 2014, p. 32.
76. See, 'India-Pakistan Bilateral Trade: Past, Present and Future", Study conducted by PHD Research Bureau, PHD Chamber of Commerce and Industry, New- Delhi, February 2013, p. 4.

77. Ayesha Kiran, "Is International Trade Reduces the External Conflicts? Case Study of Pakistan and India", International Journal of Economics and Management Sciences, Vol. 7, No. 1, 2018, p. 4.
78. Zafar Mahmood, "Moving Toward Pakistan-India Trade Normalisation: An Overview", Michael Kugelman and Robert M. Hathaway (eds.), Pakistan-India Trade: What Needs to be Done and What Does it Matter? (Washington, DC: Woodrow Wilson International Center for Scholars, 2013), p. 25.
79. Loknath Acharya and Ashima Marwaha, "Status Paper on India-Pakistan Economic Relations", prepared by FICCI, February 2012, p. 13.
80. M. Umar Farooq Baloch, op cit., p. 16.
81. Bashir Ahmad Dar, "Major Bilateral Issues between China and India", Arts and Social Sciences Journal, Vol. 5, No. 1, 2014, p. 1.
82. Vinod Anand, "Military Aspects AF-Pak Situation: An Appraisal", in Klaus Lange, Klara Knapp and J P Panda (eds.), Revisiting Contemporary South Asia: Politics, Economics and Security (New Delhi: Pentagon Press, 2012), pp. 95-6.
83. Abdul Sattar, Afghanistan: Past, Present and Future, From Jihad to Civil War (Islamabad: The Institute of Regional Studies, 1997), pp. 462-63.
84. Selig Harrison, "From Kabul to Kashmir", Indian Express (Pune), 20 November 2009 and Fareed Zakaria, "The Prize is India", Indian Express (Pune), 23 November 2009.
85. Zahid Ali Khan, "Post 9/11 Development of Indo-Afghan Ties: Pakistan's Concerns and Policy Options", Regional Studies (Islamabad), Vol. XXXI, No. 1, Winter 2012-13, pp. 80-95.
86. Safdar Hussain and Muhammad Ijaz Latif, "Issues and Challenges in Pakistan-Afghanistan Relations after 9/11", South Asian Studies, Vol. 27, No. 1, January-June 2012, p. 92.
87. Safdar Hussain and Muhammad Ijaz Latif, n. 30, p. 97.

88. Ayesha Siddiqa, India-Pakistan Relations: Confrontation to Conciliation (Islamabad: Centre for Democratic Governance, 2004), p. 1.
89. Khalid Iqbal, "Pakistan's Relations with India Since 9/11: A Pakistani Perspective", FPRC Country Specific Studies on Pakistan, New Delhi, Vol. 2, p. 75-6.
90. Kishore C. Dash and Robert K. McCleery, "The Political Economy of Trade Relations between India-Pakistan", Journal of Economic and Financial Studies, Vol. 2, No. 2, April 2014, pp. 26-27.

4

Kashmir and India-China

The present chapter analyses the critical role and the increasing influence of China both in Indian Administered Kashmir and Pakistan administered Kashmir. It would also highlight Chinese interests in Kashmir and its policy approach towards the Kashmir dispute that has remained the bone of contention between India and Pakistan. Further, the chapter discusses the emerging strategic relations between Pakistan and China. It also makes an assessment of the growing Chinese influence in Pakistan occupied Kashmir (PoK) in the recent past and its security concerns for India.

Kashmir is a region where India, China, and Pakistan all have territorial claims.[1] China's role and involvement in Kashmir issue is getting complicated with every passing years. China has over the years developed keen strategic interests in the Kashmir dispute between India and Pakistan. In fact, it is quite well known that the occupation of Kashmir is divided amidst three states, India, Pakistan, and China. As against the general understanding that Kashmir problem is related to India and Pakistan, but China is equally a part of the problem. It is due to the fact that China at present occupies 42,685 sq. kms of Jammu and Kashmir.[2]

Beijing's interests lies in both Indian occupied Kashmir as well as Pakistan occupied Kashmir (PoK). Given the rich natural resources present in Kashmir, Beijing seeks the exploitation of rich resources particularly energy and also to upset India's military superiority over the arch rival Pakistan.[3] Chinese interests and involvement in Kashmir will definitely have spill over implications on India from the short to the long-term perspective.

The state of Jammu and Kashmir at the time when India got independent from British had a total area of about 2,22,236 sq. Km. However, in 1949 when a cease fire line was drawn, Pakistan went on to occupy about one third of the area i.e. 78932 sq. km (comprising of the whole of Gilgit, Mirpur, Kotli and a part of Poonch). In the post 1962 war with India, China occupied about 64000 sq. kms in Ladakh known as Aksai Chin. Besides, 5,180 sq. km. of Jammu and Kashmir was illegally ceded to China by Pakistan under the March 1963 Sino-Pak Boundary agreement. As of now, only 101,437 sq. km is with India. China deny Aksai Chin to be a part of Kashmir.[4]

By virtue of the occupation of one-fifth of territory, China shares border with Kashmir.[5] Chinese interests in Kashmir have started to flourish in the post 1962 war. Since then, China has been calling for self-determination in Kashmir. Such a China's policy has to be seen in the context of Pakistan's continued relevance in China's strategic calculus in South Asia. China shares positive sentiments with Kashmiri people[6] By refusing to issue visa to Lt. Gen B S Jaswal serving in Indian Occupied Kashmir, Beijing has sent a clear message that Kashmir is a disputed territory left over from history. China invested heavily on energy and power generation projects on both sides of Azad Jammu and Kashmir and in Gilgit-Baltistan region. If on the one side China refused to accept Indian side of Kashmir, then, on the other side, it is continued to be actively involved in Pakistan occupied Kashmir.[7] In fact, prior to official meeting between India's Prime Minister Manmohan Singh and his Chinese counterpart Wen Jiabao in Hanoi on 29 October 2010, China's Foreign Ministry Spokesperson Ma Zhaoxu has affirmed that, "China's visa policy toward residents of the India-held Kashmir is consistent and remains unchanged."[8]

China looms large on India's unfriendly relations with Pakistan. It seeks to exploit the lack of political misunderstanding between the two South Asian neighbours to its advantage. Seeing the security scenario in the South Asian region, China has improved engagement with Pakistan thereby making strategic and economic investments in the latter. The idea is to keep the common enemy under strategic pressure for strategic purpose.[9] The last one decade has seen India gaining significant weight on the international stage by virtue of its growing economic and military prowess, which is never in the interests of China and Pakistan. Pakistan and China share a very strong desire to halt India's progress in this direction. In fact, India has been the main factor that has influenced China and Pakistan policies toward each other. The two sides have a close understanding on the need to enhance strategic coordination, advance pragmatic cooperation and work together to meet challenges in pursuit of common development. Pakistan in particular viewed India as a potential challenger leading to use China to counter Indian power in the region.

The close strategic partnership between the two countries has been based on the principles of mutual respect, mutual trust and mutual benefit. Pakistan's search for a country that can help sustain a sufficient military capacity for itself against India coalesces with China's intention that "a militarily strong Pakistan would serve their objective of keeping India preoccupied on two fronts, thereby safeguard their national security interests."[10]

Beijing is fuelling that arms race between the two South Asian rivals. It has in the past and even today helped Pakistan maintain conventional military balance between India and Pakistan by equipping the latter with JF-17 aircraft and JF-17 production facilities, F-22P frigates with helicopters, K-8 jet trainers, T-85 tanks, F-7 aircraft, small arms and ammunition. It has also built a turnkey ballistic missile manufacturing facility near Rawalpindi and helped Pakistan develop the 750-km-range, solid-fuel Shaheen-1 ballistic missile.[11] China's strategy of providing advanced arms and equipment requirements for Pakistan will continue to remain a case of serious national security concerns for India. Pakistan continues to be the major beneficiary of China's unending support to acquire nuclear materials and technology. Arms-control analysts, Gary Milhollin has very rightly pointed out that,

> "If you subtract China's help from Pakistan's nuclear program, there is no nuclear program."[12]

In the same line, another strategic affairs analysts, Robert Ross is of the perception that,

> "China continues its support for Pakistan by supplying nuclear and missile technology because China views a credible Pakistani deterrent as the most effective way to guarantee the security of its sole ally in Southern Asia against Indian power."[13]

The chapter argues that although relations between China and Pakistan may be getting stronger, but when it comes to Kashmir dispute between India and Pakistan, China is never interested in the resolution of one of the oldest disputes that exists in the world today. China's interest lies in keeping the issue intact so that India, its strategic rivalry is tied down in a long-term rivalry with Pakistan.[14]

Map 4.1

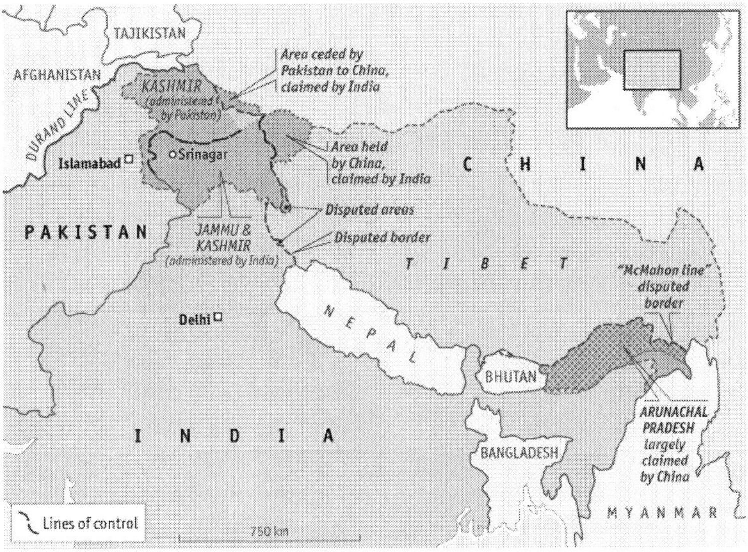

In response to China's stance on Jammu and Kashmir, Pakistan has allowed China's People's Liberation Army (PLA) to enter into Pakistan-controlled Kashmir. Lt Gen KT Parnaik, heading the Northern Command has warned that China's military presence in Pakistan-controlled Kashmir was too close for India's comfort. "It poses military challenges to India and not only along the Sino-Indian border but also along the LoC." He further added that "We hear many people who are concerned about the fact that if there were to be hostilities between us and Pakistan what would be the complicity of the Chinese. Not only because they are in the neighbourhood but the fact that they are actually stationed and present on the LoC." Besides, "The Chinese Links with Pakistan through PoK lend strength to the China-Pakistan nexus which has been of great security concern for us. It jeopardises our regional and strategic interest in the long run...the Chinese footprints are too close for comfort."[15]

The present chapter seeks to make a critical analysis

on the role and influence of China in Kashmir. The last over five decades has seen change and continuity in Beijing's policy approach towards the Kashmir dispute between India and Pakistan. It would also throw light on the more recent developments. In doing so, the chapter seeks to answer for these questions – What is China's interests in Kashmir from a long-term perspective? How does China view the Kashmir conflict? What would be the possible implications to India's sovereignty on Kashmir vis-à-vis Chinese involvement in Indian state of Jammu and Kashmir?

Geo-Strategic Significance of Kashmir for China

China's role and involvement in Kashmir has not occurred in vacuum. The geo-strategic significance of Kashmir has without any doubt attracted the attention of China towards it. One of the key distinctive feature of Kashmir is its geo-strategic location. The very location of Kashmir give China economic and strategic advantage over its long-term strategic rival India. Silk Route holds immense significance for China for it helps to maintain dominant military position over India. Silk Route connects China with Pakistan and passes through Kashmir. Through Gilgit, China can infiltrate deep into the Kashmir valley of our country. Besides Gilgit, China and Pakistan together can pose a serious threat to the security of our country via Siachen Glacier.[16]

Another significance for Kashmir lies in the fact that it shares borders with Afghanistan, a country which acts as a bridge between South Asia and Central Asia.[17]

China's Kashmir Policy: Historical Perspective

It is quite pertinent to understand the factors that shaped the China's Kashmir policy in the past decades prior to post cold war era. According to B. Raman, China's Kashmir policy has been consistent with a change in its stance on Indian-held Kashmir. It has diluted its past acceptance of Jammu and Kashmir as a de facto part of India.[18]

In the immediate years of the independence of India and Pakistan, Chinese stance has been neutral. It hesitated to taking side between India and Pakistan over Kashmir issue. Chinese hesitation were further strengthened when Pakistan joined western alliances. By remaining neutral, Chinese Premier had in 1957 gave a statement that both sides should resolve the issue bilaterally through peaceful means.[19]

The situation in which India's relations with China was at its historic low in the 1960s, Chinese leaders and people were supportive to the Kashmiri people in their claim for right to self- determination. In a piece that was published in the People's Daily on 5 September 1965, it was highlighted that,

> "...the Chinese people deeply sympathize with the just struggle of the people of Kashmir for their right to self-determination... the Chinese government and people... resolutely support... the Kashmir people's struggle for national self determination... the Kashmir people will surely realize their desire for national self-determination."[20]

The Sino-Indian war of 1962 brought about a shift in Chinese policy towards the Kashmir issue. In the post Sino-Indian war, there witnessed a perceptible shift in the Chinese position from maintaining neutral to inclination towards Pakistan's position on the Kashmir issue. This was the time when the relations between India and China started to deteriorate. Beijing supported Islamabad's position on the Kashmir issue to demonstrate solidarity with an "all weather" ally during periods of Sino-Indian estrangement and hostility.

During the visit to Pakistan in 1964, China's Prime Minister Zhou Enlai declared its commitment to support for the resolution of Kashmir dispute in accordance with the wishes of people of Kashmir as pledged to them by India and Pakistan. The very next year, President Ayub visited China and entered into a joint statement that declares the support for self-determination of Kashmiri people. In a message received from China on 16 September 1965, it is clearly mentioned that the Kashmir dispute between India and Pakistan should be settled on the basis of respect for Kashmiri people's right of self determination, as pledged by both countries. It is also stated that by China's non-involvement in the Kashmir dispute between India and Pakistan would mean allowing both sides to peacefully resolving the problem. But, non-involvement absolutely doesn't mean failure to distinguish between right and wrong; it absolutely does not mean that China can approve of depriving the Kashmiri people of their right of self determination.

Till the early 1980s, China's Kashmir policy has seen constant call for the right of self-determination for Kashmir people.[21] However, with China seeking to maintain close relations with India for the mutual benefit, Beijing seems to have changed its mind. And as the relations with India got normalised, China shifted its approach from a policy of inclination to neutrality to avoid needless alienation of India, coupled with running the risk of entrapment. For that matter, the Chinese policy got reflected in Deng Xiaoping's June 1980 statement that, "... Kashmir ... was a bilateral issue left over from history between India and Pakistan, and should be resolved peacefully..." This carried forward to the decade of the early 1990s, when China's position became unequivocal that the Kashmir issue is a bilateral matter.[22]

In the past, Pakistan took Chinese protection on the issue of Kashmir, be it in UN or giving moral support. However in the early 90's there was a change in Chinese approach, when it advocated peaceful negotiations between the two sides over the Kashmir dispute.[23] The major concern for Pakistan is in regard to China adopting a neutral position on Kashmir.[24] During Chinese President Jiang Zemin visit to India and Pakistan in late 1996, he advocated a direct dialogue between the two countries on Kashmir as well as progress towards better bilateral relations.[25] Speaking at a press conference, Mr. Zhu, said, 'China had neither any intention nor will it play any mediatory role between the two countries.'[26] Seeking to maintain a balance between India and Pakistan, Chinese Premier, Zhou Enlai had in an interview stated that, "We were on friendly terms with India; we took an attitude of non-involvement in the Kashmir issue. We... hope that India and Pakistan would settle the Kashmir issue and other problems in a friendly manner, with Pakistan. Despite, friendly terms with Pakistan, we have not given up our desire for friendship with India."[27] The neutral stand taken by China on the Kashmir issue is a result of the fear psychosis of spill over implications of ongoing terrorist violence in Kashmir into its Muslim dominated province of Xinjiang.[28]

China's Kashmir Policy in the 21st Century

From the beginning of the Kashmir problem to the end of twentieth century, China's Kashmir policy have seen four different forms. The decade of 1950s saw China remained neutral, but, the following decades of 1960s to 1970s, witnessed inclination towards Pakistan's position over Kashmir issue owing to the unhealthy relations between India and China. However, by 1980s, the policy of China return to the previous position of neutrality due to normalization in China-India relations. In the post Cold War period it changed its position and said that Kashmir is a bilateral issue between India and Pakistan and it should be resolved through peaceful means.

China's Ministry of Foreign Affairs had in 2002 declared its official position on Kashmir issue that,

"China's position on the issue of Kashmir has been clear cut. We have always maintained that the Kashmir issue is one between India and Pakistan left over by history. China hopes that the two sides should seek new ways to appropriately solve the problem through peaceful exchanges and negotiations and refrain from military conflicts".[29]

In regard to China's stand on Kashmir and the expanding relations between China and Pakistan, John Garver, has very rightly said that, from the very beginning, China started supporting the Kashmiri people's war of self-determination, a support that was translated in the following years to material support to launch an insurgency inside the state of Jammu and Kashmir (Jammu and Kashmir).[30]

China's involvement in Kashmir is getting stronger and deeper with every passing years. China's sympathy for Pakistan over the Kashmir issue, and for secessionists in the territory itself, are extremely unwelcome for India. China's Kashmir policy has to be seen within the broader contexts of its South Asia policy. It has adopted a policy seeking to serve its regional and global interests. On the Kashmir issue, seeing the nature of engagement and the understanding it has with both Islamabad and New Delhi, Beijing has supported the former's positions to demonstrate solidarity with it. India's long-term strategic rivalry with both China and Pakistan really influenced Beijing to be supportive towards Islamabad in its dealing with new Delhi over the Kashmir issue. However, when relations with New Delhi gets normalized, Beijing adopted a policy of neutrality to avoid unnecessarily alienating India and running the risk of entrapment.[31] Overall, China's policy towards Kashmir has ranged between support to Islamabad and maintaining neutrality between the two South Asian rivals.

By virtue of the fact that China shares border with Kashmir, the policy adopted has in one way or another supported the case of Pakistan in Kashmir. China's generous support is based on the rationale that a strong Pakistan in the region of South Asia which is of no threat to Beijing but is necessary to balance India from the long-term point of view. China shares some sentiments with Kashmiri people.

As part of its evolving policy, China invited Mirwaiz Umer Farooq, the president of All-Parties Hurriyat Conference in 2009 to showcase its support for the people of Kashmir. To further make the matter really worse, Beijing has invested billions of dollars on different energy and power generation projects on both sides of Azad Jammu and Kashmir and similarly in Gilgit-Baltistan region. While, on the other side, it has refused to accept Indian control of Kashmir and considers it as disputed territory.[32]

For strategic reasons, China has so far maintained that Kashmir is a disputed territory between India and Pakistan and rejects Indian claim over Kashmir as an integral part of it. There witnessed change and continuity in Beijing's policy towards Kashmir from time to time and offered different methods of resolving it. Under the so-called China's Kashmir policy, Beijing offer military assistance to Pakistan in its dealing with India which also serves its long-term interests of containing New Delhi from gaining international leverage.

Chinese Involvement in Pakistan Occupied Kashmir (PoK): Security and Strategic Concerns for India

Pakistan occupied Kashmir (PoK) comprised of both Azad Jammu and Kashmir and Gilgit-Baltistan. India's official stand has been made clear to the Pakistanis and the international community that PoK is part of the state of Jammu and Kashmir (Jammu and Kashmir), and hence an integral part of India. It has been under the illegitimate control of Pakistan since 22 October 1947.[33] The geo-political and geo-strategic significance of PoK has increased manifold after the establishment of the Karakoram highway (KKH) that connect Pakistan with China via PoK. What makes PoK really significant for China can be reflected from the fact that it shares border with Xinjiang province of the People's Republic of China to the north.[34] The KKH offers tremendous opportunities for both countries in terms of trade and transfer of arms and equipment needs including nuclear and missile material from China to Pakistan.[35]

From the Islamabad point of view, China is the most reliable and capable partners to dealing with the threat of India. Chinese involvement in PoK is quite usual when the former provide the necessary support to the latter's need whether it may be in the case of Kashmir or providing arms and equipment needs to deal with a much stronger Indian side.

Whatever may be the reasons, the Chinese presence in PoK has opened a new chapter to the prolonged strategic rivalry between India and Pakistan over the state of Jammu and Kashmir. The growing Chinese presence in the region is a case of serious concerns for our country.[36] In 2009 and 2010, India responded sharply to reports of the presence of Chinese soldiers and workers in the region. India's External Affairs Minister, Sushma Swaraj had termed the CPEC project "unacceptable" for it pass through PoK. National Security Advisor Ajit Doval raised eyebrows when he reminded an audience of BSF officers to factor in 106-km-long non-contiguous border with Afghanistan in a clear reference to Gilgit-Baltistan's Afghan frontier. She has unequivocally emphasised that entire state of J & K including Gilgit-Baltistan as an integral part of India in recent press releases. With the recent up-gradation of Karakorum Highway through Gilgit-Baltistan, the collousivity of China and Pakistan and likelihood of two front war especially along PoK and Aksai Chin increases.

The vast improvement in communication infrastructure especially in Giligit-Baltistan will enable Pakistan to sidestep forces in a much faster rate and quantum compared to India, hampered by external and poorly developed lines-of-communication. This implies that Pakistan will effectively be able to increase force-ratios in theatres to her advantage in a much reduced timeframe.[37]

By way of increasing its influence in Pakistan occupied Kashmir, China desires to secure access to the Arabian Sea and Indian Ocean. This would hold the key for its commercial, energy, and military supplies with other countries via the CPEC corridor. Gaining foothold in PoK would bring Chinese naval forces close to India's south-western waters that can prove to be effective in times of crisis with India. That's the reason why India's Ambassador to China, Gautam Bambawale has said that the CPEC corridor 'violates our territorial integrity.' Most importantly, the CPEC project undermines Indian sovereignty as it passes through a Pakistan-administered part of Kashmir.[38]

India expressed deep concern and reservation over the US$42 billion China-Pakistan Economic Corridor (CPEC) which passes through Pak-Occupied Kashmir.[39] China's growing involvement in PoK through the CPEC not only pose setback to India's sovereign claim over PoK, but, also, its role and presence distorts the balance of position in the dispute.[40] However, against the rising voice of India, China has compared its developments effort in PoK to that of India's developmental projects in Arunachal Pradesh, which according to the former is not part of India. China in cooperation with Pakistan is undergoing the transit and transport project that passes through PoK. They are of the argument that if India can carry out all sort of political, economic and military developmental projects in Arunachal Pradesh, China can do the same in PoK.[41]

The matter of concern for India is that China in the name of development efforts in PoK is carrying out its military activities in the region. Beijing has stationed its PLA troops in the region, and in particular to the 772-km-long Line of Control (LoC) running between India and Pakistan. Besides, it is also being reported that a unit of PLA soldiers is placed near the Khunjerab Pass with the negative intent of establishing its military edge in India's northern sector is pretty clear.[42] Pakistan welcomed Chinese involvement in the infrastructure and development activities in the region which serve Beijing interests of putting a pressure on India. On the other hand, by way of opening to China, Pakistan seeks to capitalize on it to counterbalance India in a crisis situation with India.[43]

India's External Affairs Minister, Sushma Swaraj had stated in response to a question raised in Lok Sabha in December 2014 that,

> '... Government has seen reports with regard to China and Pakistan being involved in infrastructure building activities in Pakistan Occupied Kashmir (POK), including construction of China-Pakistan Economic Corridor. Government has conveyed its concerns to China about their activities in Pakistan Occupied Kashmir, and asked them to cease such activities.'[44]

China-Pakistan Engagement: Historical Perspective

Pakistan's decision to develop close relations with China was influenced by the former's self-interest because 'in view of Pakistan sponsored militancy in India and passive hostility of the Afghan Government, Pakistan doesn't want another great neighbour to be its enemy. Until the late 1950s, Pakistan's relations with China was nothing special. However, with the Sino-Indian relations started declining in 1959, Pakistan was driven closer to Beijing. The Sino-Indian War proved a watershed in the Sino-Pakistan relations. In the aftermath of 1962 war, Pakistan was convinced that split between New Delhi and Beijing had come full circle. Hence the circumstances allowed 'Enemy's enemy is my friend' to perpetuate as the mode of discourse and decks cleared for future Sino-Pakistani entente-cordiale. Taking advantage of this discourse, Pakistan under a border agreement on 2 March 1963 ceded a portion of "Azad Kashmir" to China. India protested to both China and Pakistan stating its position that it would not agree to any arrangements or agreements on Indian territory which was under 'illegal occupation of Pakistan.' The Indian Government alleged that Pakistan had not given away 2050 square miles but 11,000 square miles of territory according to the data of the Survey of Pakistan. The agreement signified serious strategic implications for India and helped China to have a direct access and attack capability on Kashmir by land via the Karakoram pass and by air via direct Chinese air link to the Gilgit airfield. Islamabad presumed that any attack by India on Pakistan would bring China to its rescue. Pakistan's then Foreign Minister, Z. A. Bhutto declared on 17 July 1963 that, "An attack from India on Pakistan is no longer confined to the security and territorial integrity of Pakistan~ it now involves the territorial integrity and security of the largest state in the Asia as well."

However in the 1965 Indo-Pakistan war, despite assurances to help Pakistan, China did not offer any physical moves and only gave verbal warnings to India. Between 1965 and 1971, Pakistan received USD 200 million worth arms aid from China of which, USD 45 million worth of arms were supplied in 1971 alone.

Chinese cultivated relations with Pakistan for two reasons - one, Pakistan was looked upon as a link to the Middle East and two, in the regional initiatives, Chinese strategy was to forge closer links with South Asian countries to create a sub-regional balance to counter the Indian pre-eminence in South Asia. Pakistan sought precisely the kind of countervailing authority that China had willingly provided i.e, convince its special friends, that despite its potential resources, China would never behave like a superpower and within the regional context it was able to project an image of a weighty neighbour, particularly in South Asia.[45]

To strengthen the strategic part of the relations between China and Pakistan, both concluded a comprehensive nuclear cooperation agreement in 1986. Under the agreement, China has committed to support Pakistan in the design, construction, and operation of nuclear reactors and even assist the latter with the enrichment of weapons grade uranium. Besides, it also transferred tritium gas to Pakistan specifically meant to advance the yield of atomic bombs.[46]

In 1989 China built a 27 MW nuclear research reactor in Pakistan and Pakistani scientists were being trained in China. In the early 1990's China built an un-safeguarded plutonium reprocessing facility at Chashma, which was the chief source of Pakistan's weapon grade Plutonium. In 1995 China build another un-safeguarded reactor at Khushab. The same year China transferred 5000 ring magnets to Pakistan, after which it got exposed and there was a worldwide condemnation of China. In 1996, China transferred an industrial furnace with a casting surface in which the bomb core is cast and helps Pakistani engineers install it in Khushab. The commitment and involvement of China in Pakistan's nuclear programme leads one to believe that in the event of an Indo-Pak conflict, Chinese would align with Pakistan, so long as it remained convinced that neither the US nor the USSR would intervene.[47]

In the aftermath of the end of the cold war, if on the one side, there witnessed sharp reduction in Pakistan's strategic relevance for the United States, but on the other sides, Pakistan move closer to China to compensate for this loss. The post-Cold War global strategic developments have its impact on the relationship between China and Pakistan. Both countries enjoy a multifaceted partnership which ranges from political to economic and trade and from defence and security to nuclear cooperation. In 1996, during the state visit of President Jiang Zemin to Pakistan, the two countries decided to establish a comprehensive friendship. They signed a Treaty of Friendship and Cooperation, to the effect that "neither party will join any alliance or bloc which infringes upon the sovereignty, security and territorial integrity" of either nation or "would not conclude treaties of this nature with any third party." However, the suitable environment was created when China had equipped Pakistan Air Force with F-7P fighter in 1992. On the very same year, China also supplied to Pakistan 34 M-11 battlefield missiles, a solid-fuel variant of the Soviet Scud-B missile.[48]

The growing significance of relations between the two sides can be acknowledged from the historic speech made by Chinese President Jiang Zemin to the Pakistan Senate on December 1996 that underlines that,

> 'Our two peoples have regarded each other as friends in need and brothers bound by common fate, always sympathizing with and supporting each other. The Chinese Government .... stand ready to join the Pakistani side in further solidifying this friendly and cooperative relationship.'[49]

As the relationship gets stronger with every passing year and the Beijing's ensuring security guarantee for Islamabad has only brought significant change in the latter perception towards the former. Pakistan gives strategic importance to its partnership with China. This was very well reflected in the words of Dr Shireen Mazari, "The Peking has not only repudiated to back down on its defence pledges to Islamabad, in spite of Western pressure, but has been about especially responsible for permitting Pakistan a modicum of sufficient defence ability and nuclear development clearly makes China absolutely essential for Pakistan's survival., Pakistan has become extremely casual about its relations with China." Despite U.S. imposition of Pressler Amendment upon Islamabad, China continue to extend support to Islamabad nuclear weapons programme. China was closely working with Pakistan over the development of 9300 Mw power plant at Chasma. Moreover, China has been accused for transferring 500 ring magnets for Pakistan's nuclear facilities.[50]

Pakistan is in no way behind China when it comes to

cementing this close strategic partnership. Pakistan is making every effort to ensure that the relationship with China continue to progress unhindered. Pakistan has clout in controlling the Islamic separatist movement in China's Xinjiang Autonomous Region.[51] To show its commitment in this aspect, Pakistan not only killed Hasan Mahsum, the leader of the East Turkestan Islamic Movement (ETIM) in October 2003 but also agreed to conduct a joint anti-terrorism exercise in the province in August 2004.[52]

Pakistan attaches significant importance to its expanding relations with China from the futuristic perspective. As was very rightly pointed out by Lt. Gen. Talat Masood in a way that, "China concluded defence cooperation agreement; supplies were subject to almost no limitations, and Beijing does not look for commercial but for strategic gains from this partnership."[53] In support of what the army general has said, Shen Chun Chuan, an analysts from China is of the view that, "The partnership not only benefited Pakistan military .... China's continued cooperation has greatly contributed towards enhancing the morale of Pakistan's military establishment as also expanding military's influence and role in Pakistan's polity."[54] In fact, Pakistan believes that China provided the much needed force that is crucial to achieving its long cherished aim of capturing Kashmir by pressurising India and if necessary to contain it.[55]

Where the Kashmir issue between India and Pakistan is concerned, it serves China's interest to keep the Kashmir pot boiling, by diverting India's attention from other issues. Beijing has also equipped Islamabad with JF-17 aircraft and JF-17 production facilities, F-22P frigates with helicopters, K-8 jet trainers, T-85 tanks, F-7 aircraft, small arms and ammunition. It has also built a turnkey ballistic missile manufacturing facility near Rawalpindi and helped Pakistan develop the 750-km-range, solid-fuel Shaheen-1 ballistic missile.[56] China's strategy of providing advanced arms and equipment requirements for Pakistan will continue to remain a case of serious national security concerns for India. Details of China's major arms supplies to Pakistan are given in Table 4.1.

Table 4.1

China's Major Arms Supplies to Pakistan

Sl. No.	Years of Delivery	Weapon Designation	Weapon Description	No. Ordered/ Delivered
1	–	F-6	Fighter aircraft	100
2	–	A-5-Fantan A	Fighter/ground attack	98
3	1993	F-7M Airguard	Fighter	40
4	–	F-7P Skybolt	Fighter	40
5	2005	FC-1	Fighter	150
6	–	Super 7	Fighter	–
7	1986-90	F7	Fighter	75
8	2002	F7MG	Fighter	57
9	1986	Q5- Fantan-A	Fighter/ground attack	100
10	–	FT-7P	Fighter trainer	15

Source: Srikanth Kondapalli, "Pakistan in China's Security Perceptions", in Swaran Singh (ed.), *China-Pakistan Strategic Cooperation: Indian Perspectives* (New Delhi: Manohar, 2007), pp. 74-75.

China-Pakistan Strategic Engagement at the Dawn of 21st Century

President Pervez Musharraf during his visit to China in November 2003 said that the China- Pakistan strategic partnership was "deeper than the oceans, higher than the mountains."[57] The China's relations with Pakistan are no more bilateral, but possesses multi-dimensional character.[58] The deepness of the bilateral engagement between the two sides can be reflected from what Pakistan Prime Minister,

Shaukat Aziz had said at Islamabad's Institute of Strategic Studies on 27 September 2005 that,

> 'Pakistan and China enjoy all-weather friendship based on complete trust and confidence. Our friendship is rooted in the psyche and ethos of our people. From Khunjrab to Gwadar, the symbols of Pakistan-China friendship dot the landscape. The mega projects that we have undertaken with China's help are like anchors that hold two countries together in trusted friendship.'[59]

Continuing in the two countries' anti-India stance, Pakistan's Foreign Minister Shah Mehmood Qureshi said in 2010 that "Pakistan and China strongly feel that India should not become a permanent member of the United Nations Security Council, as it would disturb the balance of power in the region."[60] Out of the deepening relations, Islamabad expect China to support in its political and military dealing with India and its position on Kashmir. As committed China is providing Pakistan with the much needed help for its national security needs by way of aid and investment. That's the key reason as to why Islamabad attaches significant importance to its engagement with its close ally China.[61]

The events of 11 September 2001 were, however, a turning point in India-United States relations. Since then, the security understanding between the world's two largest democracies has improved significantly. The United States offered civil nuclear cooperation to India and rejected similar cooperation with Pakistan. It has also encouraged India to play a significant role in the reconstruction of Afghanistan, which detracts from Pakistan's objective of gaining strategic depth in that country. For Pakistan, this increases the value of the Chinese friendship that today Islamabad considers China to be the cornerstone of its foreign policy.[62]

In April 2005 China and Pakistan signed a Treaty of Friendship, Cooperation, and Good Neighbourly Relations. The agreement binds the two countries to desist from joining "any alliance or bloc which infringes upon the sovereignty, security, and territorial integrity of the other side."[63] Pakistan's Information Minister Sheikh Rashid Ahmad stated in a TV interview that Pakistan would stand behind China if the United States ever tried to "besiege" it. From Pakistan's perspective, China is a far more reliable partner than the United States, given that the latter in the recent past has been much more committed to strengthening its ties with India.

During President Pervez Musharraf's visit to China in 2006, Beijing committed itself to equip Pakistan with JF-17 (Thunder) aircraft. On 23 May 2006, Pakistan clinched a $600 million defence deal with China, which included the construction of four F-22P frigates for the Pakistan Navy (three to be built in Shanghai and the fourth at the Karachi dockyard), upgrading of the Karachi dockyard, and transfer of technology for the indigenous production of a modern surface fleet.[64] In a move that would further strengthen the already stronger ties with Pakistan, China during the visit of Pakistan's Prime Minister Yousuf Raza Gilani in May this year, has agreed to provide 50 JF-17 thunder aircraft equipped with more sophisticated avionics on easy loan terms.[65]

Since the dawn of the current century, the two countries have committed themselves to further strengthening their economic ties. The visit of Pakistan's Prime Minister Shaukat Aziz in December 2004 and the subsequent visit by the Chinese Premier in April 2005 to Pakistan paved the way for future cooperation. The two sides signed a number of agreements and memoranda of understanding (MoU), after which China provided Pakistan a preferential credit of $500 million, out of which $150 million was for Phase II of the Chashma nuclear power plant. Also, a new Pakistan consulate was opened in Shanghai. The two sides have also taken initial steps towards establishing a free trade area, by cancelling tariffs on 767 items. China-Pakistan trade has expanded rapidly from $1.4 billion in 2001 to $5 billion in 2006.[66] China is engaged in 120 projects with Pakistan such as heavy engineering, power generation, mining and telecommunications, and expects its investment in Pakistan to grow from $4 billion in 2007 to $15 billion by 2010.[67] During the visit of Premier Wen Jiabao to Pakistan in 2011 the two sides signed agreements for thirty-five new pacts. These pacts may bring $30 billion investment to Pakistan over the next five years from China.[68]

On the other side, India-China trade volume has improved significantly, from $2.9 billion in 2000 to $61 billion in 2010, compared to $1.16 billion to $7 billion over the same period with Pakistan.[69] Nevertheless, China's long-term interest of restraining India from gaining international space is certain to prevail over the short-term interest of expanding trade and other ties with India.

Chinese Nuclear Cooperation with Pakistan and Proliferation Concerns

By entering into a civilian nuclear agreement, the United States has not strengthened India's missile and nuclear programmes because India has agreed to separation of civilian facilities from that of the military facilities, thereby voluntarily placing all the civilian facilities under the IAEA safeguards. By entering into the civilian nuclear initiative, India's interests do not lie in undermining the non-proliferation regime, but to strengthen the regime. India's commitment to preventing the proliferation of Weapons of Mass Destructions (WMDs) is justified by its impeccable record of not transferring any of its nuclear related technology and materials to the third countries.[70] Regardless, China supported Pakistan in its ambitions of acquiring nuclear and missile programmes by violating international commitments. Even after joining the Nuclear Non-

Proliferation Treaty (NPT) in 1992 China has engaged in nuclear and missile cooperation with Pakistan.[71] Pakistan continues to be the major beneficiary of China's unending support to acquire nuclear materials and technology. Arms-control advocate Gary Milhollin has very rightly pointed out that, "If you subtract China's help from Pakistan's nuclear program, there is no nuclear program."[72]

By supporting Islamabad in its nuclear weapons programme, Beijing has sent an indirect message to Washington that if you can do this for your partner (India) then why I should desist from doing the same for my long time ally (Pakistan). Shen Dingli, a nuclear security expert and Vice President of Institute of International Studies at Fudan University accused Washington of "contributing to nuclear proliferation" as "New Delhi can now devote its resources and energy to the research and development of nuclear weapons...Wouldn't it be possible for other nuclear states to cooperate with Pakistan in the development of nuclear energy? Pakistan...has a need to develop civil nuclear energy and the right to do so..."[73]

Pakistan, it may be noted, has an execrable record of nuclear proliferation. China's Foreign Ministry spokesman Qin Gang has repeatedly dismissed such concerns by claiming that "Civilian nuclear energy cooperation between China and Pakistan is completely in line with international obligations of non-proliferation, and is completely meant for peaceful purposes."[74]

It was during his visit to India, retired Israeli Army General, Shalom Harari has alleged Pakistan for nuclear proliferation in the Arab World. He said that,

> "Israel recently got information that Pakistan was supporting the nuclear weapons program of Syria by supplying it some of the key components." He further added that "Pakistani and its nuclear scientist A Q Khan were involved in Libyan

> nuclear program. Khan was involved in the Uranium program by supplying them atomic detonators. Pakistan is actually the main proliferators of atomic bombs in the Middle East to Islamic states."[75]

In future too, the possibility of Pakistan proliferating nuclear components and technological know-how cannot be ruled out. Therefore, China should think twice before moving ahead for any kind of nuclear cooperation with Pakistan, because it would face a serious threat to international peace and security.

Conclusion

China looms large on India's relations with Pakistan. India has in recent years gained significant weight on the international stage by virtue of its growing economic and military prowess, but Pakistan and China share a very strong desire to halt India's progress in this direction. In fact India has been the main factor that has influenced China and Pakistan policies toward each other. The two sides have a close understanding on the need to enhance strategic coordination, advance pragmatic cooperation and work together to meet challenges in pursuit of common development. Pakistan in particular viewed India as a potential challenger leading to use China to counter Indian power in the region.

China's position on Kashmir can't be delinked from its ever expanding relations with Pakistan. Although, the China's positions on Kashmir have not always been characterised by pro-Pakistan, but with expanding involvement in PoK, it can be expected that China would support its close ally ahead of India with which both Pakistan and China doesn't enjoy close relations.[76] By considering Kashmir as disputed territory between the two South Asian neighbours, China seems to reject Indian claim that Kashmir is its integral part. This tacit help of China emboldens and assures Pakistan to continue fuelling the terrorism in Jammu and Kashmir. Thus it may be concluded that China's support to Pakistan is detrimental to improving Indo-Pak relations.

References

1. Kerry B. Dumbaugh, "Exploring the China-Pakistan Relationship", Roundtable Report Prepared by CNA China Studies, June 2010, p. 5.
2. Aditi Malhotra, "The Red Shadow in Pakistan Occupied Kashmir", Scholar Warrior, Autumn 2011, p. 74.
3. Syed Waqas Haider Bukhari and Tahira Parveen, "China's Approach Towards Kashmir Conflict: A Viable Solution", Journal of Professional Research in Social Sciences, Vol. 1, No. 1, July 2014, p. 14.
4. Anil Kamboj, "Creation of Pakistan Occupied Kashmir and Present Scenario", World Focus, Vol. XXXVIII, No. 7, July 2017, p. 10 and Kewal Krishan, "India, Pakistan and China Border Dispute With Special Reference to Jammu and Kashmir", Journal of Global Research and Analysis, Vol. 3, No. 2, December 2014, p. 4.
5. Ibid., p. 15.
6. Jabin T. Jacob, "China and Kashmir", p. 19, available at *<https://www.ideals.illinois.edu/bitstream/handle/2142/15471/China_and_Kashmir.pdf?sequence=2>.*
7. Syed Waqas Haider Bukhari and Tahira Parveen, n. 1, pp. 15-16.
8. Prashant Kumar Singh, "Revisiting China's Kashmir Policy", IDSA Comment, available at *<https://idsa.in/idsacomments/RevisitingChinasKashmirPolicy_pksingh_011110>.*
9. Mohan Malik, "The China Factor in the India-Pakistan Conflict", Parameters, Spring 2003, pp. 35-6.
10. Refer to, "India and Future Global Order", Paper produced at the Section for Policy Planning in the Department for

Security Policy, Norwegian Ministry of Defense, November 2009, pp. 17-18, available at <*http://www.regjeringen.no/upload/FD/Dokumenter/India-studie_ssek_301109.pdf*>.

11. Lisa Curtis, "China's Military and Security Relationship with Pakistan", Testimony before the U.S.-China Economic and Security Review Commission, 20 May 2009, available at <*http://www.heritage.org/research/testimony/chinas-military-and-security-relationship-with-pakistan*>.

12. Harsh V. Pant, "The Pakistan Thorn in China-India-U.S. Relations", Washington Quarterly, Vol. 35, No. 1, Winter 2012, pp. 85-6.

13. T.V Paul, "Chinese-Pakistani Nuclear/Missile Ties and Balance of Power Politics", The Nonproliferation Review, Vol. 10, No. 2, Summer 2003, p. 24.

14. A S Chonker, " An Eye For an Eye - The Answer to the Chinese Predicament in Jammu And Kashmir", Claws Article, No. 1835, 8 December 2017, available at <*http://www.claws.in/1835/an-eye-for-an-eye-the-answer-to-the-chinese-predicament-in-jammu-and-kashmir-as-chonker.html*>.

15. Quoted from "Chinese Troops Around Kashmir Posing Threat", Canadian Asian News, Vol. 15, No. 197, 15-30 April 2011, pp. 1 and 3.

16 Syed Waqas Haider Bukhari and Tahira Parveen, n. 1, p. 16.

17 Bahauddin Foizee, 'Kashmir's Geopolitical Significance is Growing Day by Day', Geopolitical Monitor, 24 May 2018, available at <https://www.geopoliticalmonitor.com/kashmirs-geopolitical-significance-is-growing-by-the-day/>.

18. B. Raman was quoted in Banyan, "China and Kashmir – The Chinese Connection", The Economist, 29 August 2010, available at <*https://www.economist.com/banyan/2010/08/29/the-chinese-connection*>.

19. J. Korbel, Danger in Kashmir (New Jersey: Princeton University Press, 1966), p. 331.

20. Monika Chansoria, op cit., pp. 75-6.
21. Syed Waqas Haider Bukhari and Tahira Parveen, op cit., pp. 19-20.
22. Monika Chansoria, "China's Current Kashmir Policy: Steady Crystallisation", Claws Journal, Winter 2016, pp. 68-9.
23. Ahmad Bhatty Maqbool, "China's Emerging Role in the World", Peace Initiatives, Vol. V, No. III-VI, May -December 1999, p. 163.
24. The Hindu, 14th January 2002.
25. Kissing Contemporary Archives, (London, 1949), p. 104.
26. Aziz Qutubuddin, "Relations between Pakistan and People's Republic of China", in Ahmed Sherwani Latif, (ed.), Foreign Policy of Pakistan (Karachi, 1964), p. 82.
27. Pervaiz Ali Mahesar, Ali Khan Ghumro, Ghulam Mushtafa Khuskh and Abdul Hamid Mahesar, " International Journal of Scientific Research and Innovative Technology, Vol. 3, No. 3, March 2016, p. 23.
28. Farzana Shakoor, "The Kargil Crisis: An Analysis", Pakistan Horizon, Vol. 52, No. 3, July 1999, p. 61.
29. Syed Waqas Haider Bukhari and Tahira Parveen, op cit., p. 21.
30. John Garver views on China's Policy towards Kashmir was quoted in Savita Pande, "Sino-Pakistan Strategic Relationship: Implications for India", Scholar Warrior, Autumn 2015, p. 19
31. Jingdong Yuan, "China's Kashmir Policy", China Brief, Vol. 5, No. 19, September 2005.
32. Syed Waqas Haider Bukhari and Tahira Parveen, op cit., pp. 15-16.
33. See, 'Pakistan Occupied Kashmir: Changing the Discourse', IDSA PoK Project Report, New Delhi, May 2011, p. 9.
34. Ibid., p. 11.

35. Anil Kamboj, "Creation of Pakistan Occupied Kashmir and Present Scenario", World Focus, Vol. XXXVIII, No. 7, July 2017, p. 11.

36. Aditi Malhotra, "The Red Shadow in Pakistan Occupied Kashmir", Scholar Warrior, Autumn 2011, p. 74.

37. Jaiveer Singh Negi, "Gilgit-Baltistan-China-Pakistan-Economic Corridor: Implications for India", in Sanjay Kumar et al. (eds.), India-Pakistan Relations: Past, Present and Future (New Delhi: G B Books Publishers and Distributors, 2018).

38. Bahauddin Foizee, n. 17.

39. M. Ganapathi, "Contours of India's Foreign Policy: An Overview", Indian Foreign Affairs Journal, Vol. 12, No. 1, Jan-March 2017, p. 49.

40. Avinash Godbole, "India-China Relation: Enhancing Engagement Promises Better Future", which featured in a debate titled, 'Future Trajectory of Sino-Indian Relations', Indian Foreign Affairs Journal, Vol. 11, No. 1, Jan-Mar 2016, p. 16.

41. Monika Chansoria, "China's Current Kashmir Policy: Steady Crystallisation", Claws Journal, Winter 2016, p. 70.

42. Ibid., pp. 71-72.

43. Anil Kamboj, op cit., p. 12.

44. Netajee Abhinandan, "Turbulence in PoK: The China Factor", World Focus, Vol. XXXVIII, No. 7, July 2017, p. 53.

45. O. P. Gulia, "History of India-Pakistan Relations Through Chinese Prism", in Sanjay Kumar et al. (eds.), India-Pakistan Relations: Past, Present and Future (New Delhi: G B Books Publishers and Distributors, 2018).

46. Aparna Pande, Explaining Pakistan's Foreign Policy: Escaping India (New York: Routledge, 2011).

47. O. P. Gulia, op cit.

48. Ahmad Faruqui, "The Complex Dynamics of Pakistan's Relationship with China," Islamabad Policy Research Institute, Summer 2001, *<http://www.ipripak.org/journal/summer2001/thecomplex.shtml>*.

49. Jiang Zemin Speech titled, "Carrying Forward Generations of Friendly and Good Neighbourly Relations and Endeavoring Towards a Better Tomorrow for all", Islamabad, 2 December 1996.

50. Muhammad Ishaque Fani, "Pakistan-China Security Relations and Mutual Ventures", JRSP, vol. 46, No. 2, 2009, p. 81-6.

51. Urvashi Aneja, "Pakistan-China Relations: Recent Developments (Jan-May 2006)", IPCS Special Report 26, June 2006, p. 2, *<http://www.ipcs.org/pdf_file/issue/136564802IPCS-Special-Report-26.pdf>*; also refer John W. Garver, "The Future of the Sino-Pakistan Entente Cordiale", n. 6, pp. 389-90.

52. Tariq Mahmud Ashraf, "Future Sino-Pak Relations and the War on Terrorism", *<http://www.grandestrategy.com/2008/04/future-sino-pak-relations-and-war-on.html>*.

53. Talat Masood, "Guns vs. butter: Finding the balance," The News (Islamabad), February 18, 1996.

54. Shen Chun-Chuan, "Peking's Relations with India and Pakistan", Issues & Studies, Vol. 25 No. 9, September 1989, p. 32.

55. Rakesh Datta, "The Kargil War-China Factor", in Rajendra Nath (ed.), Musharraf's War (New Delhi: Lancer's Books, 2003), p. 236.

56. Lisa Curtis, "China's Military and Security Relationship with Pakistan", Testimony before the U.S.-China Economic and Security Review Commission, 20 May 2009, *<http://www.heritage.org/research/testimony/chinas-military-and-security-relationship-with-pakistan>*.

57. Robert G. Wirsing, "The Enemy of my Enemy: Pakistan's China Debate", Asia-Pacific Center for Security Studies

Special Assessment, December 2003, p. 4, *<http://www.apcss.org/Publications/SAS/ChinaDebate/ChinaDebate_ Wirsing.pdf>*.

58. Kerry B. Dumbaugh, "Exploring the China-Pakistan Relationship", Roundtable Report Prepared by CNA China Studies, June 2010, p. 2.

59. Swaran Singh, "Introduction", in Swaran Singh (ed.), China-Pakistan Strategic Cooperation: Indian Perspectives (New Delhi: Manohar, 2007), p. 22.

60. See "India in UNSC? No Way, Say Pakistan, China", *<http://www.rediff.com/news/slide-show/slide-show-1-pak-china-unite-against-indias-unsc-bid/20101113.htm>*.

61. Kerry B. Dumbaugh, n. 43, p. 4.

62. "U.S.-China Relations: Seeking Strategic Convergence in Pakistan", n. 7, p. 1.

63. See "Text of Pak China Joint Statement", October 17, 2008, n. 5.

64. Urvashi Aneja, n. 14, pp. 3-5.

65. Sanjeev Kumar, "PM Gilani Visit to China: Symbolic or Substantive", Indian Council of World Affair, New Delhi, 26 May 2011, *<http://www.icwa.in/pdfs/VPGilaniVisit.pdf>*.

66. Bhatty, "China's Peaceful Rise and South Asia", n. 4, p. 33.

67. Jamal Afridi, "China-Pakistan Relations", *<http://www.pakistan talk.com/forums/strategic-issues/3953-china-pakistan-relations.html>*.

68. R.N. Das, "China's 'All-Weather Friendship' with Pakistan: Implications for India", IDSA Comment, New Delhi, 4 January 2011, *<http://www.idsa.in/idsacomments/Chinasallweather friendshipwithPakistanImplications forIndia_ rndas_040111>*.

69. Isaac B. Kordon, "China and Pakistan: Emerging Strains in the Entente Cordiale", Project 2049 Institute, Arlington, Virginia, 25 March 2011, p. 11.

70. Devki Nandan, "Sino-Pak Nuclear Nexus and India's

Concerns", Centre for Air Power Studies Issue Brief, 16 July 2010, pp. 1-3.

71. Upendra Choudhury, "The Indo-USA Nuclear Deal and its Impact on India's Ballistic Missile Programme", South Asian Strategic Studies Institute Research Report 17, June 2008, pp. 16-17, *<kms1.isn.ethz.ch/serviceengine/Files/ISN/99928/.../RR+No+17.pdf>*.

72. Harsh V. Pant, "The Pakistan Thorn in China-India-U.S. Relations", Washington Quarterly, Vol. 35, No. 1, Winter 2012, pp. 85-6.

73. Sherry W. Wangwhite, "China's Reactions to the India Deal: Implications for the United States", Thesis Submitted to the Naval Postgraduate School, Monterey, California, December 2007, pp. 63-4.

74. Issam Ahmed, "China-Pakistan Deal Raises Fears of Nuclear Proliferation", *<http://www.csmonitor.com/World/Asia-South-Central/2010/0701/China-Pakistan-deal-raises-fears-of-nuclear-proliferation>*.

75. Refer to "Pakistan Supporting Syrian Nuclear Programme: Ex-Israeli Army Gen", Indian Express, 13 November 2011, available at *<http://www.indianexpress.com/news/pak-supporting-syrian-nuclear-programme-exisraeli-army-gen/875154/>*.

76. Jabin T. Jacob, n. 6.

5

Military Intervention in Pakistan-Politics and Contours of India-Pakistan Relations

Present chapter is an Etiological Investigation of Military Intervention (Praetorianism) in Pakistani Politics. It focuses on the chronological account of Military Intervention in Pakistan's Politics, its Causes and impact on India's Security.

There was always a question striking in my mind that: "Why there has never been a military dictatorship in India while twin Pakistan has observed and experienced Four Military Coups d' état since its birth?"

So Present chapter is a humble attempt to investigate the Military Coup-generating conditions prevailing in the Pakistan.

In fact, the Civil–Military Relations in Pakistan and India remained in Stark Contrast since the partition of the British Indian Empire in August 1947 into separate nation–state as Pakistan and India. Both adopted contrasting pathways according to their domestic compulsions and circumstances.

Unfortunately, the founding father -Quaid-i-Azam M.A. Jinnah (1876-1948) died on 11 September 1948 by Cancer of the lungs. It caused an irreparable tragedy for a newly-born nascent Pakistan resulted into severe *political instability* and *political vacuum* which experienced the quick succession of *Seven P.Ms.* from 1950 to 1958. Pakistan took nine (9) years to draft its constitution, and failed to hold a free and fair national election, while in India, Democracy quickly took root and only after two years India drafted her Constitution and enforced it on 26 January 1950 and held a successful nationwide free and fair elections based upon universal adult franchise.

The prevailing political instability and leadership syndrom provided military a chance to think about the possibility of military intervention in Pakistani politics. General Ayub Khan was the C-in-C of armed forces as well as Defence Minister saw the shortcomings and weaknesses of political system very closely and therefore Pakistan witnessed its *first military coup in 1958.*

On the other hand, in India P.M. Nehru has abolished the post of the Commander-in-Chief (C-in-C) during the initial phase of his tenure, as contrast to India, the post of C-in-C was abolished by the civilian leader Zulfikar Ali Bhutto on 3rd March 1972, appointing General Tikka Khan as the first COAS (Chief of Army Staff) of Pakistan and the tenure of COAS was also reduced to three years from previously fixed at four years. The naval HQ was also shifted to Islamabad from Karachi. In this way Z.A. Bhutto cut the powerful wings of Pakistan Military after the debacle of 1971 War of Secession of East Pakistan.

The first military coup of Pakistan (1958) became the Precedence and paved the way for further Military Coups in Pakistan. Infact, Z.A. Bhutto was the first democratic civilian leader of Pakistan who courageously suppressed the dominance of Pakistan Military prone to intervene into the matters of elected civil authority.

Genesis of Pakistan

The word *'Pakistan'* was coined by Choudhary Rahmat Ali in a pamphlet titled as *'Now or Never: Are we to Live or Perish Forever?'* published on January 28, 1933.

Later an eminent Muslim poet and philosopher Alamma Dr. Muhammad Iqbal (1875 - 1938), Quaid-i-Azam Muhammad Ali Jinnah (1876 - 1948), and A.K. Fazal-ul-Haq (Sher-e-Bengal) picked up the idea on which the resolution for creation of PAKISTAN was based during All-India Muslim League (AIML) convention on 23rd March 1940. Muslim League under direction of M.A. Jinnah passed the 'Pakistan Resolution' at its Lahore Convention that demanded creation of Pakistan. These developments deeply pained the Indian National Congress (INC) and Mahatma Gandhi. British authorities too had infused a lot of fuel into M.A. Jinnah's formation that the Muslims were different than the rest of Indians in the terms of religion, social, cultural and economic identity and demanded a *'Separate Homeland or Nation'* for Muslims and argued the *'Two-Nation Theory (TNT)'*.

On August 14, 1947, British Rule in India ends with the creation of Pakistan into two parts east wing and west wing at a distance of 1000 miles on the religion basis.

Both nations suffered a severe birth-pains as millions of people on both sides turn refugees and suffered large scale killings, lootings, rapes and abductions (kidnappings). Unfortunately, the founding father M.A. Jinnah died on 11 September 1948 by Cancer of the lungs just about 13 months after the creation of nascent Pakistan. Jinnah's ideas and vision of Secular Democracy were immediately forgotten by a thankless nation. Due to *Political Instability,* Pakistan quickly falls under the control of military-bureaucracy nexus instead of elected representatives of its people on democratic pattern.

The literally meaning of the term Pakistan is a *'land of pure'*, contradictory to its meaning, Pakistan had turned into the *'land of impure'* where impurities such as *Conspiracies, Assassinations* and *Political instability* had become the common incidents, frequently occurred into the day-to-day life of Pakistani people. A few examples of VVIP's are being cited here: The Rawalpindi Conspiracy against P.M. Liaquat Ali (1951), the Agartala Conspiracy case against Sheikh Mujibur Rehman and 34 others; Assassination of first P.M. Liaquat Ali on October 10, 1951 by a hired Afghan youth, Assassination of first woman P.M. Mrs. Benazir Bhutto considering her as pro-US and pro-democratic lady on 27 December 2007 and due to having a vision of good-relations with India. On 4 January 2011, Punjab Governor, Salman Taseer was slain/killed by his official bodyguard, Malik Mumtaz Hussain Qadri. due to misuse of Blasphemy law against a poor Christian labourer Aasia Bibi and Minister for Minority Affairs, Shahbaz Bhatti was also assassinated in Islamabad on 2 March 2011 regarding falsely accused outspoken against Blasphemy Law, and *'Judicial Murder'* of Z.A. Bhutto committed by General Zia-ul-Haq on April 4, 1979, at Rawalpindi Jail etc, etc. Political Instability just after the sad demise of Jinnah caused a quick succession of seven P.Ms. from 1950 to 1958. Pakistan experienced four Military Coups d' e'tat within a period of 40 years (from 1958 to 1999) at an average of ten years per coup.

Pakistan army remained India-centric and suffered with parity-syndrome, insecurity complex and obsession of Kashmir factor.

The third Military Regime (from 1977 to 1988) under general Zia-ul-Haq was the most disastrous period in which*Islamization, Radicalization* and *Sectarian Violence* were prevalent and its repercussions and dire consequences were seen in the forthcoming future.

After the Al-Qaeda's terrorist attack on US-Soil on 11

September 2001 (known as 9/11), Pakistan turned into the sanctuary of Taliban and al-Qaeda terrorists subsequently becoming a failing state. Strong nexus of Pakistan Army and I.S.I. constantly exporting, sponsoring and nurtured cross-border terrorists into the Indian soil.

Military Coups of Pakistan and its Typology

Whether it is 'soft coup' or 'hard coup', the coup had remained a common thing in the short history of Pakistan. Pakistan has suffered nine (9) Coups overall since her independence on August 14, 1947 upto October 12, 1999.

Four (4) successful military 'Coups d′ État' were occurred by Gen. Ayub Khan in (1958), Gen. Yahya Khan in (1969), Gen. Zia-ul-Haq in (1977) and Gen. Pervez Musharraf in (1999).

Apart from four successful Military 'Coups d′ État'; five (5) failed/ unsuccessful military coup-attempts or conspiracies (including Agartala Conspiracy Case) were also occurred in Pakistani Politics.

Therefore, the military coups of Pakistan may be classified into the two main categories mentioned as under:

1. Successful Military Coups, and
2. Failed Military Coup-attempts or Conspiracies.

Four successful military coups of Pakistan are being described as under:

(i) First Military Coup occurred on 27 October 1958: Maj. Gen. Iskander Mirza, the first President of Islamic Republic of Pakistan was deposed in 1958 bloodless 'Coup d′ État' by General Ayub Khan and took control over the country, becoming President as well as P.M. simultaneously upto 25 March 1969. This coup was often locally called the *'October Revolution'*.

(ii) The Second Military Coup on 25 March 1969:

This coup took place when senior commanders forced Ayub Khan to hand over power to General Yahya Khan. Ayub Khan resigned under pressure from opposition and handed over power to Gen. Yahya Khan. It was also a bloodless coup and political power was transferred peacefully.

(iii) The Third Military Coup was carried out by Gen. Zia-ul-Haq, when he ousted Z.A. Bhutto on 5th July 1977 coup, which was also a peaceful. Gen. Zia as a COAS declared martial law throughout the country, took over as the Chief Martial Law Administrator (CMLA). The 1973 Constitution was suspended (not abrogated). Federal and provincial cabinets, national and provincial assemblies were dissolved. The coup, later described as *'the operation fair play'*, did not surprise any one, Bhutto himself had not ruled out the possibility of a 'Coup d´ État'. He was so deeply trapped in the political crisis that he had no option but to capitulate. The rightist-party PNA (Pakistan National Alliance) welcome the coup and celebrated the removal of Bhutto by the military. The P.M., Cabinet members and leading opposition leaders were arrested and placed under protective custody. The President of Pakistan, Fazal Ilahi Chaudhary was allowed to continue titular head of state and chief-justices of provincial High Courts were appointed acting governors of their respective provinces.

Gen. Zia-ul-Haq took de facto control over the country by leading the 1977 'Coup d´ État'. He served as CMLA until 1979. He was killed in a plane- crash on 17 August 1988.

(iv) The Fourth Military Coup was taken place on 12 October 1999, when the COAS and Chairman of the JCSC of Pakistan Army, Gen. Pervez Musharraf overthrew elected P.M. Nawaz Sharif. It was a bloodless 'Coup d´ État'. On 14 October 1999, Musharraf declared *a state of emergency* and issued a Provincial Constitutional order. Musharraf designated himself as Chief Executive of the Islamic Republic of Pakistan, suspended the Parliament and Provincial assemblies of the four provinces, and suspended the constitution, although the president Muhammad RafiqTarar shall continue in office.

Causes of the Fourth Military Coup

Indian Prime Minister Atal Behari Vajpayee travelled to Lahore in February 1999 for better relations with Pakistan, at the same time Pak Army, Gen. Musharraf and his Coterie of generals were planning the covert (indirect) military operation in the Kargil mountain range on the LoC. In the aftermath of the Kargil misadventure (May-July 1999) differences between Nawaz and Musharraf had turned into a very strong and mutual antipathy (deep dislike). Nawaz has alleged that the Chief architects of the Kargil operation–Gen. Musharraf, Gen. Aziz, and Gen. Mahmood – began to plot to topple his government simply to cover their tracks since the Kargil fiasco was their doing. On the other hand, Musharraf, has accused Nawaz for corruption through rampant misuse of power. On 12 October 1999, Nawaz removed (dismissed) Musharraf as CAOS and nominated the ISI D.G, Lt. Gen. Zia-uddin Butt of the Engineers Corps as COAS in his place. Musharraf was informed about his dismissal while he was, at that time, on an official visit to Sri Lanka, on a PIA (Pakistan International Airlines) flight back to Karachi from Colombo. In an attempt to prevent Musharraf's return to Karachi, Sharif first ordered the plane to be diverted to India and then Nawabshah (in Sindh). When this failed, Sharif ordered the Karachi airport to refuse to allow the plane to land; the airport used civil aviation planes to block the runway. The Pakistani Army, under directions from Lt. Gen. Muzaffar Usmani, seized the control tower and allowed the plane to land. Musharraf was lucky, Nawaz's strategy backfired as key military allies got wind of what was happening and rallied what transpired (which Musharraf has mentioned in his memoir – *In the Line of Fire*), "Lt. Gen. Mahmood Ahmed, the corps commander at Rawalpindi, and Lt. Gen. Mohammad Aziz, chief of General staff, were playing tennis when they heard about Sharif's decision. The two Generals rushed to the GHQ to mobilize their forces for the *Counter Coup.* The situation was delicately balanced. Loyalties were not clearly defined. Entrenched in the P.M. House, Gen. Zia-uddin was issuing orders and making new appointments. He was desperately trying to garner the support of the commanders. He sacked both Gen. Aziz and Gen. Mahmood. But it was too late. Brig. Satti's 111 Brigade had already moved to seal the P.M. house.

After this, troops took control of the state-run TV station in Islamabad, encircled the PM house, gained control of International Airports, and cut International phone-lines. There was utter confusion in the country as the state-controlled Pakistan TV went off the air." The entire military High Command refused to follow the orders of newly appointed Zia-uddin Butt as COAS.

The corps commanders took over all key state buildings throughout the country, placed the entire cabinet including the PM and his powerful brother under House arrest, arrested Nawaz Sharif and Zia-uddin Butt and announced the dismissal of Nawaz Sharif as PM.

"The Supreme Court of Pakistan declared the coup to be legal, but ordered that the army rule be limited to three years. Nawaz was tried by Pakistan's Anti—Terrorism Courts which, in 2000, handed down a life sentence on him for kidnapping, attempted murder, hijacking, and corruption – the hijacking charges were based on Nawaz allegedly not allowing the plane to land at Karachi. Rumours were in the air that the death sentence would be passed on him but since Nawaz enjoyed considerable goodwill with the Saudi Royal family, who intervened on his behalf, the court passed a sentence of life imprisonment on him. Later the military government agreed to exile him to Saudi Arabia. Nawaz has made the incredible assertion that he was willing to go to prison but, as a Muslim, being sent to the holy land in exile was a blessing he could not refuse and so he accepted that option. Nawaz reportedly gave an undertaking that he would abstain from politics for the next ten years, but he does not mention any such deal".

Failed Military Coup-attempts or Conspiracies

Apart from four overt successful Military Coups occurred in 1958, 1969, 1977 and 1999, Pakistan had also experienced at-least four failed Coup-attempts/Conspiracies since her independence August 14, 1947, mentioned as under:

1. Rawalpindi Conspiracy Case against P.M. Liaquat Ali on 23 February 1951.

The Rawalpindi Conspiracy was an attempted Soviet-backed 'Coup d′ État' against the govt. of Liaquat Ali Khan, the first P.M. of Pakistan in 1951. The coup was planned by Major-Gen. Akbar Khan to overthrow the then Govt. at his residence on 23 February 1951 alongwith other military officers and left-wing activists e.g. prominent poet-intellectual Faiz Ahmed Faiz and Syed SajjadZaheer (Secretary Gen. of Pakistan Communist Party). Eleven (11) military officers and Four (4) civilians were involved in the conspiracy. The master mind behind the Rawalpindi conspiracy, Maj. Gen. Akbar Khan was the chief of Gen. staff of the Pakistan army. He was disagreed with P.M. Liaquat Ali Khan on his policy on Kashmir and believed that a military solution of the problem was possible. Although he was in service, he openly advanced his views and developed ties with the communists.

P.M. Liaquat Ali announced the foiling of the coup on March 9, 1951. The Govt. passed the Rawalpindi conspiracy (Special Tribunal) Act to set up a special tribunal to investigate the conspiracy. The secret trial was conducted in 18-months in secrecy. It was held for the 15 individuals accused. There were three main causes of this coup such as:

1. Some of the Pakistan's army officers were not satisfied by the performance of the Liaquat Ali Khan's Govt., they consider it as corrupt and incompetent.
2. Most of the high ranking Pakistani Generals thought the continuing presence of British army officers in the Army as a security threat, as well as a hindrance in the path of their speedy promotions.
3. The immediate cause was their discontent with Liaquat regime's handling of the Kashmir war with India (1948). Army officers thought Govt's acceptance of UN mediation/Ceasefire, as a *'tame surrender'* and *'flouting an opportunity to capture whole of Kashmir'*. Several Pakistan Army officers who had fought the Kashmir war, were ethnic Kasmiris and owned land over there.

During the 1947 war, Maj. Gen. Akbar Khan had led Pakistani forces under the pseudonym (changed name) of 'General Tariq' also known as the hero of the Kashmir war. Maj. Gen. Akbar Khan's wife, Naseem Shahnawaz Khan, was also believed to have motivated her husband to undertake this plot. Maj. Gen. Akbar Khan and Faiz Ahmed Faiz were both convicted and sentenced to long terms of imprisonment. Their defence lawyer was the notable Bengali Muslim politician Huseyn Shaheed Suhrawardy, when H.S. Suhrawardy became the PM of Pakistan in 1957, he obtained a reprieve for most of the conspirators.

2. Failed Coup-attempt against Z.A. Bhutto on 30 March 1973

Due to the creation of FSF (Federal Security Force) and as the reform policies were unfolded, some junior, and middle-ranking army and air force officers began to meet to discuss the situation to overthrow the govt. of Z.A. Bhutto, but through Military Intelligence (MI), the plot was foiled and several officers were arrested on 30 March 1973.

There was a resentment against president Z.A. Bhutto among some junior and middle-ranking army and air force officers because Bhutto had retired Yahya Khan and his close associates, but retained many senior commanders who were involved in the East Pakistan debacle including Gen. Tikka Khan. Secondly, their dissatisfaction grew, over the months, as the (land) reform policies unfolded (were not stopped). In 1972, Bhutto retired Brigadier F.B. Ali, who taken the leading role in the officer's agitation that resulted in Yahya Khan and his stepping down. It added to the frustration of the brigadier's admirers in the armed forces. Thirdly, the creation of the FSF convinced them that Bhutto was on the way to consolidating a personal authoritarian rule and dictatorship. Initially FSF was established directly under civilian control to assist the govt. deal with smugglers, black-marketeers, and other criminal elements, but in practice, it served as *'Bhutto's Private Army'*.

"Consequently, they began to meet to discuss the situation, but were penetrated by military intelligence and the plot was foiled, resulting in the arrests of several officers on 30th March 1973.

The arrested men were put on trial in Attock Fort. Bhutto selected Maj. Gen. Muhammad Zia-ul-Haq to head the military tribunal to try the alleged conspirators. As a balancing gesture, Bhutto undertook a set of measures purported to appease the military – for example, he increased their pay scale and permitted the army to expand its recruitment and Defence Expenditure was increased, in nominal terms, from '3725 million in 1971-72 to '8210 million in 1976-77.

3. Failed Coup-attempt against to topple Benazir's Government in 1989.

(*Operation Mid-Night Jackal*)

It was a high profile political scandal during the first

term government of P.M. Benazir Bhutto to topple her government in 1989. The mastermind of the plot was a ISI rogue agent Brig. Imtiaz Ahmed "the cat" Ahmed. The judge Advocate General Corps launched the full-fledged military inquiry against the Brig. Imtiaz Ahmed and Major Amir Khan, subsequently ending their military careers. The investigations revealed that some members of the establishment wanted to pay hefty bribes to the senior leadership of Benazir Bhutto's peoples Party to bring the vote of no-confidence movement in the parliament. The military lawyers of prosecution also reported that the objectives of the *'Midnight Jackal'* were to support Nawaz Sharif as the establishment was said to have "liked" or preferred Sharif as a country's P.M., and was a part of his political camp. Major Amir Khan told his military lawyers that: "Nawaz Sharif was more acceptable to the Pakistan Army than Benazir Bhutto, and the establishment was against of every leader who had people's mandate behind them. They prefer weak leaders like Sharif, which the Army could control", Major Amir Khan maintained. A videotape was obtained from Intelligence Bureau (IB) containing a conversation of two active-duty army officers and a rogue ISI operative regarding toppling down Benazir Bhutto's government. The videotape exposed the conversation of a rogue agent Major Amir Khan, who revealed that COAS Gen. Mirza Aslam Beg, with the backing of the conservative President Ghulam Ishaq Khan, had ambitions topple the Benazir Bhutto's govt., and to bring a more conservative Nawaz Sharif and other conservatives in power instead. Due to lack of sufficient evidence against the COAS, his court martial could not take place. Allegedly, in 1989, the Al-Queda leader, Osama bin Laden, offered money to members of Parliament, including those from the PPP, to pass a no-confidence vote to make Benazir's govt. fall. When some of them informed her about the conspiracy, Benazir used some of them as *'Trojan horses'* in the *'ISI-IJI'* camp. Benazir wrote: "I used another group to videotape Brig. Imtiaz Ahmed asking my members to defect because *"the army"* did not want me." The no-confidence vote failed and Benazir continued in office.

This assertion of Benazir's- subsequently confirmed by Brig. Imtiaz during an interview on 'Dunya TV' was called operation Midnight Jackal. Imtiaz revealed that COAS General Aslam Beg wanted to replace her as her policies were deemed to be contrary to those of the army. (The Daily Times, 28 August 2009)

The Pakistan Military, as well as IJI (Islami Jamhoori Ittehad) were against and critical about Benazir's following policies:

1. At the 4th SAARC summit in Islamabad in December, 1988, Benazir and the Indian P.M. Rajiv Gandhi, seemed to have struck a friendly rapport. Benazir was of the view that Pakistan should re-orient its foreign policy towards democracy and, since India was a democracy, relations with that country should improve.
2. During their meeting, it was agreed that the two countries would not attack each other's nuclear facilities.
3. Some understanding also emerged on increasing trade and resolving the dispute over the Siachen Glacier. (Shafqat, 1997; 234-35)

In any case, a Rumour began to circulate after the SAARC Summit that Benazir had, handed over the names of the Khalistani Sikhs who had, hitherto, received sanctuary in Pakistan.

4. Failed Coup-attempt to overthrow Benazir's Government in September 1994

"In September 1994, the M.I uncovered a plot to overthrow Benazir's govt. The masterminds of the Conspiracy were Maj. Gen. Zaheer-ul-Islam Abbasi, Brig. Mustansar Billa,

Col. Azad Minhas, and some other officers, to assassinate Benazir Bhutto, Gen. Kakar, Senior Cabinet Minister and top commander in the GHQ and to declare *Pakistan a Sunni Religion state"*.

'The new director of the ISI, Lt. Gen. Javed Ashraf Qazi did his job with determination and courage to punish the plotters. The ringleaders and their followers were court-martialed and sent to jail, others were retired.'

Benazir's reputation continued to be tainted by Rumours that she and her spouse (A.A. Zardari) were relentlessly looting the national treasury once again. Her brother Murtaza's daughter (Fatima Bhutto) has affirmed the corruption charges in ample measure, giving many examples. Benazir's appointment of 21 new judges of the Punjab High Court caused considerable controversy on 20 September, 1996, Benazir's brother, Murtaza Bhutto, was gunned down in a spray of bullets, Murtaza had established a separate PPP faction. According to Benazir, Murtaza and she had reconciled their differences two months earlier. However, the Intelligence agencies began spreading RUMOURS that her husband Zardari, had masterminded the murder. A judicial inquiry set up to investigate the crime, Benazir informs, cleared Zardari of any involvement.

Etiology of Military Coups of Pakistan

1. Political Instability

The Etiology of Military Coups d' etat of Pakistan is a *multi-factorial* which cannot be explained through a *mono-causal theory.*

'Political instability' in Pakistan prevailing since its birth from 14th August 1947, is responsible for the occurrence of its military coups but 'political instability' is itself caused due to a number of *other actors and factors* which can be identified as under:

i. Pakistan leadership after the death of Quid-i-Azam, M.A Jinnah on 11 September 1948 and first P.M. Liaquat Ali on 16 October 1951 shifted to the shoulders of inapt, inefficient, inexperienced, divided, corrupt, feudal landlords who never allow a sustainable democracy in Pakistan to safeguard their vested interests.

ii. **Illiteracy:** Illiteracy played a major role in destroying the roots of nascent and fragile democracy of Pakistan. *'The literacy rate in FATA is for example 17.5 percent compared with the Pakistan average of 44%.'* About Pakistan's fragile democracy, Gen. Musharraf's views are similar to that of Gen. Ayub Khan that democracy is not workable in illiterate masses of Pakistan. Pakistan is a largely feudal society with a *high illiterate population* inherently unable to practise unfettered democracy. Gen. Ayub Khan expressed his views in favour of controlled democracy in place of unfettered democracy: 'Our people are mostly *uneducated* and our politicians not so scrupulous (absolutely honest). The people are capable of doing great things, but they can also be easily misled.'

Grinding Poverty: Pakistan is a very poor country. 'In Pakistan, where it is variously estimated that between 30% and about 50% of people in the rural and urban areas live *below* or just barely on the *Poverty Line (BPL)* sharp disparities become a glaring contradiction of progress on other fronts.'

According to Human Development Report on South Asia, at least 28 million (2.8 Crores) people in Pakistan live *below the poverty line* (BPL), two-thirds ($2/3^{rd}$) of its adult population is *illiterate* basic health facilities are available to *only half* the population. *(Ayesha Siddiqa, 2005, Pakistan: Political Economy of National Security)*

Rampant Corruption: Democracy in Pakistan could

not take deep root due to rampant corruption. According to Javed Jabbar, (2012) 'In its Corruption Index for 2010, Transparency International (TI) placed Pakistan at no. 143, in its index of 180 countries. *In other words: out of 180 countries surveyed, Pakistan is ranked as the 38th most corrupt country out of 180.* It is disturbing to realize that the Index gives countries like Nigeria (134) and India (87) better ratings than Pakistan even though both the above two countries are widely perceived to have *as much corruption,* if not more, as exists in Pakistan.'

2. Leadership Crisis after the death of M.A. Jinnah and Liaquat Ali

Pakistan had witnessed *'leadership vaccum'* after the death of founding father of Pakistan Quaid-i-Azam M.A. Jinnah on September 11, 1948, only 13 months after he had assumed the office of Governor-General. Like Mahatma Gandhi, Jinnah had also the such charismatic leadership qualities which none other Pakistani leaders possessed. After Jinnah, leadership had gone into the hands of Jinnah's loyalist and trusted fellow Liyaquat Ali Khan as the first P.M. of Pakistan. Unfortunately he was assassinated by a hired Afghan agent on October 10, 1951, in Rawalpindi for his authoritarianism and bias, further augmenting the leadership deficit of newly born Pakistan. The inter-party rivalries and intra-party power politics in the Muslim League caused to a succession of *Seven P.Ms* from 1950 to 1958. The prevailing political instability of the country gave military a chance to think about the posibility of *military intervention (praetorianism)* and change in the political system. As being the C-in-C of armed forces, Gen. Ayub Khan took the charge of Defence Minister also since 1954 and remained very close with political system and being aware about its shortcomings and weaknesses. The quick succession of seven P.M.s gave the message among Pakistan army and the public that Pakistani politicans were too weak, corrupt, divided, inefficient, ill-experienced, quarrelling and were looting the country with both hands, therefore the Parliamentary System was flawed. *Tolerance of opposition is the essense of democracy,* this intolerance in the mindset of leaders of opposition encouranged military to intervene into the politics. Gen. Ayub Khan and generals loyal to him forced Maj-Gen. Iskander Mirza, President of Pakistan to resign through a peaceful coup d' etat on October 27, 1958 and Ayub Khan took the charge of President and P.M.

Strong Nexus among Army, Civil Bureucracy and ISI: The Punjab form 60 percent of Pakistan population and 80 percent of its army. The feudal lords of Punjab have always been dominating force in the upper hierarchy of civil and military establishmetn of Pakistan. West Punjab is called the *grain bowl of Pakistan* because of its highly fertile plains. As characterised by the British, the Punjabi's are considered a *Martial Race*. Therefore, the military does not hesitate to *intervene* Whenever its peoples' intersts are challenged or threatened. First Governor-General of Pakistan M.A Jinnah and P.M. Liaquat Ali Khan relied very heavily on Civil Servants. It is rightly often said that *Politicians may come and may go but the bureaucrates control the real power in their hands.* Jinnah appointed Chaudhary Mohammad Ali as the Secretary-General of the Govt. of Pakistan which became an overlord of bureaucracy with vast powers. According to AtaurRehman Khan, 'a powerful clique in the bureaucracy did not want democracy to function in Pakistan and to take roots in the Country'. Gen. Ayub Khan too have no faith in political parties and politicians and became heavily dependent on the bureaucracy. Gen. Ayub appointed a civil servant, named Akhtar Husain as the head of the *Land Reforms Commission*. *Half-heated attempts* were made to appease feudal landlords; elites class of military and civil bureaucrates and corrupt politicians. Ultimately the nexus of civil bureaucracy with military junta became a permanent feature of Pakistans political system.

3. Delay in Constitution-Making & Weak Enforcement of the Law

While India had drafted and enforced her Consitution on 26 January 1950 *but contrary to India,* the task of Constitution making in Pakistan took about nine (9) years as it could be framed upto February 1956. Till the new Consitution could be framed, Pakistan was to be governed in accordance with Government of India Act of 1935 with certain modifications to meet the needs of newly born free Pakistan. The first and the most difficult task faced by framers of the Constitution was to decide the exact role of Islam in the State. *A second difficulty* in evolving a Constitution for Pakistan was the problem of nationalities, becuase Pakistan was founded under the *two-nation theory* i.e. separate homeland for Muslims and Hindus. These nationalities were a product of the history and geography which devided them from one another. The two wings of Pakistan, *east and west* were separated by more than a 1000 miles speaking entirely different languages, differing widely in their dress, manners and customs and people having conflicting interests. On language issue the Interim Report of the BPC (Basic Principles Committee) said that only *Urdu* shall be the national language. While the BPC report remained silent, but both the modified BPC report and the 1956 Consitution gave *Bengali and Urdu* co-equal official status. The 1956 Consitution had a very short span of life as Governor-General Iskander Mirza abrogated the Constitution on 7 October 1958. A fortnight later Gen. Ayub Khan made a coup against Mirza and brought Pakistan under Martial Law and appointed, an eleven member commission, headed by justice Muhammad Shahabuddin of the Supreme Court of Pakistan to frame a new Constitution for Pakistan. The Consitution prepared by the commission was approved by Gen. Ayub Khan with *some changes* and promulgated on 1 March 1962. It was called *'Basic Democracy'* Constitution and provided for indirect election of the President and members of the National and Provincial Assemblies by 'Basic Demorats' who were members of local councils in villages and towns. The 1962 Constitution lasted only 11 years. Due to secession of East Pakistan, Bangladesh emerged as a new Nation on the world map in December 1971. Ultimately Z.A Bhutto was able to get the Fourth Constitution passed in the National Assembly on 10th April 1973. Which came into force on 14 August 1973. Gen. Zia-ul-Haq overthrew Z.A Bhutto's civil Govt. through a Coup and assumed complete powers of the Govt. on 5 July 1977 but unlike earlier Coups, this time the Constitution was not abrogated but some parts of 1973 Constitution were held in abeyance.

In the absence of a permanent Constitution, the roots of sustained democracy in Pakistan could not be proliferated. And this situation was favourable to the feudal landlords and elite class of Military and bureaucracy.

Zia-ul-Haq imposed Martial Law and the 1973 Constitution was held in abeyance. Its revival took eight (8) years (1985) and that too with the addition of the 8th Amendment that included ***Article 58(2)(b):*** It empowered the President to dismiss the Prime Minister (P.M.) and the National Assembly if the situation so warranted. The President was also given *discretionary powers,* besides others, to appoint the Services Chiefs and the chairman of the Joint Chiefs of the Staff Committee (JCSC). The enhanced powers of the President created two power centres. The seeds of conflict were planted. During the period 1985-1996, three successive Presidents invoked *Article 58(2)(b)* on four different occassions and dismissed four elected P.Ms. Viz. Junejo (1988), Benazir (1990), Nawaz Sharif (1993) and Benazir (1996). The repeated use of the President's discretionary powers created uncertaintly in the country and started a national debate on *Whether Article 58(2)(b) was legally valid, politically justified, and insitutionally appropriate. The issue was agitated in Supreme Court of Pakistan under Consitutional Petition No. 60/1996. The Supreme Court held that this article had (infact shut the door on Martial Law which had not been imposed since 1977.)* The Apex

Court further state that the 8th Amendment, including Article 58(2)(b), was a valid piece of legislation and it was open to the Parliament to amend it, if so desired.' The controversial part of the 8th Amendment were *deleted* from the Statute Book by the Parliament by a unanimous vote.

Military rulers not only delayed the process of Constitution-making but they amended the Constitution according to their own wishes and convinience. According to Satish Kumar "Gen. Zia-ul-Haq amended 61 articles and inserted 20 to the 1973 Constitution. Similarly, Gen. Pervez Musharraf amended the Constitution drastically prior to the October 2002 generals elections. In the words of *Asma Jahangir, a human rights and women's rights activist of Pakistan....... The addition of Musharraf's amendments will convert the peoples Constitution of 1973 to a Consitution of the generals, for the generals, and by the generals" (Jahangir 2002:45)*

4. Praetorian Army of Pakistan

Roy Macridis and Steven Burg (Introduction to comparative politics, p-139) points out that the *'Armies* that intervene in politics in the contemporary era and *states* in which army intervention occurs are thus called *Praetorian Armies and Praetorian States',* and thus they define *Praetorian States* not only as states 'in which the army has the potential to dominate the political system' but also has the disposition to dominate.

Newly born Pakistan went through eleven years (from August 1947 to October 1958) of *political instability and uncertainty.* Frequently shifting of seven P.Ms. from 1950-58 encouraged to develop a praetorian mindset of army with the help of bureaucracy. More than half of its history Pakistan has been subjected to Military Coups d' etate. The Intelligence Agencies such as ISI and MI played a pivotal role in suppressing the institutions of democracy in Pakistan, and remained notoriously involved in engineering the *rigging of various elections* according to the preferences of each military dictator. For example in the elections of the 2002, Gen. Musharraf used all the means to achieve the desired results.

Army's Motive behind Praetorianism: Some reasons and causes for military intervention in politics of Pakistan are identified as under:

i. To allocate *'Lion's share'* for defence budget under the pretext of perceived threat from India, Kashmir obsession, and parity with India being anti-India-centric.

ii. Pakistan Army is the *final arbitrator* in the policy-making system, defence and foreign policy matters including Kashmir issue. Army manages its *vetopower* against any political decision which diminishes its interests.

Whenever any civil govt. has become weak and unmanageable due to its mal-administration, failed in maintaining law and order or corruption or the combination of all, the omnipotenet nexus of the Army and senior bureaucracy along with covert or overt support and sympathy of the leaders of opposition parties have engineered the downfall / overthrow of the civilian govt. and replaced it either with a new civil govt. or with their own rule; or, after the military themselves have been in power for a few years, they have managed a transition from their own rule back to civilian rule; and the whole cycle of *Patronage* has begun again. As the *Partonage* and *Kinship* (blood relation) form the basic elements of the Pakistani political system and *corruption* is an integral part of the system as a whole.

iii. **A Taste of Politics:** Vice-Chief of Army staff (during Gen. Zia's Military Rule) *Gen. Khalid Mahmud Arif* presented a depth analysis of the factors which influenced Military Intervention (Praetorianism)

> in the political field. He opined that Gen. Ayub Khan acquired a taste for politics when he included in the federal cabinet in 1954 as a Defence Minister, while retaining the post of the Army Chief. It became an opportunity enabled him to judge the political weaknesses from the inside, and *plan a Military takeover. This taste of politics made the army to reluctant to relinquish the military rule and prolonged it in the future.*

He identified some reasons which shifted the Role of Military from external security into internal Politics such as: acquiring a ladder of quick/swift Promotions from junior to senior ranks, to get extensions in service. The tenures of the services chiefs in Pakistan had a term of 4 years. But this tenure was generally extended. For example:

a) The first Pakistani incombent, Gen. Ayub Khan served this for seven and half ($7\frac{1}{2}$) years.

b) Gen. Muhammad Musa, the second Army Chief, served in this appointment for eight (8) years, because he was loyal to his patron (Gen. Ayub) and he was incapable of posing a threat to Ayub Khan.

c) The third Army Chief, Gen. Yahya Khan Military Regime ended with the tragic humiliating defeat in 1971 war againt India resulting the further division of country into Bangladesh.

d) While the next Army Chief Gen. Gul Hassan Khan, had a short tenure of only three months due to a personality clash between him and the then P.M. Z.A Bhutto caused his forced retirement.

e) General Zia-ul-Haq overthrew Z.A Bhutto in 1977 through a coup and remained the Army Chief throughout his military regime until his death in plane-crash.

Gen. K.M. Arif viewed that the grant of extensions to

the Army Chiefs was a *political blunder*. He stated: "The country might NOT have faced the pain of the 1958 Martial Law, if Gen. Ayub Khan had retired from Military Service in 1955, after completing his full term of four years as the Army Chief. *The history of* the country might have been differently written." *The Feudal Lords* were the most dangerous threat against to spread the roots of sustainable democracy and political stability in Pakistan. As Gen. Arif stated that irrespective of their political divide, the feudal lords (elite) act in unison (and perfect unity) when it comes to protecting the immense powers, privileges and influence exercised by them in the rural areas where 70 percent of the population lives. They have vigorously resisted the feeble (weak/fragile) attempts made in the legislatures to carry out *land reforms* that might loosen their landownership and control on the people. The Feudal elite class was responsible for the delay in making-Constitution. So it was a curse for common man of Pakistan.

Zia's Islamization, Redicalization and Sectarian Violence

"Villian" became the *"Hero"* of the West: Gen. Zia-ul-Haq was lucky because despite being as a *"Villian"* of the brutal judicial murderer of a populist leader Z.A. Bhutto on April 4, 1979, the Soviet Intervention of Afghanistan on 24th December 1979, made Zia the *"Hero"* of the west, particularly of the US, in supporting the Jihad against the soviet invaders of Afghanistan. As history repeats itself but in reverse gear, as post 9/11 Gen. Musharraf supported the US war on terror aginast Al-Qaeda and Taliban in Afghanistan under strong US pressure on Musharraf. Allah's Gen. Zia-ul-Haq believed that Pakistan could not survive except as an Islamic state. In 1976, he changed, the motto of the Pakistan army to *'Jihad fi Sabil Allah'*. He believed that only Islam could resurrect a force traumatized in combat with its mortal foe, India. But Zia's step to use religion in state politics became very disastrous towards nation-building and maintaing

peace, harmony, law and order.

Amongst four Military Regimes of Pakistan; Zia-ul-Haq's military rule (Martial Law, 1977 to 1988) is regarded as most dangerous/disastrous and of Creating Conflict-Generating Conditions.

Some of the most disastrous steps taken during Zia's military rule can be listed below under Islamisation which caused overtly or covertly political inistability and sectarian violence in Pakistan:

i. Proliferation of Madrassas,

ii. Islamization of the education system,

iii. Islamization of the military,

iv. Growth of sectarian violence between Sunnis and Shias during Zia's regime.

v. Introduction of Blasphemy Laws and its misuse against the small Christian & Hindu minorities and other weaker sections of the society.

vi. The Hudood Ordinances and introduction of an Islmaic judicial system based upon the Quran and the Sunnah& set up a Federal Sharia Court to decide whether any judicial law was contraty to that of Islam.

vii. Widespread Discrimination against Ahmadiyyas and declared them as Non-Muslims and Kafirs.

Soviet invasion in Afghanistan during 1980s and simultaneous Military regime of Zia-ul-Haq in Pakistan multiplied Pakistan problems. Pakistan's drift towards religious extremism and jihad militancy converted this *region into a hub and epicentre of terrorist activities*. Sectarian intolerance and hatred promoted killings, blasts, armed attacks and suicide bombings in which thousands of innocent civilians of Pakistanis have lost their lives.

i. ***Proliferation of Madrassas:*** Well-armed Islamic radical groups used the Madrassa students as *'street power'*. The Islamization of Pakistan during Zia's regime led to the rapid growth in the number of Madrassas. In 1971, there were 900 Madrassas in Pakistan, but by the end of the Zia era in 1988, there were 8000 registered, and over 25000 unregistered Madrasas." Zia had also recognised the *Sanad (Certificate)* awarded by these Madrasas as equivalent to University Degree.

ii. ***Islamization of the education system:*** During the time of Gen. Zia, Social Studies, which comprised of 'History' and 'Geography', were replaced by *Pakistan Studies,* which was made a *Compulsory Subject for all students from the IXth grade through the first year of college including Engineering and Medical schools.* Curriculum changes, institutionalised during Zia's *Islamisation Campaign,* required that all students also take a series of courses under the title *Islamiyat,* and memorisation of Quranic verses. To guide students towards the ultimate goal of Pakistan – the creation of a completely Islamised State." Islamisation of Pakistani Social Studies Text books; Rupa. Co. in association with ORF (Observer Research Foundation) Ansari Road, Daryaganj, New Delhi-110002. Standard 'Pakistan Studies' Text books rarely include chapters that discuss the culture and histories of *Balouchis or Pathans or Sindhis.* So the people and intellectuals of these provinces protested against this move of Zia silently. According to Avril Powell, Professor of History at the University of London, History by erasure can have its long-term negative repercussions. These Text books were manipulated by omission. See an example of this is the manner in which *the Indo-Pakistan war of 1965* is discussed in Pakistani Text books: "There is no mention of *'operation Gibralter'*, even after four decades and its repercussions of that ill-planned military adventurism which resulted in India's attack on Lahore. In Pakistani Text books the story is told that 'the Indian Army, unprovoked, inexplicably attacked Lahore' and that 'one Pakistani Jawan (soldier) equals ten Indian Soldiers', who, upon seeing the fierce Pakistani, 'drop their *banduks*(rifles) and run away'. Many people in Pakistan still think this, and several mentioned this assumed *cowardice of the Indian Army* in discussions while the fighting was raging in Kargil (1999)"[12]

iii. ***Islamization of the military*:** However the traditions of the British Indian Army were a Professional, Secular, border protector, internal security provider and subordinated under the control of civilian democratic rule *but under Zia, the Pakistan Military became a staunch defender of Islam.* Islamic philosophy and the prayer at the regimental mosques on Friday became mandatory. *Promotions* were partly based on demonstrated *piety* (i.e. devotion to God and respect for religious principles), and non-pious Muslims and non-Muslims found their promotion to senior ranks forcefully blocked. Under Islamization process some measures were introduced such as: banning of drinking of alcohol in the officer's mess – which had been a cherished tradition since British times, the setting aside of time for *prayer* and fasting and the introduction of the *Study of Islam* into the education of the officer corps. Religious Indoctrination of recruits from middle and lower-middle class backgrounds strengthened the alliance between the military and the religious conservative radicals. Many troops attended *Jamaat-i-Islami* meetings and joined Islamic missionary groups. They became powerful in the ISI. Former D-G, ISI Hamid Gul and his successor, Gen. Javed Nasir, both supported the more extreme mujahideen groups in Afghanistan and the jihadi groups in Kashmir. Both opposed the US and wanted Pakistan to undergo an Islamic Revolution that would free the country from the western Culture and political influence of the US.

iv. ***Growth of sectarian violence between Sunnis and Shias:*** As far as ethnic demography of Pakistan is concerned, Muslim population in Pakistan is 97% remaining 3% are minorities such as Hindus, Christians etc. Sunnies and Shias Constitute roughly 80 and 20 percent of the population. Pakistan is a Sunni majority state. Saudi Arabia is a major patron and close friend of Pakistan also is a Sunni majority Muslim state. Iraq is also Sunni majority Muslim state but Iran is a Shia majority Muslim state.

There was a very little overt sectarian violence in Pakistan between Sunnis and Shias until the 1980s. The sectarian violence was began to emerge during Zia's regime, and it was fuelled by the rivalry between the new Revolutionary Shia state of Iran, under the leadership of Ayatollah Khomeini; (after Iran Revolution in 1979), and the Wahhabi fundamentalist monarchy of Saudi Arabia (a Sunni Muslim State). To check the export of Shiate Islamic revolution from Iran, the Sunni dominant Saudi Arabia began to use sectarian violence as an instrument of policy. Americans had also encouraged Sunni Islam in their war against soviets in Afghanistan. The famous Iran-Iraq war (1980-88) was viewed as the war between the Shias of Iran and the Sunnis of Iraq. Iraq's Saddam Hussain had mobilized Pakistan's Sunnis against Shias of Iran during the eight years long war with Iran. The Iranian Saudi proxy war, in the context of Pakistan, meant sectarian terrorism between Pakistani Shias and Sunnis.

Saudi Arabia supported the radical Sunni groups in Pakistan in order to counter the influence of his enemy-the Shia state of Iran. As being the long and deep relationship, Pakistan had recived more aid from Saudi Arabia than from any other country. In return, Pakistan provided Saudi Arabia with military aid, assistance and expertise. The Saudi strongly supported Zia's attempt to turn Pakistan into a strongly authoritarian Sunni state. During Iranian Revolution in 1979, Iran's Shia leader Ayatollah Ruhollah Khomeini had overthrown the Shah (pro-US) and established with Shia grounded Islamic Law. Islamization under Zia encouraged *aggressive Sunnification* and Zia imposed *'Zakat tax'* on Shias, Shia law, however, maintained that the tax would be paid by the individual and not collected by the state. Pakistani Shias, like Shia minorities in other countries, greatly welcomed the Iranian Revolution (1979), which encouraged them to stand up for their own religious rights. Khomeini allegedly warned Zia that if he attempted to suppress Shias in Pakistan, he *'would do to him what he had done to the Shah'*.

In July 1980, Shias assembled from all over Pakistan in Islamabad, demanded that *'Zakat'* not be imposed upon them by the state. Zia became demoralized against Shia's huge demonstration and quickly exempted Shias from aspects of the Islamization process that contradicted Shia law and practices. An anti-Shia, Sunni terrorist organization named as *the Sipah-e-Sahaba (Army of the Prophet's companions)* was emerged first time during the rule of Zia. This organization was founded in 1985 in the district of *Jhang* in the centre of the Punjab province. It advocated a strong *Sunni State* in which *Shiites* would be classified as *Kafirs,* as such, would be considered a non-Muslim minority in Pakistan, similar to the *Ahmadiyya.Sipah-e-Sahaba* also wanted the *ban* the *Muhurram processions* on the grounds that they insulted the early Islamic leaders who was revered by *Sunnis.* However, on 12 January 2002, the organization was banned by Gen. Pervez Musharraf for its alleged involvement in terrorist activities. The growth of sectarian violence between Sunnis and Shias during the 1980s which escalated during the 1990s, now become a feature of contemporary Pakistani politics. History will not forgive Zia-ul-Haq for the blunders committed through Islamizationprogramme to legitimize his military regime and committing 'judicial murder' of his predecessor Z.A. Bhutto.

The Military dictator Gen. Zia-ul-Haq is held responsible for changing the Pakistan from a religiously tolerant state into the state of widespread sectarian violence. Zia attempted to use the oppression of Ahmadiyya to woo the Muslim votes. Terrorism (within and outside) and sectarian violence are the two major problems to which Pakistani resilient and tough society is facing today.

"One of the most disastrous consequences of Zia's policies (under Islamization) was the rapid growth of sectarian violence between the *Sunni majorityand the Shia minority* which was to lead to a terrorist war between the two sects which is currently still ongoing"[14]

v. ***Introduction of Blasphemy Laws and its misuse:*** The blasphemy laws have been criticized by human right activists and campaigner *Asma Jahangir* in Pakistan and abroad because they have been repeatedly *misused* in order to settle personal vendettas and to persecute Pakistani's tiny population of Christians, comeout from very impoverished background. For example; on 4 January 2011, A policeman of Islamabad, Malik Mumtaz Hussain Qadri murdered 66-year-old SalmaanTaseer – the controversial Governor of Punjab province who was a member of Pakistan's nominally secular ruling PPP. Qadri justified the reason for Taseer assassination as a *'punishment' for a 'blasphemer'* because he alleged that Taseer was a blasphemer as he had courageously defended a poor Christian Woman, AasiaBibi (Noreen) who had allegedly insulted the *Prophet Muhammad* during a row (quarrel) with her Muslim neighbours. Qadri's lawyer claimed that over 800 lawyers had volunteered to defend Qadri without charging a fee and that all sections of the population of Pakistan believed that his killing was justified.[14] On 2 March 2011, Pakistan's Christian Minister for Minorities, *Shahbaz Bhatti* was assassinated in Islamabad for advocating reform of the blasphemy laws.

vi. ***The Hudood Ordinances:*** Set out very cruel or brutal and inhuman punishments laid down in the Quran and Sunnah such as: cutting off hands of thieves and execution by stoning for severe crimes. Although these punishments were never actually carried out, public floggings (beating) and harsh imprisonment certainly were. Pakistani Soceity became more intolerant and sectarian. Under Zia's rule, women were pressurized to dress modestly and to wear the *Hijab* (head covering cloth) in public. Strict government censorship was applied to all TV programmes and movies. Women's rights were severely restricted by the Hudood Ordinances, particularly in respect to *rape,* where an unfortunate rape victim could be *flogged* (beaten) and jailled for *sexual misbehaviour,* unles she could prove her innocence.

Kashmir Factor: According to some Pakistani Scholars and diplomats the major the irritant towards the betterment of India-Pakistan relation is *Kashmir dispute.* The views of two top leaders of Pakistan and India are quoted here:

"Kashmir runs in our blood. No Pakistani can afford to sever (cut) links with Kashmir. The entire Pakistan and the world know this. We will continue to extend our moral political and diplomatic support to Kashmiris. We will never budge (change opinions/attitude) an inch from our principled stand on Kashmir." *(Gen. Pervez Musharraf, address to the Nation, January 12, 2002)*

"We wish to state once again that Jammu and Kashmir is an *integral part* of India. It will remina so.... For us, Kashmir is not a piece of land; it is a test case of *'Sarva Dharma Samabhava' – Secularism. India* has always stood the test of a secular nation. Jammu and Kashmir is a living example of this." *(Prime Minister Atal Bihari Vajpayee, Independence Day, address, August 15, 2002)*

The four wars of 1947-48, 1965, 1971 and 1999 did not deliver Kasmir to Pakistan and Political leaders of both the countries know very well that it is not possible for Pakistan to forcibly take Kashmir from India and it is not possible for India to give Kashmir to Pakistan on a platter (dish). Due to Kashmir obsession, Pakistani Army, ISI, and other Islamic radicals shifted their policy on Kashmir: in place of Conventional War with India, they started waging proxy war, Low-Intensity Conflict, Cross-border Terrorism to fight against India covertly with strategy of Indirect approach. Pakistan's Army and ISI decided to make *'Terrorism as an instrument of its state policy against India'* Pakistani Military as well as civilian rulers maintained a *double face* or *dual policy* on Kashmir issue and towards the betterment of Relations between India and Pakistan. Under international pressure, particularly of the US, Pakistan started to propagate that they want to have a *composite dialogue* with India on the issue of terrorism. On the other hand, *Pakistani non-state actors* with the underhand support of Pakistan Army and ISI started to intensify terrorist activities across the border, Consequently ModiGovernmet replied that *dialogue and terrorist activities cannot be carried out parallel and simultaneously.* Fruitful dialogue can only be possible in a peaceful and friendly environment. Prime Minister NarendraModi took initiative and visited Nawaz Sharif's home as a goodwill gesture on 25 December 2015 for better relationship with Pakistan during his returning journey from Afghanistan. But Pakistani Army, ISI and Islamic radicals want the *Kashmir Issue* alive because it is needed for their survival and to safeguard their own vested interests to allocate *'lion's share' in National budget for defence affairs.*

Hypocritically Pakistan Army had been projecting an image of being the *'Saviours of the Nation'* to seek legitimacy and justification of its various military rules and frequent Praetorianism due to lacklustre (dull and uninspiring) performance of the civilian governments as and when they were elected to power. In May 2014, present COAS, Gen. Raheel Sharif also expressed the similar views on Kashmir Issue as Gen. Pervez Musharraf opined on January 12, 2002, and stated that: *"Kashmir is Jugular Vein of Pakistan"*. Due to Kashmir the Army will avail *lion share* within resourceless Pakistani economy. An eminant military expert of Pakistan and major researcher in Pakistan, *Ayesha Siddiqa* has opined her views in her famous book: *'Pakistan Military Inc'"that even if India will hand over Kashmir to Pakistan in a Silver Plate, there is hardly any guarantee that animosity between both rivals will end. For the time being both countries must sustain the dialogue process on Kashmir till its final resolution and in the meanwhile cooperate on the areas where there are hardly any divergences like trade and commerce."*

Munir Akram, Pakistani's former Ambassador to the

UN, has opined his pessimistic views over the betterment of India-Pakistan Relations. He stated that despite cultural, linguistic and ethnic affinities, the mutual hostility (and antagonism) between Hindus and Muslims of the Sub-Continent is real and endemic. It was the *raison d' etre* (reason for justification) for the creation of Pakistan.

Geo-Demographic Asymmetry, Inequality and Discriminatory Behaviour of Federal Government with Balochistan Poses and Prone - to the Second Secession of Pakistan:

Pakistan has a population of over 170 million (i.e. 17 crores) in 2011. The Federation of Pakistan comprises four Provinces namely: Punjab, Sindh, Khyber-Pakhtunkhwa (KP) and Balochistan. Punjab has the largest share of the population at about 55%. Sindh has a share at about 30%. K.P has a share of about 11 percent. But Balochistan has a population of *only 4% of the total.*

See the asymmetry!, the Province with the smallest share of population (i.e. 4%) – Balochistan–has the largest land mass of all the four Provinces; i.e. over 45% of Pakistan's territory. On the other hand, the Punjab alone, has more People (Population i.e. 55%) than all the other 3 (three) Provinces combined.

This Asymmetry poses substantial problems of *equity, participation and governance.*

The Baloch people have always demanded decisive control over the pricing and exploitation of natural resources as gas and other minerals found in their province. Development project of Gwadar Port by China is neglecting the economic rights of Balochis. Therefore, there is a substantial dissatisfaction among Balochi peoples against the federal govt. of Pakistan which is making wide discrimination and suppression to them which led to the *Second Secession of Pakistan like East Pakistan in 1971.*

Conclusion & Policy- Implications For India and Pakistan

Despite having mandate P.M. Nawaz Sharif was under limitations because of Democracy in Pakistan is still fragile and controlled by the Pakistan Army. Army is the final arbiter and *'single-decision maker'* pertaining to foreign policy, defence policy, Kashmir issue and framing relations with India and Afghanistan.

After getting defeat in four wars of 1947-48, 1965, 1971 and 1999 Pakistan is using *'terrorism as an instrument of state policy'* against India. Pakistan Army is protecting him and providing patronage to so-called *'Good Taliban'* and playing double game with US war on terror against al-Qaeda and Taliban. Pakistan's strategy of using terrorism as an instrument of state policy has also affected its ability to fight terrorism and sectarian violence at home.

Pakistan Army did not target so-called *'Good Taliban'* who are considered as *'Strategic Assets'*.The three groups of good taliban are the *Haqqani network under Hafiz Gul Bahadur,* the *TTP in North Waziristan* and *Mullah Nazir's group* active in wana a region of *South Waziristan.* The major dilemma for Pakistan army was-how to conduct the military operation during US war on terror *without* harming the *Haqqani Network* and so-called good taliban.

Pertaining to Pakistan's sponsored state-terrorism, Mrs. Hillary Clinton, during her forthcoming Presidential election campaign recently stated that: "If you pet the snakes in your court-yard, it will not make any discrimination between you and your neighbour in biting." Till the military in Pakistan remains as the most important and dominating player in Pakistani politics; no shift in foreign policy is expected towards better relations between India and Pakistan in near future. Civil-Military-Relations in Pakistan will improve only through sustainable political stability and establishment of strong democratic pattern and four pillars of democracy i.e. Legislation, Execution, Judiciary and Free & Fair Mass Media will work together with full cooperation, proper coordination, as well as controlling the *praetorian* (intervening) *role of almighty Pakistani Army* which hypocritically projecting its image of being the *'Saviours of the Nation'* but every time the interest of the common people of Pakistan is always sacrified and neglected due to the vested interests vis-a-vis a coterie of feudal lords. The Process of Islamisation during Zia-ul-Haq's Military regime is being held responsible for the intensification of 'Sectarian Violence' between Shia and Sunni and the collapse of harmonial society of Pakistan due to wide religious Islamic discrimination among minority groups like Christians, Hindus, and Ahmadiyyas. Misuse of the Blasphemy laws further intensified the 'Sectarian violence' and radicalization of orthodox extremism and use of terrorism as a tool of state-policy against India as a mortal-foe.

After investigating the Pakistani political dynamics, it has become clear that the secession of Pakistan into Bangladesh in 1971 was occurred due to its *'own weight'* and wrong policies adopted by military ruler General Yahya Khan and PPP autocratic leader Z.A. Bhutto through dis-honouring the democratic mandate and 'Six-Point Progamme' of Sheikh Mujibur Rahman of Awami League Party of East Pakistan.

Feudal, corrupt, inapt, divided, inefficient and inexperienced political leaders of opposition provided the chance and opportunities to intervene the military in Pakistani politics. Once the Military Rule was established, the Military Rulers became reluctant to relinquish the authority through prolonging it either under the guise of maintaining 'law and order' or even amending and abrogating the then Constitution and resisting the Movement for the Restoration of Democracy (MRD) by political leaders. This Vicious circle remained continue for decades in Pakistani politics.

In the eyes of World Media, the image of Pakistan is

as 'the most dangerous country in the world'. Who made it? Of course, All this is done in the name of Islam!. Misuse of religion in state-politics have its own consequences, Pakistan's political, social and religious life today is completely contrast to what the founding fathers–Quaid–i–Azam Muhammad Ali Jinnah (1876-1948) and and eminent poet and thinker Dr. Muhammad Iqbal (1877-1938)-had aspired and dreamed it to be. The ground realities of today's Pakistan would be disappointing to both. They (both) imagined Pakistan as an Islamic State at tolerance, and respectful of Non-Muslim citizens and their faiths, enabling them to live in Pakistan as equal citizens, suffering from no legal or political discrimination. Both of them expected Pakistan to be a Democratic State under the rule of law, not to be periodically ruled by Martial Law. Pakistan was expected to be a prosperous state, where science and technology (instead of theology and orthodox ideology) were to flourish. Pakistan was to be a beacon of enlightment and progress in the Muslim world. But Alas! the dream could not be fulfilled till today. Jinnah's liberal and humane political philosophy became brightly visible after Pakistan had come into existence in August 1947. His liberal political vision filled with secular democratic values has been expressed in his address which he delivered to the Constituent Assembly of Pakistan on 11 August 1947; he articulated (speak clearly and distinctly) the notion of Pakistani nationalism which combined religious freedom, political equality, and the state's detachment from religious and sectarian squabbles with emphasis he added: "You are free; you are free to go to your temples, you are free to go to your mosques, or to any other place of worship in this state of Pakistan.............. you may belong to any religion or caste or creed-that has nothing to do with the business of the state................ we are starting in the days when there is no discrimination, no distinction between one community and another................ "

(Speeches of Quaid-i-Azam Muhammad Ali Jinnah as

Governor-General of Pakistan (Karachi: Sindh Observer Press, 1948). pp.4-5.)

Jinnah died on 11 September 1948 by Cancer of the lungs. If Jinnah had survived for another period of three years, he certainly would have led the Constitution Assembly to complete a democratic Constitution for Pakistan. Jinnah was a barrister and leading lawyer of Bombay High Court. Unfortunately Jinnah's Ideals and vision of secular democracy were forgotten and pay no heed to his message after the death of charismatic leader. Jinnah was perhaps aware and had foreseen that radical Islamism may take Pakistan on the road to disaster. Today's Pakistan is definitely not Jinnah's Pakistan what he dreamt.

Drifting away from Jinnah's ideals brought the Pakistan into the quagmire of political instability, periodical martial laws, sanctuary of dreaded terrorist groups like al-Qaeda and Taliban, ultimately towards a failed state. Cross-border Terrorism has done irreparable damage to the India-Pakistan Relationship. Pakistan must abandon its strategy of 'Terrorism as an Instrument of foreign policy'. Pakistan's foreign policy with India is harmful and not practically fruitful. Considering its size, population, area, economic development, India's defence preparedness is China-Centric, it is not Pakistan-Centric. India is big brother of Pakistan, therefore, Pakistan not need to bother any parity with India.

Pakistan Army and I.S.I. are 'State within State': Due to PM Modi's sound foreign policy and under US pressure, PM Nawaz Sharif has assured the action against the perpetrators of terrorist attack on Pathankot Air Base and Mumbai attack on 26 November 2008, but the main obstacle in the betterment of Relations between the two neighbours is the nexus of Pakistan Army, I.S.I. and radical orthodox islamists, so-called 'good terrorists'. It is rightly said that Pakistan is controlled by "3As" i.e. Allah, Army and America. All 'three As' are almighty, omnipotent, omniscent, and omnipresent in Pakistan.

A Pakistani analyst, Mosharraf Zaidi writes a relevant remark pertaining to Pakistan Army as a big hurdle towards the betterment of India-Pakistan Relationship. "If Pakistan and India become normal neighbours, the military's influence in Pakistan automatically decreases. The hawks (i.e. Pakistani Army) clearly won't go easily." Ishaan Tharoor has cited from the 'Washington Post' on August 29, 2014 regarding Pakistan Army's legitimation as: 'The Pakistani Military, a half a million (i.e. 5 Lakh) – strong standing army finds something of a *'raison d' etre'* (reason for justification) in its historic rivalry with India.' The country have fought four wars since their Independence from Britain in 1947......"

Pakistan will not change overnight but it will certainly change because Pakistan itself perceive that present policy of terrorism, parity with India, projecting hatred and anti-India feelings is harmful for Pakistan itself. Pakistan will not collapse through so-called external threat but internal threats and challenges *within home* are most dangerous for Pakistan's survival and existence. A Shayar (poet) has mentioned a relevant statement pertaining to Pakistan : *"Iss Ghar Ko Jalaa Diyaa, Ghar Ke Chiraag Ne"*

Keeping controversial issues like *'Kashmir'* aside and forwarding towards trade, commerce, games, cultural heritage, film & cinema, educational exchange, people-to-people contact are so many wide areas where India and Pakistan come together under peaceful co-existence and tolerance which are the basic teachings of real Islam. After that we hope the sustainable Peace and Tranquillity will prevail in south-Asian sub-continent.

As far as India is concerned, the Indian government is moving in right direction under PM Modi's charismatic leadership, statecraft and statesmanship which can be seen through achieving growing popularity during the two years of his first tenure as Prime Minister. His endeavours, vision, and clear intension will yield certainly fruitful in nation-building for both India as well as Pakistan. India is hopeful that goodwill and five-senses will prevail to Pakistan and Pakistan will abandon the policy of 'cross-border terrorism' and will come out with good and positive intention for Comprehensive bilateral dialogue with India to sort-out all controversial issues through peaceful means in order to strengthen economic development of this region.

In the last, but not the least the common-man (people) of both neighbours is hopeful for the establishment of political stability and sustainable democracy in both countries, particularly in Pakistan, so that Civilian Government may not work under the pressure of *'praetorian army of Pakistan'* and its ally I.S.I. and they (both) will remain upto the limits of their professional duties subordinated under the civilian authority. Despite the constant endeavors and repeated demands of India to take a tangible action against the perpetrators of 26/11 Mumbai attackers, attack on Pathankot Air Base and other frequent incidents of cross-border terrorism from the Pakistani Soil into Indian territory; all perpetrators of terrorist activities are playing their role without any fear and guilt under the patronage of Pakistani military establishment and intelligence agencies nexus which consider them as strategic assets for extending strategic depth in Afghanistan on both sides of Durand Line at the time of crisis and call them non-state actors of proxy war against India. Therefore, neither India nor the Pakistan's duly elected democratic government can hope for peace, stability, economic development and better Indo-Pak Relations *unless and untill*praetorian military of Pakistan firmly decided to abandon applying *'terrorism as an instrument of state-policy'.*

Options Open For India

The writer does not support Pessimistic and Idealstic views and have an approach of thinking in pragametic, positive and realistic manner. It has now become the crystal-clear fact that praetorian military of Pakistan will not abandon its status of *"State within State"* and *"Terrorism as an instrument of State-policy"*. Therefore, following options are open for India to follow *Track-II Diplomacy* to eliminate Cross-Border Terrorism between India and Pakistan. Appropriate measures are divided into two categories:

1. Preventive Measures
2. Operational (Military) Measures

1. Under Preventive Measures the below mentioned effective options are open for India under Statesmanship & Statecraft of Prime Minister NarendraModi:

i) It is right step of India to withdraw the status of MFN given to Pakistan in1996, and increasing 200% duty on commodities importing to India from Pakistan.

ii) Abrogation of *Indus Water Treaty*(19 Sept. 1960) signed by the then P.M. J.L. Nehru and Pakistan's President Gen. Ayub Khan and World Bank as mediator, and manage 100% water of three eastern rivers *Ravi, Beas and Sutlej*. India have to establish infrastructure for water transportation (first phase from Delhi to Prayagraj), construction of dams and Canals for irrigation etc.

iii) Isolate Pakistan from International platforms (like OIC, SAARC, G-20, ASEAN, APEC, BIMSTEC, OAU, UNSC, UNGA etc.) and expose her as epicenter of terrorism as Pakistan is exporting, patronaging and funding terrorism in her soil. Gov. of India is doing well in this direction e.g.

a) OIC has invited India as a guest of honour, while Pakistan who is the founding member of OIC did not attend the OIC.

b) UNSC pressurised Pakistan and rejected Hafiz

Saeed's (founder of LeT now could JuD) plea on removal from terror list. He was the mastermind of Mumbai Attack (26.11.2008)

c) USA has objected Pakistan why F-16 fighter plane was used against India after Balakot Air Strike by I.A.F. on 26 Feb. 2019. Indian Pilot of Mig-21 Abhinandan targeted and destroyed it.

d) UNGA must prepare a comprehensive definition of terrorism and enforce strict laws to punish perpetrators of terrorist acts.

e) All members of UNGA collectively stand to end International Terrorism as their first priority.

iv) Economic Santions, political and diplomatic Isolation should be promoted collectively against the nations which support the acts of terror universally.

Role of Finance, because *"Money is the engine that derives terrorist acts"* correct information about the Sources, Methods and Channels which are involved in Financing and funding of Terrorism should thoroughly be investigated. Money is flowing through *Hawala, Money laundering, Black Money, Drug Trafficking, Smuggling, Narcotics, Petro-dollars, Donations and Ransoms etc.* Large amount of money is collected in the name of *Charity, Zakat* for terrorist organizations. Pakistan's terrorist organizations are providing money to stone throwers on security forces in Kashmir Valley. Money of any person or group or organization must be frozen who helped directly or indirectly to any terrorist outfit.

v) India should support Secessionist Insurgencies at Balochistan, Gilgit & Baltistan, Sindh as done in Bangladesh in 1971

vi) Article No. 370 & 35-A should be abolished so that the Demography (ratio of population) can be shifted in the interest of integration and integrity of India as Pakistan has already done in Gilgit & Baltistan.

2. Under Operational (Military) Measures: India has suffered a lot from the plight of terrorism, the list is very large, e.g. Two PMs on 31 Oct. 1984 (Indira Gandhi), 21 May 1991 (Rajiv Gandhi), Punjab C.M. Beant Singh 1995, Attack on Parliament on 13 Dec. 2001, suicide attack on the gate of Legislative Assembly of Kashmir on Oct.1, 2001, Mumbai attack on 26 Nov. 2008, Attack on Pathankot Air Base on 2nd Jan. 2016 (02:50 A.M.), Fidayeen Terrorist Attack of JeM on URI Army Brigade Headquarters on 18 Sep. 2016 at 05:35 A.M. To retaliate it, Indian Army conducted *Surgical Strike* on mid-night of 28-29 Sep. 2016 across the LoC and destroyed seven Pakistani terrorist training camps and launching pads of infiltrators. About 40 terrorists were killed on the spot. Again on 14 Feb. 2019 Fidayeen terrorist attacked on the convoy of CRPF Bus and 40 CRPF Jawans were martyred at *Pulwama* in South Kashmir. On retaliation, the Indian Air Force has conducted an Air Strike in the midnight of 25/26 Feb. 2019 at *Balakot* and other terrorist training camps of Pakistan.

From the above Air Strike (26 Feb. 2019) and Surgical Strike (29 Sep. 2016), India demonstrated that she is no more a *Soft State* but is a *Hard State.* India should reply to Pakistan into its own language: and follow the policy of Tit-for-Tat.

References

1. Oxford Advanced Learner's Dictionary (1989), Oxford University Press; p. 272.
2. Coup d′ État – Wikipedia, the free encyclopedia.
3. Oxford Advanced Learner's Dictionary (1989), Oxford University Press; p. 272.
4. The International Relations Dictionary-by Plano & Olton (1969), western Michigan University, p. 55.

5. A Sage Professional Paper by William R. Thompson – "*The Grievances of Military Coup-Makers- Comparative Politics Series, Series Number; 01-047 Volume 4; 1973*".

6. Coup d′ État by Edward Luttwak (1968, 1979), p. 667.

7. "World Military Coups since 1945 : A short Note on Data Collection"; Milton Leitenberg. p. 385.

8. Coup d′ État, A Practical Manual, published by Arms and Armour Press Limited, Link House West Street, Poole, (Great Britain).

9. Huntington S.P. (1968) Political Order in Changing Societies, New Haven and London: Yale University Press, pp. 192-264.

10. Hussain, Zahid, 2010, *Frontline Pakistan : The Path to Catastrophe and the Killing of Benazir Bhutto*, London and New York: I.B. Tauris& Co. Ltd. P.P- 5-6.

11. Ishtiaq Ahmad (2013) : *The Pakistan Military in Politics : Origins, Evolution Consequences*, Amaryllis, New Delhi. pp– 297-298.

12. Ibid – pp–209-210.

13. Source – Wikipedia, the free encyclopedia & Ishtiaq Ahmad (2013).

14. Abbas, Hassan, 2005, *Pakistan's Drift into Extremism: Allah, the Army, and America's War on Terror*, New Delhi: Pentagon Press. pp – 152-153

15. Talbot Ian, 2012, 2013, *Pakistan : A New History*, London, C. Hurst & Co. (2012) & New Delhi, Amaryllis, Munjal Publishing House Pvt. Ltd. (2013) & Marketed by Pentagon Press, p-280.

16. Ahmed, Ishtiaq, 2013, *The Pakistan Military in Politics: Origins, Evolution, Consequences*, New Delhi: Amaryllis, p-111.

17. Jabbar, Javed, 2012, *Pakistan : Identity and Destiny*, New Delhi-110020, Har-Anand Publications Pvt. Ltd, pp-135-136.

18. Ibid, pp-136-137.

19. Dogra C. Deepak, 2016, *Pakistan : Caught in the Whirlwind,* Lancer Publishers & Distributors, New Delhi-110016, p-143.
20. Ibid, p-277.
21. Malik Hafeez (Editor), 2001, *Pakistan : Founders' Aspirations and Today's Realities,* Karachi, New York, Oxford University Press, pp-89-90.
22. Kukreja, Veena and Singh M.P., (Editors), 2005, *Pakistan : Democracy, Development and Security Issues,* New Delhi and London, Sage Publications, p-229.
23. Malik Hafeez (Editor), 2001, *Pakistan : Founders' Aspirations and Today's Realities,* Karachi, New York, Oxford University Press, p-115.
24. Murphy Eamon, 2013, *The Making of Terrorism in Pakistan : Historical and Social roots of extremism,* London and New York, Routledge, p-91.
25. Rosser Y.C., 2003, *Islamisation of Pakistani Social Studies Text books,* Published by Rupa. Co, New Delhi-110002, In Association with Observer Research Foundation, p-8.
26. Ibid, p-55.
27. Murphy Eamon, 2013, *The Making of Terrorism in Pakistan : Historical and Social roots of extremism,* London and New York, Routledge, p-98.
28. Ibid, p-12.
29. Ibid, p-4.
30. General Pervez Musharraf, address to the Nation, January 12, 2002.
31. *Prime Minister Atal Bihari Vajpayee, Independence Day,* address, August 15, 2002.
32. Jha N.N. and Singh Sudhir, (Editors), 2016, *Modi's Foreign Policy : Challenges and Opportunities,* New Delhi: Pentagon Press, in association with Society for Social Empowerment and ICWA, P-289.

6

Conclusion, Suggestions and Recommendations

Since the partition of the Indian sub-continent, the South Asian security dynamics has been hit hard by the contradictory threat perceptions and the prolonged security dilemma that exists between the two neighbours, India and Pakistan. Such a conflicting scenario has undermined the scope of bilateral relations due to increased mistrust, economic, military, and diplomatic asymmetries. The subsequent opposing security policies goals adopted by both sides were influenced by intrinsic antipathy, mutual distrust and the long-lasting rivalry to the present day.[1]

Even after more than seven decades of their inception, the relations between India and Pakistan has never been cordial. Both sides have never enjoyed a decade of peaceful and friendly relations. The fact remains that India-Pakistan relationship has seen less improvement, rather it remains complex. There are limited people-to-people contacts that may contribute to overcoming the negative perceptions that many Indians and Pakistanis have for each other. The relations between the two sides are marred by decades old misperceptions, distrusts and divergent orientations to bilateral issues.[2]

Instead a protracted confrontation has been witnessed between two nations. There witnessed a scenario of hostile and insecurity environment and an armed rivalry between the two neighbours that has resulted to wars of 1948, 1965, 1971 and Kargil conflict of 1999. Besides, there also witnessed violations of ceasefire along the Line of Control, allegation of spying and ferocity on embassy staff at both sides are the some of the prominent evidences of antipathy between the two nations. Throughout the history, two nations remained in a continuous conflict and have limited bilateral relations.[3] This has seriously affected the development of cordial ties between the two.

The complexities of India-Pakistan relations have always been hard to comprehend and difficult to unravel. Mutual suspicions have arisen out of the bitter history of partition, disparity in geographical size, population, military strength, economic resources and technical expertise. This has been compounded by the nature and working of domestic political structures, and the impact of international political alignments on India-Pakistan relations. The political and military tussle between India and Pakistan over the Kashmir has had adverse effects on their security and relations between them.

The problem of Jammu and Kashmir is one of the major problems confronting our nation today. The border issue continues to remain one of the most intimidating and ferociously contested border problem in the world. Without any doubt, India is a dominant player in the conflict ridden South Asian region. However, its position is being increasingly challenged by the growing influence of China in the region plus the all weather partnership between China and Pakistan which is primarily aimed at containing India at the regional and global level. India on its part seeks to develop closer politico-security and economic engagement with Pakistan, but Pakistan's alleged involvement in cross border terrorism in Kashmir has only delayed the prospect of closer ties.[4]

India and Pakistan are exercising their diplomatic efforts to resolve the Kashmir issue and pave the way to a secure environment. Given the divergent stand taken by India and Pakistan on the number of issues including the key issue of Kashmir, future prospects for peace and stability in the bilateral relations are miserable in foreseeable future. In the short to long term view point, there seems to be no hope for improvement in relations. Pakistan's unresponsive attitude and the hard stand taken by India plus the ideological rivalry makes it really difficult to come to the agreement. Pakistan's ideology is contradictory to that of India and Pakistan's domestic opinion is steeped in that ideology. The Indian government has taken a clear stand that there can be no talks till Pakistan stops instigating terrorism across the border into India. Former Pakistan President, Musharraf has many years back argued that hostility would continue even after resolution of the Kashmir issue, seems to imply that the aim of the Pakistani establishment, is not just to get Kashmir, but the destabilisation of the Indian state. While from the Indian side, the successive leaders have reiterated that unless Pakistan occupied Kashmir (PoK) is returned to India we will not talk to Pakistan.[5] The hard stands of the two sides have so far prolonged the resolution of the Kashmir issue and caused the failure of the past peaceful efforts. In fact, even the third party mediation or assistance did not work in facilitating a permanent solution to the oldest dispute.

On several occasions, both sides have made concerted efforts to resolve the issue on a bilateral basis. For instance, the Tashkent Declaration of 1966, Shimla Agreement of 1972, Lahore Declaration of 1999 and the subsequent Agra Summit of 2001 and many more peace process have been undertaken as a means and methods of confidence building to settle the Kashmir issue. But, none has worked as a settlement till date. However, the Agra Summit specifically reiterated to continue to abide by the spirit of the Simla Agreement in bilateral negotiations between the two countries.

From the preceding analysis, it can be observed that the Kashmir issue and the problem of cross border terrorism pose a serious challenge to India's bilateral engagement with Pakistan. It is an unprecedented threat to overall development requiring political will and commitment on the part of the both sides on a sustained basis. It is imperative for both South Asian neighbours to engage in dialogue and discussion with each other if they want to attain peace and prosperity in the region. With the formation of the new government in both countries, there is a dire need for common understanding between the two sides over the need to closely engage with each other for mutual benefits. Both sides will need to maintain transparency in their policies with each other in order to bridge the gap of distrust and hostility and to maintain regional peace and trust-worthy bilateral relations.

The key challenge ahead of India and Pakistan would be as to how in spite of the conflicting geo-political and geo-strategic interest, both side have cast aside their difference on a series of issues and concerns of the past and make way for cooperating in the areas where their interests converge. For instance, economic cooperation offers tremendous scope for cooperation wherein Pakistan has a lot to gain. Bilateral trade between the two countries can prove to be an effective tool in order to increase mutual dependency for sustainable and stable bilateral relations.[6] The Indian Prime Minister Narendra Modi and the Pakistani counterpart Imran Khan have huge responsibility of restoring peace process between India and Pakistan. Besides, the present government of both countries will need to explore opportunities and areas where their interests converge.

When would the time come for both India and Pakistan

to realize the need to reduce the trust deficit that continues to serve as the key roadblock to constructive bilateral engagement? From the geo-strategic, political, economic point of view, it is imperative for both the countries to have close and cordial relations. Establishing cordial relations between these two can contribute a lot in making this strategically important region prosperous.[7] However, it is very difficult to make a prediction of how the relations between India and Pakistan would look alike in the coming years or so. But one thing is sure, for bilateral relations between any two countries to improve, it becomes imperative for a positive response from them. India and Pakistan will need to first change the perception about each other as strategic rival. In doing so, Pakistan has to change track on its 'Kashmir first' policy and shifting gear to a process of building co–operation and confidence in other areas. Similarly, India too, has to show a big brotherly attitude and offer some liberal concessions to the Pakistan without compromising any security needs. Such a positive attitude will reduce tension and ease the way for cordial relationship between the two countries. Ayesha Siddiqa, a well known scholar from Pakistan has very rightly pointed out two factors which hinder the prospect for peace between India and Pakistan – first, outstanding political/territorial disputes between the two countries; and second, historical perceptions of each other, especially Pakistan's perception of India.[8]

The two countries have maintained a patchy ceasefire over the LoC in Kashmir since 2003. Current spate of ceasefire violations began in January, 2013; by the close of year such incident could be around 200, far exceeding last year's total of 117. Things came to a crisis situation is September, 2013 when, just short of high-profile talks between Nawaz Sharif and Manmohan Singh on the sidelines of 68th UNGA session, militants of unknown identity killed eight Indian security personnel and a civilian. The attack was deliberately timed, and follows a pattern of attempts by vested interests to frustrate the bilateral peace process. Dr Singh, despite domestic electoral compulsions, could not be provoked to the level of calling off the talks. However, the bilateral was grossly de-scaled from a breakfast meeting to a display of glass of water. Narendra Modi, the BJP's prime ministerial candidate, had advised Dr Singh to skip his meeting with Nawaz Sharif.[9] Pakistan and India are neighbouring countries whose future is entwined and dependent upon each other. It is up to the two countries to find a way that leads to peace and prosperity of not only the two countries but also of the region.

Pakistan's unresponsive attitude has compelled India to freeze the composite dialogue, thereby putting a pressure on Islamabad to addresses India's grievances. India has demand the complete dismantling of the terrorist infrastructure available in Pakistan that play a crucial role in advocating terrorist elements targeted against India.[10] From the Indian side, it has been made clear to the leaders of Pakistan that terror and talks can't go together. For engaging in a fruitful talks, Pakistan will need to reconsider its stand on cross border terrorism. In this regard, there witnessed mixed response from the academician and analysts in our country. Former Army Chief, V.P. Malik is of the perception that, 'India can afford to be patient. Our primary effort should remain focused on the economic agenda and to keep our house, including Jammu and Kashmir, in order. If we keep our house in order, political bullying or the terrorists' guns from across the border are meaningless. We have the resilience and hard and soft power to ignore them, or to respond, if that becomes necessary.'[11]

The influence of military establishment in Pakistan's domestic and foreign policy has severely affected the bilateral relations between the South Asian neighbours. It is never in the interests of Pakistan military that there is a peace process between the two countries. It has so far derailed the entire peace process with India. The military organization in Pakistan is wary of achieving any peace landmark with

India as it would diminish their significance in the political landscape of Pakistan. Hence, the need of the hour is to strengthen the democratic forces and institutions in Pakistan to rein in the adventurous military to achieve the major breakthrough in normalizing the relations, thereby serving the mutual interests of both countries.[12]

One of the hypothesis of the study are that without a settlement of the Kashmir conflict, which focuses and magnifies all the historical, religious and political hatreds between the two conflicting countries, the perilous stalemate will continue indefinitely, expose to dangerous rise of war at any time. With no hope for resolution of the Kashmir dispute in the distant future, the relations between the two countries continue to remain unpredictable and the possibility of the future conflict cannot be ruled out.

Another hypothesis set out in the study are that India-Pakistan peace process halts because of cross border Terrorism actions i.e, Mumbai attack has a worse impact on the bilateral relations that bring both countries to an end of peace process. The hypothesis has tested to be positive in that the relations in the post 26/11 has failed to turn back to the normalcy. Since then, India has tightened its approach by making clear that terror and talks can't go together. India has put a pressure to the Pakistan in regard to its alleged involvement in cross border terrorist activities in Kashmir side of our country.

It was also hypothesised in the study that the Indo-Pakistan conflict has also hampered the development of economic and trade cooperation between them. Owing to lack of political understanding and the conflicting scenario that exists between the two, the economic and trade relations is still struggling to find the momentum. It has so far failed to reach the actual potential. Lack of political understanding and mutual distrust causes massive opportunity costs, not least the absence of significant economic ties.

As regards the dispute over the Kashmir, India is in no way ready to reverse its firm stand that the State of Jammu and Kashmir is an integral and an inalienable part of our country. Time and again such India's stand has been made clear to Pakistan and the international community. To keep the issue intact, Pakistan has adopted the strategy of supporting cross border terrorism which pose a serious threat to the peace and stability of Jammu and Kashmir. When Pakistan government despite several commitments in the past have failed to curb the issue, India has made it clear that there can be no meaningful dialogue as long as it supports and sponsors terrorism against our country. India have demanded Pakistan to stringent action gainst terror groups like the Lashkar-e-Taiba, Jamaat-ud-Dawa, the Jaish-e-Mohammed, and others.[13]

Option to Resolve Kashmir Dispute

Any permanent solutions to the Kashmir Dispute is less likely to happen in near future. Over last seven decades many solutions have been tried ranging from resolution in UN Assembly, bilateral talks, covert mediation by third parties, Military solutions, people to people contacts, track II Diplomacy and attempts to resolve Kashmir problem internally. However all attempts have failed due to intricacy of the problem, hard stand by each stake holder and proxy war by Pakistan. The situation today is that of an impasse. India wants Pakistan to dismantle terrorists infrastructure and stop proxy war before resumption of the talks. Pakistan on other side due to influence of the deep state (Army) still thinks to take Kashmir by use of the policy of "Death by thousand Cuts".

There are however various options which, if adopted, have the potential to resolve the Kashmir Dispute and Indo-Pak relation. Based on deep research in this Thesis, three major options emerge as under :-

(a) Option I : Third Party Mediation.

(b) Option II : Bilateral Engagement through Dialogue.

(c) Option III : Resolve Kashmir Problem Internally.

Option I : Third Party Mediation

India's stand has been to resolve the Indo-Pak Relation through bilateral dialogues whereas Pakistan has been in favour of involving third party, a country or UN. In International context mediation is defined by Jacob Bercovitch as

> "a process of conflict management, related to but distinct from the parties' own negotiations, where those in conflict seek the assistance of, or accept an offer of help from, an outsider...to change their perceptions or behaviour, and to do so without resorting to physical force or invoking the authority of law."

There have been attempts by the big powers US, Russia, China, UK to play the role of a mediator in past. Though many times the third party mediation succeeds when the confronting parties/nations adopt a very rigid stand and are not ready to talk to each other. The option has been analysed in detail and following are the advantages and disadvantages to India if it is adopted :-

Pros

(a) A neutral mediator has the trust of both confronting parties.

(b) A dialogue is facilitated.

(c) It moderates the rigid stand taken by both parties.

(c) Provides a neutral and balance perspectives and creates an atmosphere of cooperation.

Cons

(a) There is no truly neutral nation and bias of third party will affect the outcome of mediation.

(b) US, UK, Russia, China – all are influential countries for mediation but they all have their own interest in the region which may be detrimental to the interest of India.

(c) The UN wants plebiscite in Kashmir which is against the stand India adopted since long time.

(d) It will internationalise the issue and it will no more remain a bilateral dispute.

Option II : Bilateral Engagement Through Dialogue

In today's international environment use of force to resolve contentious issues is not an option. The International community will step in if any such situation emerges between two nations. Therefore, solution to all the problems are to be discussed across the table and that is the preferred approach.

This has been the Indian approach since 1947. India has made several attempts some direct one to one and others on the side lines of international foras like SCO, SAARC etc. The bilateral agreements like ceasefire agreement of Dec 1948, The Tashkent Agreement in 1965, Shimla Accord in 1972, Lahore Declaration in 1998 and Agra summit in 2002 were all great steps forward but were sabotaged by Pakistan on one pretext or other. The option has its own pros and cons which are enumerated below:-

Pros

(a) As India is rising power in the sub-continent and at world stage, resolving the issue bilaterally will enhance India's image as a mature and responsible nation.

(b) Any third party is kept out who may serve their own agenda which will not be in favour of India or Pakistan.

(c) It vindicates India's stand to resolve the issue

bilaterally.

(d) It is the most preferred peaceful solution world over.

Cons

(a) Though the option is most preferred but it has been experienced that Pakistan sabotages it time and again.

(b) It has been experienced that Pakistan buys time in garb of peace process, consolidates and rejuvenates the terrorist infrastructure to wage a renewed proxy war.

(c) The gains made by security forces in neutralising the terrorists and bring the situation under control will all go in vain.

(d) Pakistan will take it as a sign of weakness.

Option III : Resolving Kashmir Problem Internally

This is an option which India may adopt to resolve the issues with Kashmir people and politicians. It is to establish peace and stability in the state by adopting a hard approach towards terrorists and cross border terrorism and conciliatory approach with the "AWAM" (People of Kashmir). Simultaneously keep pressure over Pakistan internationally to shun the path of violence through state sponsored terrorism. Strengthen economically and militarily and then talk to Pakistan from a position of strength. The option has been analysed in detail and following are the pros and cons:-

Pros

(a) The solution is entirely internal. It does not need support of any outer forces.

(b) Once peace and stability is ensured in Kashmir, India can talk from a position of strength.

(c) Pakistan is put under international pressure which

will stop the military and financial aid.

(d) Likely to get support from international community fight against terrorism which Pakistan is aiding and abetting.

Cons

(a) It may be a short term solution. For long term peace and stability Pakistan has to be engaged.

(b) India may be seen as hard liner not ready to talk to Pakistan.

(c) Solutions to Kashmir problem internally is not easy. It has several stake holders and it may not be possible to satisfy all.

Recommendations

Over last seven decades a number of attempts have been made by both countries, international community and track II diplomacy to resolve the issue. In addition researchers world over have also suggested numerous plausible solutions ranging from all out military solution to people to people contacts. However none has succeeded, No single solution has the capability to satisfy all the parties. The Kashmir Dispute is a very complex and intricate issue. All stake holders have different aspirations which are divergent from each other. Therefore, one single formula or model may not see the light of the day. It has to be a mix of all the above mentioned models. The low hanging fruits may be plucked first to show some progress while simultaneously continuing the effort to resolve more contentious issues. It is on these lines, I have framed my recommendations which are enumerated in succeeding paragraphs. A likely solution must satisfy the following conditions :-

(a) It should be within the framework of the Indian Constitution.

(b) It should meet the aspirations of the people.

(c) It should not compromise on the unity and integrity of the Nation.

(d) It should bring peace and development to the Valley.

(e) It should have maximum local participation in its implementation.

(f) It should deal effectively with the threat posed by terrorist groups.

(g) It should clear India's image effectively as regards accusations of Human Rights abuses.

Short Term (Till 2024)

The short term recommendations for next five years, till the tenure of current dispensation at centre, is based on the current situation in Pakistan and in Kashmir. Pakistan is at its worst situation economically and diplomatically. Its economy is down, there is no domestic production/ manufacturing to revive/survive the economy. The foreign exchange reserves have depleted to the level that it is not able to meet its interest obligations on international loans. It has to borrow from IMF or other international financial institutes who have put conditions which will make Pakistan further vulnerable. On international front Pakistan is slowly feeling the heat of pressure applied by its major allies to dismantle the terrorist infrastructure and support global war on terrorism. Its all time ally USA is leaning towards India, the Arab countries are distancing themselves. It has a war like situation on its borders with Afghanistan and Iran in addition to India. Internally there is complete unrest. The deep state (Army) is still dictating the terms even though there is an elected govt at centre. The Baloach are continuously at war path and want to secede, the Sindhis want to have greater autonomy, the entire KPK region is in turmoil due to Talibans and Pushtun war lords. The railway system is vintage and almost defunct. The power situation is precarious. There is a scarcity of water for a predominantly agrarian economy.

Internally the situation in Kashmir saw a period of stability from 2007 to 2015. There have been however, recent spurt of violence which is being brought under control. The separatists are losing ground support. The state is under governor's rule which is good for a short time to curb the militant activities. The elections are likely to be held by end of year 2019 and a democratically elected Govt will be in place. The Central Govt has executed various plans to develop the region and provide employment to youth. The security forces are once again seem to have upper hand. The terrorist and separatists funding is under scrutiny and sources of foreign funding are drying up.

It is, under these circumstances, recommended that India should not plead for Bilateral Dialogue with Pakistan. It should consolidate the gains made in Kashmir and make all out effort to resolve all issues with Kashmiri AWAM (people and politicians). In next five years Pakistan is going to be further weaker economically, militarily and in international foras. Make Kashmir stable and then offer to talk to Pakistan from a position of strength. To achieve this the following is recommended:-

(a) **Resolve Kashmir Problem Internally**

(i) Strong posture by security forces to curb all kind of violence perpetrated by militants.

(ii) Ensure peace and violence free situation so that Govt organisation and political process function freely.

(iii) Take hard decisions to resolve major issues like providing more autonomy, removing of article 370 and 35A of constitution.

(iv) Alienate the separatists (APHC) by exposing them and squeezing their financial support.

(v) Economic development of the state by bringing in industries, providing employment to youth and growing the business.

(vi) Encourage Kashmiriat and Sufism to wean away support to militants.

(vii) Perception managent through media and all other resources at the disposal of Govt.

(viii) Hold elections at the earliest and install a democratically elected Govt in state.

(ix) Transformation of education system to eradicate fundamental teaching.

(x) Keep a very strong posture at LOC to deny any infiltration of terrorists from Pakistan.

(b) **Approach towards Pakistan**. As recommended in earlier paragraphs, no bilateral talks with Pakistan during this period. The approach recommended to be taken is as follows :-

(i) Diplomatically isolate Pakistan at International forums for its support to terrorism.

(ii) Strengthen own Military capabilities to a Punitive Deterrent level.

(iii) Develop own economy to $5 trillion by 2025 vis a vis Pakistan's collapsing economy.

(iv) Develop good relations with Iran and Afghanistan to isolate Pakistan.

(v) Support the internal discontentment among people of Balochistan and Sindh. Keep the unrest in KPK simmering.

(vi) Encourage and strengthen democracy. The influence of deep state (Pak Army) must be diminished for a long lasting solution.

(vii) Continue people to people contact, track II

diplomacy and cultural exchanges.

(viii) Be proactive to any Pakistan sponsored terrorists attack in India. Carry out punitive action on Pakistan.

(ix) Strengthen the regional forums like SAARC.

(x) Engage China economically and diplomatically to reduce its collusivity with Pakistan in case of a conventional war.

(xi) Pakistan to be brought under pressure by abrogating the Indus Water Treaty and sharing of waters of other river if it continues the proxy war.

Long Term Recommendation

The long term recommendation pertain to a period of 2025 and beyond. As suggested in previous paragraphs, India should stabilize Kashmir by that time, bring peace and stability in the valley. Pakistan must be weakened economically, militarily and isolated diplomatically if it does not stop support to terrorists. Under these circumstances Pakistan may be offered to come for a bilateral dialogue and talk from a position of strength. It is envisaged that a democratically established strong Govt in Pakistan will see the sanctity of peace and prosperity and likely to cease hostility with India and negotiate a peaceful solution to Kashmir.

In the present geo-political situation it is unlikely that borders will be redrawn. It is envisaged that four point solution proposed by Musharraf is more plausible. However India must continue to claim its legitimate stand i.e integration of entire Kashmir including Pakistan Occupied Kashmir and territory under control of China. A weakened and isolated Pakistan may accept the conditions put by India.

Conclusion

Any permanent solution to the prolonged issue of

Kashmir is less likely to happen in the distant future, India on its side must ensure that internal stability and development in the state is preserved. The ongoing security scenario in the state is fully in control. This will help in dealing the external factor in an efficient manner. We should take firm measures against the rising militancy and the terrorist violence which pose a serious threat to the peace and stability in the state. The ongoing internal security in the state of J&K needs to be managed much more efficiently so that the people of the state are with the rest of the country. Feeling of alienation needs to be reduced by taking care of the grievances of the people. Past experience has shown that the people will cooperate when they are convinced that their life, identity, and future are safe in Indian hands.

On the other hand India must continue to strengthen economically and militarily and be prepared for a conventional confrontation if forced upon by Pakistan and ensure victory. In the mean time she must make efforts to put Pakistan under pressure through international forums to shun support to terrorists. The efforts to strengthen democracy in Pakistan and reduce the influence of deep state (Army) must continue. It is under these circumstances a weak, isolated Pakistan will accept a solution for permanent peace and stability in Kashmir.

References

1. Zulfqar Khan, "India-Pakistan: Emerging Trends in Strategic Dynamics", The Korean Journal of International Studies, Vol. 13, No. 3, December 2015, pp. 577-79.

2. Surender Singh, "India-Pakistan Peace Process: Problems and Prospects of Confidence Building Measures (CBMs)", *Ph. D Thesis Submitted to the Department of Political Science,* Kurukshetra University, Kurukshetra, 2015, p. 2.

3. Noshina Saleem, et al., "Indo-Pakistan Trade Relations: A Critical Discourse Analysis of Daily Dawn", A Research

Journal of South Asian Studies, Vol. 29, No. 1, Jan-July 2014, p. 309.

4. Sachinkumar Manikrao, "Areas of Contestation and Debate between India and Pakistan: A Critical Study", Ph. D Thesis Submitted to the Department of Political Science, Sahyadri Arts College, Kuvempu University, Karnataka, 2014, p. 238.
5. Ajay Pratap Singh, "Indo-Pak Relations Since 1990", Ph. D Thesis Submitted to the Department of Defence and Strategic Studies, T. D. P. G. College, V. B. S Purvanchal University, Jaunpur, 2001, pp. 15-16.
6. "Pakistan-India Relations: Challenges and Prospects", Foreign Policy Roundtable Series, No. VI, Centre for Pakistan and Gulf Studies, Islamabad, May 2014.
7. Safdar Hussain and Muhammad Ijaz Latif, n. 30, p. 97.
8. Ayesha Siddiqa, India-Pakistan Relations: Confrontation to Conciliation (Islamabad: Centre for Democratic Governance, 2004), p. 1.
9. Khalid Iqbal, "Pakistan's Relations with India Since 9/11: A Pakistani Perspective", FPRC Country Specific Studies on Pakistan, New Delhi, Vol. 2, p. 75-6.
10. Sachinkumar Manikrao, , p. 241.
11. Ibid., p. 242.
12. Sachinkumar Manikrao, p. 244-45.
13. M. Ganapathi, "Contours of India's Foreign Policy: An Overview", Indian Foreign Affairs Journal, Vol. 12, No. 1, Jan-March 2017, p. 47.

Appendix-1

Kashmir: A Historical Timeline

A chronicle of key political events that undergird the Kashmir emerged as an "international dispute" in 1947, but looking at the Kashmir question exclusively from that prism privileges India-Pakistan state-centric perspectives while erasing Kashmir's own distinct political history. To begin to understand the Kashmiri aspiration for self-determination, it is important to trace the major events that have shaped Kashmiri political subjectivity. Kashmir's political history is a complex and volatile interaction between external forces and internal struggles. Keeping this in mind, I present this timeline as a resource for those curious about what drives the Kashmiri movement for self-determination despite the tremendous odds it faces. To be clear, the timeline is **not** the history of Kashmir, but **a chronicle of key political events.** In being so, the timeline falls squarely within the long tradition of Kashmiri chronicle writing. I start with the year 1586 because many Kashmiris see the arrival of the Mughals as the first tragic entanglement of Kashmir with South Asia.

1586

Apart from the brief periods, when it was part of the

Buddhist empires of Ashoka (~300 BC) and Kushans (~130 AD), Kashmir had remained more or less independent under a series of regional dynasties, including Hindu-Buddhist Karkotas and Muslim Shah-Miris. The centuries of complex interaction between indigenous peoples of Kashmir and Aryan settlers, and later preachers from South India, Central Asia and Iran, had led to mass conversions to Buddhism, Shaivism, and eventually Islam. In 1586, Mughal Emperor Akbar attempts a conquest of Kashmir, but is thwarted by the last native Kashmiri Muslim ruler, Yusuf Shah Chak. Under the pretext of negotiations, Akbar takes Chak as a prisoner and makes Kashmir a part of his Afghan principality. Never allowed to return to Kashmir, Chak's grave is in present-day Indian state of Bihar.

1750s-1846

As the Mughal empire weakens, Kashmir first falls under the Afghans and then under the Sikhs from Lahore.

1846

In the aftermath of Anglo-Sikh wars in the 1840s, the British East India Company rewards a Dogra chieftain, Gulab, who had betrayed his Sikh overlords during the war, with control over Kashmir. Signed on **9 March 1846**, the Treaty of Amritsar allows Gulab to claim the title of Maharaja of the state of Jammu and Kashmir, which now includes the kingdom of Ladakh that had been incorporated into the previous Sikh empire in **1834**. In return, Gulab agrees to serve British interests as a buffer state (primarily against the Tsarist Russia) and send Kashmiri soldiers to join British campaigns as and when called upon. A brief rebellion against the treaty by the Sikh-appointed Muslim governor of Kashmir Imam-ud-Din is suppressed. Despite most of their subjects being Muslim, Dogras turn the state into a Hindu kingdom. Except for the period from 1889 and 1905, when the British curtailed some Dogra powers, the Dogra maharajas enjoyed almost full sovereignty over

Kashmir. Dogra rule is marked by oppression, forced labor, and heavy taxation. Several artisans' revolts have been forcibly put down. In particular, the Kashmiri Muslims, who form the majority of the state's subjects, are systematically impoverished, disempowered and exploited, while the minority upper-caste Hindus become part of the ruling establishment.

1931

On July 13, during the trial of Abdul Qadeer, who is accused of inciting Kashmiris to rebel against the Dogras, people assemble in the capital Srinagar. The Dogra troops shoot 22 Kashmiris dead. Widespread protests erupt all over the country against Maharaja Hari Singh, but the revolt is brutally suppressed. Dozens of Kashmiris are shot dead during the next few days in Islamabad (Anantnag) and Kupwara. In the hilly regions of Poonch, a rebellion erupts which will continue for years.

1932

Kashmiri Muslim leaders petition the British and the Dogra rulers for reforms. Several of them launch the All Jammu Kashmir Muslim Conference (MC) with a goal to fight for governmental reform, education, and representation for Kashmiri Muslims in the government. The Maharaja's subsequent efforts to redress the grievances, including establishing Praja Sabha ("Subjects' Assembly") turn out to be empty as Muslim representation remains disproportionately minimal. A group of radical Kashmiri youth led by Sheikh Abdullah emerges as a popular faction within the Muslim Conference.

1939

MC splits over political approach. Sheikh Abdullah names the major faction the Jammu Kashmir National Conference (JKNC or NC), signaling that their goal is a secular independent state and an end to feudalism. NC mobilizes Kashmiri peasantry.

1940s

Several small new Kashmiri parties emerge, including the Worker-Peasant Party. Some socialist and communist organizations also begin to grow. NC grows in popularity for its defiance of the Dogras, while Chaudhary Ghulam Abbas revives the old Muslim Conference and builds significant support among the Muslims of the Jammu province.

1944

NC adopts the "New Kashmir Resolution," proposing radical socio-economic transformation, the end of monarchy and feudalism, turning Kashmir into a democratic republic, and granting full citizenship rights to all the people of Jammu and Kashmir.

1945

With older roots in Islamist social reform, JamaatIslami holds its first convention in Kashmir. Influenced by its parent body in British India, which opposed the creation of Pakistan, JamaatIslami in Kashmir takes a stand against both NC's secular nationalism and MC's Muslim nationalism.

1946

NC launches "Quit Kashmir" movement and MC starts a campaign of action; both are against the monarchy. Sheikh Abdullah and Chaudhary Ghulam Abbas are arrested. Over the years, Abdullah has grown closer to Indian Congress leaders and is opposed to Jinnah's Muslim League. Yet, he agrees Kashmir should remain its own entity. The Muslim Conference leans toward Jinnah.

1947

Between **August and October**, Kashmir is independent. With Pakistan now a reality, Jamaat Islami activists want Kashmir to join Pakistan if it becomes an Islamic state, yet their parent body in British India has opposed Jinnah. Muslim

Conference passes a resolution to join Pakistan. The Socialist Party also wants to join Pakistan. But NC is opposed to the idea. The British withdrawal and the partition of British India into India and Pakistan leads to violence in Bengal, Delhi, Punjab and elsewhere. Kashmiris have been fighting against the monarchy and don't see their struggle as part of South Asian secular, Hindu, or Muslim nationalisms, but the British ask "Princely Rulers" to accede either to India or to Pakistan based on geographical contiguity and religious demography. According to this Partition logic, Kashmir should have gone to Pakistan, as the state has a close to 77 percent Muslim population. In September and October 1947, Hindu militias and Dogra troops attack Jammu's Muslims, killing tens of thousands. In Poonch, along the border with newly-created Pakistan, rebels create an independent state called "Azad (Free) Jammu Kashmir (AJK)." As ethnic cleansing of Jammu Muslims continues, many flee to AJK and to Pakistan. Much of Muslim Conference leadership and members are displaced. According to census reports from the time and later research, upwards of 200,000 Muslims are dead and an equal number become refugees. After what will come to be known as the "Jammu Massacre," Jammu becomes a Hindu-majority city. Meanwhile, the Dogras lose control of GilgitBaltistan province in the north. With their leader, Sheikh Abdullah, in prison, NC remains dormant. In September, troops from the neighboring state of Patiala and Hindu nationalist paramilitaries of the RSS arrive to bolster the Dogras. Pakistan blocks supplies into Kashmir. Indian Congress leaders put pressure on the Dogras to accede to India and release Abdullah. The Dogra maharaja wants to remain independent and has signed a Standstill Agreement with Pakistan, but India has refused to sign. As rebellion continues along the borders, on October 22, 1947, members of Afridi and other Pashtun groups begin to converge along the border and enter Baramulla to aid Kashmiris but falter without any clear leadership. The Maharaja flees the Kashmir valley and asks India for help. Indians demand he sign the Treaty of Accession and give power over Kashmir's defense, foreign affairs, and communication to India. Abdullah is made Emergency Administrator and he sees Pashtuns as a threat. On **October 26,** Indian troops arrive in Srinagar and the next day Maharaja signs the treaty. Indian invasion pulls Pakistani troops in too. The first India-Pakistan war over Kashmir breaks out. On **November 21**, Nehru says: "I have repeatedly stated that as soon as peace and order have been established; Kashmir should decide about accession by plebiscite or referendum under international auspices such as those of United Nations."

1948

By the middle of the year, the war has entered a stalemate. India takes the case of Kashmir to the United Nations. Kashmir is officially recognized as a disputed territory. The United Nations Security Council passes a resolution (UNSC Resolution 47) providing for 1. Ceasefire, 2. Withdrawal of Pakistani and Indian troops, and 3. Plebiscite in Kashmir (under international supervision with minimal Indian military presence). UN Commission on India and Pakistan (UNCIP) is created.

1949

Ceasefire is proclaimed under the UN auspices. India is in control of two-thirds of the historic Kashmir state while Pakistan has control over one-third, including the AJK.

1950

India backtracks on its promise of the plebiscite, even though Nehru would continue to make statements about India's pledge to Kashmiris until 1959. Indian Constitution comes into effect and Article 1 proclaims the entire state of J&K as a part of the territory of India. Article 370 gives a "special" status to the State of J&K, more or less corresponding to the terms of the Instrument of Accession. Pro-Pakistan

Kashmiri leaders are arrested, and many are sent into exile.

1951

Elections are held in the state. The UNSC passes a resolution (UNSC Resolution 91) saying elections will not be a substitute for the plebiscite. Sheikh Abdullah wins the elections, mostly unopposed, and becomes the Prime Minister. Abdullah carries out land reforms and adopts measures such as debt relief. The Jammu Kashmir Constituent Assembly is created to draft the constitution for the state. In India, Hindu nationalists begin agitation over giving special status to Kashmir. They demand "one country, one constitution, one flag."

1952

Land reforms, while benefitting impoverished Kashmiri Muslims and under-caste Hindus, lead to resentment among erstwhile members of Dogra royalty and Hindu feudals, who assemble under the aegis of a Hindu nationalist party, PrajaParishad. Abdullah sees them as a threat but is unable to control their influence. He begins to shift positions between endorsing Kashmir's accession to India and supporting the right of self-determination for Kashmiris. He signs the Delhi Agreement, but does not confirm the accession of Kashmir to India. The Delhi Agreement says: 1. except in three matters listed under Instrument of Accession, sovereignty will reside in Jammu and Kashmir; 2. Kashmiris will be citizens of India, but the elected Kashmir government will decide permanent residency requirements in the state; 3. Kashmir will have its own flag and constitution; 4. Kashmir will have a Prime Minister (wazirazam) and President (sadr-e-riyasat). JamaatIslami separates from its parent body in India.

1953

As Hindu nationalist groups coalesce against Abdullah, the Indian government claims he is conspiring with the Chinese, the Arabs, and the Americans to create an independent Kashmir. In August, Abdullah is arrested (he will spend the next decade in prison). One of his aides and the deputy prime minister until then, G.M. Bakshi, is installed as the Prime Minister. Abdullah's loyalists are removed from the government and the NC.

1954

Bakshi gets the accession formally ratified in 1954. India passes a "Presidential Order" using Article 370 which effectively gives the Indian parliament many more powers than were part of the Instrument of Accession and the Delhi Agreement. This is the start of the "erosion of autonomy," which will continue in the years to come. All dissent in Kashmir is crushed.

1955

Afzal Beg, a lieutenant of Abdullah's, forms the Plebiscite Front, which becomes the principal opposition to the governments led by India-loyalist Bakshi and his successors.

1956

The J&K Constituent Assembly adopts a new constitution, declaring the state an integral part of the Indian Union. Kashmiri activists, including those from Plebiscite Front, reject the declaration, and continue to insist on the promised self-determination.

1957

The UN passes another resolution (UNSC Resolution 122) affirming that only the "will of the people expressed through the democratic method of a free and impartial plebiscite conducted under the auspices of the United Nations" will determine Kashmir's final status, and states that the J&K Constituent Assembly's actions, including administrative or legal changes, are invalid and would not constitute a final disposition of the state.

1962

India and China fight a war. India loses control over large tracts of land in Ladakh, especially Aksai Chin that had been part of the State of Jammu and Kashmir.

1963

A holy relic—believed to be a strand of hair from the Prophet's beard—is found missing from the Hazratbal shrine in Srinagar. Popular agitation erupts across Kashmir Valley and continues until the relic is mysteriously recovered in January 1964. Protests expand against extension of Indian powers to Kashmir including Indian president's power to dismiss Kashmiri governments.

1965

Second India-Pakistan war breaks out after Pakistan sends infiltrators across the ceasefire line in August. The war ends in a ceasefire on **September 23**. The status quo remains. India removes the title of Prime Minister and Sadr e Riyasat from its loyalist Kashmiri officials, instead using the term Chief Minister.

1966

Small Kashmiri armed revolutionary groups emerge, some in the shadow of the Plebiscite Front. These groups call for complete independence of Jammu and Kashmir. One of these groups is Jammu Kashmir National Liberation Front (JKNLF) created by MaqboolBhat and others. Another is Al Fatah, which builds a strong underground network. Most are arrested and will spend years in prison.

1971

India and Pakistan fight a war, resulting in the secession of East Pakistan and the formation of Bangladesh.

1972

India and Pakistan sign the Shimla Agreement, which

recognizes the ceasefire line of 1949 as the Line of Control (LoC). The Shimla Agreement includes a clause stating that the final settlement of Kashmir will be decided bilaterally. Kashmiris see themselves as being further sidelined in future negotiations over their own country.

1974

Sheikh Abdullah is allowed to return to Kashmir. Many Kashmiris welcome him. But on Indira Gandhi's insistence, he disbands the Plebiscite Front. Abdullah agrees to give up the demand for self-determination.

1975

Abdullah accepts the much diminished position of Chief Minister. In **June**, Prime Minister Indira Gandhi plunges India into an Emergency. Abdullah supports her and does not oppose when the Emergency is extended to Kashmir ten days later. Abdullah and his aide Beg win by-elections, but Syed Ali Geelani, who is a JamaatIslami legislator, claims election rigging. Abdullah bans JamaatIslami and closes down dozens of its schools across Kashmir. Revolutionary armed groups that had risen in the shadow of the Plebiscite Front are in a disarray, even though Abdullah drops long-standing cases against Al Fatah members.

1976

Maqbool Bhat, having spent years in Indian and Pakistani jails (in Pakistan, for being suspected as an Indian spy), is arrested again in Kashmir, where a death warrant has earlier been issued against him for the murder of a bank official at the hands of one of his associates.

1977

On **May 29, 1977** Amanullah Khan, Abdul Khaliq Ansari and few others from the Azad Kashmiri diaspora in Britain form the Jammu Kashmir Liberation Front (JKLF) in Birmingham. Maqbool Bhat is proclaimed to have joined the new organization. Sheikh Abdullah wins elections in 1977. With the Indian establishment's backing, the opposition to his NC is decimated. The old JamaatIslami, having contested the elections since 1971, wins only one seat in the Assembly.

1979

Iran's Islamic revolution and the execution of Pakistan's former Prime Minister, Z.A. Bhutto, on the orders of General Zia ulHaq, causes widespread ripples across Kashmir. JamaatIslami members, seen as supporters of General Zia, are attacked by NC cadres as well as by some Islamic preachers in the countryside, especially in Islamabad (Anantnag) where JamaatIslami's support among the salaried classes is growing.

1982

On **September 8**, Sheikh Abdullah dies.

1983

Massive election rigging creates dissensions within NC and conflicts begin among Abdullah's heirs. Indian PM Indira Gandhi, campaigning in Jammu, ignites Hindu passions against Kashmiri Muslims.

1984

On **February 11**, MaqboolBhat is hanged in Tihar Jail. Indian authorities refuse to return his body to his family. Small groups of Kashmiris cross the LoC to plan armed movement and return to form underground cells. In **April**, the Indian Army captures the Siachen Glacier region of Kashmir from Pakistan. In **June**, the Indian military's assault on the Golden Temple, the spiritual center of Sikhs in Amritsar, leaves hundreds of Sikhs dead. Many Sikh activists cross the Punjab border into Pakistan to get arms training. In **July**, the Indian governor in Kashmir openly interferes in Kashmiri politics. Farooq, Abdullah's son and heir, is dismissed as the Chief Minister and his opponent in the NC and brother-in-law, Ghulam Muhammad Shah, is installed in his place. Small new Islamist groups begin to emerge in Kashmir, mostly led by Kashmir University students. In **October**, Indira Gandhi is shot dead by her bodyguards.

1986

Mujahideen war against the Soviets in Afghanistan is at its peak. India loyalist and Farooq Abdullah's brother in law, Ghulam Muhammad Shah, is dismissed as Chief Minister, after Farooq gives assurances to Indian PM Rajiv Gandhi that he will crack down on the growing unrest in Kashmir. Farooq forms a coalition government with the Indian National Congress in Kashmir.

1987

A number of opposition parties join to form an alliance against the NC. They are called the Muslim United Front (MUF). There is blatant poll rigging. Young polling agents of MUF, among them Yasin Malik, are arrested and tortured. Farooq Abdullah is allowed to win the elections and becomes Chief Minister. The MUF wins only four seats—despite a clear wave of support for the party—including one by Syed Ali Geelani of the JamaatIslami and QaziNisar, the Mirwaiz (head preacher) of South Kashmir. MUF contestants, like Yusuf Shah, are arrested.

1988

Repression in Kashmir increases. Protestors demanding basic things, like electricity, are shot down. Several groups of young Kashmiri men, including Hamid Sheikh, Ashfaq Wani, Javaid Mir, and Yasin Malik (now out of jail), cross the LoC for arms training. Later known as the HAJY group (acronym of the first letters of their names), they join the JKLF. Busy fighting the Soviets in Afghanistan, Pakistan however sends them back without promises. Pakistan cuts even minimal support as General Zia dies in a crash and Benazir Bhutto becomes the prime minister, who invites Indian PM Rajiv Gandhi to Pakistan. JKLF declare armed struggle against India, exploding several small bombs in Srinagar. JamaatIslami opposes armed struggle in its publication Azan and insists on the 1985 amendment to its party constitution that calls for resolution through constitutional means and dialogue.

1989

The judge who had sentenced MaqboolBhat to death is shot dead. Indian operations to capture JKLF members become intense. Hamid Sheikh has been captured. In **November and December**, JKLF successfully uses a high-profile kidnapping to negotiate the release of their members, including Sheikh. Vast crowds of Kashmiris come out in support of JKLF and to welcome the rebels. With Soviet withdrawal from Afghanistan, Pakistan turns attention to Kashmir, but seems interested in creating its own group, one that could profess a pro-Pakistan ideology. Among several such groups, HizbulMujahideen (HM) is founded by a JamaatIslami activist and schoolteacher known as Master Ahsan Dar. Yusuf Shah, also from JamaatIslami, joins the HM and uses the nom de guerre Syed Salahuddin.

1990

Indian military forces carry out several massacres across Kashmir in January. Protests intensify, and thousands of Kashmiris publicly resign from pro-India parties. The four MUF legislators resign have resigned as well. On **January 17**, India dismisses Farooq Abdullah's government and imposes central rule. A Hindu nationalist bureaucrat, Jagmohan, is installed as the governor. He claims that "Kashmir is sick, and I am its nursing orderly," and ominously threatens Kashmiris. Jagmohan swiftly launches widespread military crackdowns on urban neighborhoods. Intense curfews are imposed. Armed groups carry out assassinations of government officials, NC activists, and intelligence agents. While many of these (~200) are Kashmiri Muslim, a significant number (~70) are Kashmiri Hindus, who have held top positions in the government and constitute three percent of the population. Thousands of Hindu families leave Kashmir on **January 19** and head to Jammu in the south. (Years later, many Hindus would claim they left because they were afraid for their lives and that militant groups had threatened them, while many Kashmiri Muslims would blame Jagmohan for convincing Hindus to leave, facilitating their journey, and telling them they would be back after the winter when the rebellion was crushed in the Valley. According to Indian government sources, between 1989 and 2004, 219 Kashmiri Hindus were killed by armed militants, and one since then, while about 165,000 Hindus left Kashmir.) On **January 21**, an estimated 55-65 unarmed protesters are killed by Indian troops near Gawakadal in Srinagar. Later that day, Jagmohan imposes a long curfew and a military siege leading to widespread misery in the middle of an icy winter. On **January 25**, Indian forces kill 21 protestors in Handwara town. On **March 1**, Indian soldiers kill around 50 Kashmiri protestors near Tengpora in Srinagar. In **early March**, an estimated one million Kashmiris take to the streets for several days. Indian soldiers kill dozens. On **March 30**, JKLF chief commander AshfaqWani is killed during an attack. Considered the main architect of the armed struggle, his death is the first big blow to the movement. Tens of thousands attend his funeral. Hundreds of young Kashmiris cross the LoC and return to join the JKLF. HM also recruits several activists. While the JKLF professes to be "secular" and wants "unification and independence" of Kashmir, the HM professes to be an "Islamic" organization with the goal of Kashmir's "merger with Pakistan." On **May 21**, an estimated million people attend the funeral march of the slain chief preacher of Kashmir, MirwaizMaulvi Farooq. An HM activist is blamed for the assassination. Some Kashmiris claim that the HM activist had been released from prison for this purpose. Indian paramilitaries kill 60 mourners and injure 200 near Hawal in Srinagar. Thousands of armed Kashmiris return from AJK training camps and enjoy widespread public support. Indian government replaces Jagmohan with GirishSaxena as the governor. India continues to send troops into the region. There are more than 300,000 active duty Indian soldiers in Kashmir now. By summer, India imposes the Armed Forces Special Powers Act, which gives a free hand to the military.

1991

As repression continues, armed groups in Kashmir proliferate. JKLF is still the most prominent, but HM, the favorite of Pakistan, has now more trained cadres, better weapons, and has been adopted by JamaatIslami as its armed wing. The Indian military is unable to crush the rebellion. Thousands of Kashmiris are dying in the war. On **February 23**, Indian soldiers enter two villages in north Kashmir, Kunan and Poshpora, and rape dozens of Kashmiri women. Indian government denies the charge. (Later, a Press Council of India committee would declare the women to be lying, but Kashmiri activists would argue the PCI committee hadn't even met the victims.)

1992

HM starts to gain more recruits in the countryside, especially where JamaatIslami influence is predominant. HM ranks—now in thousands—are also filled by Afghan war veterans and Pakistanis. JKLF is still influential, but its main commanders are either dead or in prison. Yasin Malik, its second chief commander, has been in prison since 1990. Tensions between JKLF and HM grow as HM seeks dominance. Master Ahsan Dar is expelled from HM by now Pakistan-based Syed Salahuddin because of Dar's criticism of HM's attacks on the JKLF. Dar forms a smaller group named Muslim Mujahideen. Half a million Indian forces are deployed in the Kashmir Valley during this period. Prominent Kashmiri human rights activist and trade unionist H. N. Wanchoo is shot dead.

1993

All Parties Hurriyat Conference (APHC) is formed. It

is an amalgamation of dozens of Kashmiri political groups. Its express goal is Kashmir's "right to self-determination" but keeps the question of independence or merger with Pakistan open. As armed movement continues, Indian military repression grows. In response to a JKLF attack in northern Kashmiri town of Sopore in **January**, Indian paramilitary Border Security Force (BSF) massacres more than 100 unarmed civilians and burns down several neighborhoods. In **April**, a prominent Kashmiri heart surgeon and JKLF sympathizer, Abdul Ahad Guru, is shot dead. (Later a key Indian bureaucrat in Kashmir, WajahatHabibullah, will blame Indian security agencies to have conspired with an HM activist to kill Guru.) In **October**, BSF kills 55 Kashmiris who had assembled after Friday prayers in Bijbehara town in South Kashmir. Despite several accords, intergroup rivalry leads to frequent clashes between the JKLF and the HM. Better trained HM cadres kill dozens of JKLF members.

1994

On **February 22**, the Indian Parliament passes a resolution that claims Kashmir to be an "integral part" of India and therefore non-negotiable. More forces are sent to Kashmir to subdue the armed insurgency and to conduct elections. In **May**, JKLF commander Yasin Malik, on bail from prison, declares a unilateral ceasefire and claims JKLF to be an unarmed political organization that would work for independence of Kashmir. His decision causes a split in the JKLF. One JKLF faction refuses to declare a ceasefire, but its leaders are quickly decimated by Indian forces during a siege in Srinagar. In **June**, former MUF legislator and head preacher of South Kashmir, QaziNisar, is shot dead in Islamabad/ Anantnag. Many blame the HM. Pan-Islamic groups like HarkatulMujahideen are also now present in parts of Kashmir. With JKLF no longer a competitor, HM targets members of smaller groups. Among these are groups like Muslim Mujahideen and IkhwanulMuslimeen, many of whom surrender to the Indian forces. Nisar's killing has also led to disenchantment with Jamaat, who are seen as HM's patrons. With support from Indian intelligence agencies, surrendered militants form a new group, Ikhwanul Muslimoon, or simply "Ikhwan." Muslim Mujahideen (MM), out of Ahsan Dar's control, retains its name but now works for Indian forces. Ikhwanis and MM kill dozens of JamaatIslami members in the countryside, forcing many to run away to Srinagar. An HM vs Ikhwan/MM fight ensues, leading to intense bloodshed. HM loses ground due to persistent Ikhwani/MM assaults.

1995

Foreign armed mujahideen, especially those aligned with HarkatulMujahideen (later HarkatulAnsar) become a formidable force in the Kashmir war. Their goals are unclear, but their presence causes further confusion. They claim to be fighting a jihad, yet some of them seem to be collaborating with the Ikhwan/MM. On **July 4**, a faction of Harkat, known as Al Faran, kidnaps five western tourists in South Kashmir and after several months—as revealed later by journalists Adrian Levy and Cathy Scott in their book The Meadow—hands them over to an MM commander, who is believed to have killed them.

1996

On **March 8**, prominent Kashmiri human rights activist and lawyer JalilAndrabi is abducted by an Indian military officer Avtar Gill. Andrabi's body is later recovered from a river. In **September**, India holds elections in Kashmir. NC is contesting. Jamaat is boycotting. Members of Ikhwan/MM form political fronts to contest. There is hardly any participation. NC is declared a winner, and Farooq Abdullah is Chief Minister.

1997

Under intense pressure from the Ikhwanis, JamaatIslami declares end to ties with the HM. HM launches systematic attacks on the Ikhwan is and decimates them.

HM returns to dominance in the countryside, but Indian military has also regained enormous ground.

1998

On **January 25**, 23 Kashmiri Hindus are killed in a massacre in Wandhama village. India blames Islamist militants. In two other incidents, in Prankot and Champanari in Jammu, several Hindus are killed in April and June. Insurgency spreads to the Muslim districts of Jammu province. In the Kashmir valley, the Indian counterinsurgency war continues. Hundreds of Kashmiris are killed year after year. In **May**, India and Pakistan conduct nuclear tests.

1999

War between India and Pakistan breaks out in Kargil, a border district on the LoC. India blames Pakistani soldiers for infiltrating into positions on the Indian controlled side of the LoC. Hundreds of soldiers die in the battles. By **July**, international pressure compels Pakistan to withdraw its forces. Pakistan PM Nawaz Sharif accuses General Pervez Musharraf of launching the operation without informing the government.

2000

On **March 20**, just before US President Bill Clinton's visit to India, 35 Kashmiri Sikhs are killed by unidentified gunmen in the village of Chattisinghpora in South Kashmir. The government blames Islamic militants, but Kashmiris and prominent Sikh leaders (and later US officials) blame Indian government agencies for orchestrating the attack to seek US sympathy. The perception of the Indian role in the massacre becomes reinforced when a few days after the Chattisinghpora massacre, Indian forces abduct, kill, and mutilate the bodies of five local Kashmiris, claiming they are the foreign Islamist militants responsible for killing the Sikhs. A week after, at Brakpora in Islamabad/Anantnag, Indian forces kill nine protestors demanding an impartial investigation. Despite attempts to fudge the DNA by the NC-led government, subsequent tests of the exhumed corpses prove that the five dead "foreign militants" were actually local civilians.

2001

In **July**, Indian and Pakistani leaders meet but fail to arrive at a settlement on the Kashmir issue. However, plans for free trade, demilitarization, and shared autonomy in Kashmir are discussed. However, in **September**, in the wake of the 9/11 attacks in the US, Indian PM Vajpayee requests US President Bush to extend his "War on Terror" to Kashmir as well. The APHC and the JKLF denounce this as opportunistic. The US demands Pakistani support in Afghanistan and declares Pakistan to be a "major non-NATO ally." Pakistan drastically cuts support to Kashmiri groups. After an armed attack on the Indian Parliament in **December,** which India blames on Pakistan-backed groups Lashkar-e-Tayyiba (LeT) and Jaish-e-Muhammad (JeM) operating in Kashmir, Indian police arrest five Kashmiris, even though all the attackers are dead and are claimed to be from Pakistan. India starts a year-long build-up of military forces on the border, threatening war with Pakistan.

2002

On **May 21**, prominent APHC leader, Abdul Ghani Lone, is assassinated by unidentified gunmen. India blames the Pakistani ISI and the hardline factions of the APHC, while many in Kashmir blame Indian agencies. In **October**, former Indian Home Minister of Kashmiri origin, Mufti Syed, and his newly-created Peoples Democratic Party (PDP), win elections and form a coalition government with the Indian Congress. PDP ran its campaign on the idea of establishing "self-rule" in Kashmir. NC ran on the promise of re-establishing the pre-1953 "autonomy" for Kashmir. The remnants of the Ikhwanis are absorbed into regular Indian and local police forces.

2003

The APHC splits in Kashmir. Syed Ali Geelani blames sections of the APHC for fielding proxy candidates in the local elections despite election boycott calls. In **April**, India launches a major operation in the Jammu province against Muslim insurgents. Dozens are killed. In **May**, India and Pakistan declare ceasefire along the LoC, restore diplomatic relations, and later start a "Bus service" between Lahore and Amritsar.

2004

Geelani forms Tehreek-e-Hurriyat, leaving his formal position within JamaatIslami. In **September**, Indian PM Manmohan Singh and Pakistani President Pervez Musharraf meet in New York to discuss Kashmir.

2006

India and Pakistan hold peace talks. Musharraf proposes **4-Point Formula** for peace. The plan includes: 1. free cross-LoC movement for Kashmiris; 2. self-governance for Kashmirs on both sides of the LoC; 3. phased withdrawal of troops; 4. a joint India-Pakistan mechanism to implement these and create a future path toward the final resolution. Geelani's faction opposes the 4-Point Plan and come to be known as the "Hardliners." The APHC group led by Mirwaiz Umar Farooq support the plan. Based on their stance, they are known as the "Moderate APHC." The JKLF-led by Yasin Malik demands inclusion of Kashmiris in the final settlement of Kashmir.

2007

The JKLF launches the Safar-e-Azadi mass contact program to put pressure on India and Pakistan to include Kashmiris in the talks. Geelani claims. the 4-Point Formula is an attempt to freeze the Kashmir Dispute.

2008

The Indian governor and members of the PDP-Congress government give 100 acres of land in Kashmir to the Amarnath Shrine Board, a non-Kashmiri entity, to build permanent infrastructure for Indian pilgrims. The "land deal" contravenes protection of land guaranteed under Article 370 and Article 35A, which limit ownership of land only to the permanent residents of Kashmir. The land deal also puts an ecologically fragile mountainous region under threat. Many Kashmiris see it as an attempt to change Kashmir's demography. By **June**, widespread protests emerge across Kashmir. The protests are led by a Coordination Committee comprised of APHC factions, JKLF, and several civil society groups. Hundreds of thousands of Kashmiris join weekly protests. Indian reprisal is swift. More than 100 protestors are killed over the next few months and thousands are injured. The land deal is cancelled. In Jammu, angry Hindu nationalists impose an economic blockade on Kashmir for weeks, closing the only highway into Kashmir. During a procession headed toward the LOC to open the border to relieve suffering due to the Jammu blockade, Indian forces kill prominent Kashmiri leader and key APHC leader Sheikh Aziz, along with 20 others. The killings lead to an upsurge of young Kashmiris coming into the streets and confronting Indian soldiers with stones. India puts Kashmir under curfew for months. PDP-Congress coalition government falls. Meanwhile in Pakistan, the months-long "Lawyers Protest" has led President Musharraf to resign. The 4-Point Plan loses its prominent backer. Differences among APHC's "Moderate" and "Hardline" factions remain. In **November**, the LeT attacks in Mumbai lead to a formal end of peace talks between India and Pakistan. LoC artillery shelling resumes, causing dozens of Kashmiri deaths on both sides.

2009

In May, the rape and murder of two Kashmiri women in Shopian leads to widespread protests across Kashmir.

Independent investigations show Indian forces are involved; doctors establish rape. The Indian government claims the two drowned in a stream and closes the investigation. Widespread protests last months. The chief minister of Jammu and Kashmir, and Shiekh Abdullah's grandson, Omar Abdullah, who had previously served as a junior minister in the Hindu nationalist BJP government in Delhi, makes a U-turn from his initial support for the victims and also concludes that the two women had drowned in the shallow stream. A Kashmiri human rights group discovers 2700 unmarked mass graves across three districts of the highly-militarized North Kashmir. The graves contain some 2900 unknown bodies, many believed to be among the 8000 enforced disappearances that have taken place in Kashmir since 1989.

2010

In **April**, the Indian military kills three Kashmiri civilians in Machil, Kupwara, and claims them to be "foreign terrorists." In **June**, eight-year old TufailMattoo is killed in Srinagar when Indian forces hit his head with a teargas shell. His death catalyzes intense new protests that last months. Indian forces impose a curfew and kill more than 100 young Kashmiris during "stone-pelting" protests. Though the protests are led by youth, Geelani emerges as a key leader and his faction issues "protest calendars." Geelani demands demilitarization, release of political prisoners, and a clear path toward implementing the right to self-determination. India appoints three "interlocutors," but Kashmiri leaders claim they have no mandate and reject them. By **late fall**, Geelani calls off the protests. Disappointed, dozens of Kashmiri youth disappear and join armed militant ranks of HM, which is still operating but in a much diminished state.

2013

The Indian government hangs a Kashmiri man, Afzal Guru, in prison since the 2001 attack on the Indian Parliament, on **February 9**. Several Indian civil society groups had claimed that the evidence of his role in the attacks was thin. Guru had claimed that he was set up by Indian agents in Kashmir. The Indian Supreme Court had infamously declared in its verdict that Guru must be hanged "to satisfy the collective conscience of the Indian society," provoking shock and criticism across the world. Guru's body is not returned to his family and is buried next to Maqbool Bhat's in Delhi's Tihar Jail.

2014

The APHC faction led by Mirwaiz Umar splits as several of its constituents claim the amalgamation to be ineffective. Several of them join Geelani's faction, known as APHC (G). The NC, which has been in government in coalition with the Congress since 2008, loses elections.

2015

In March, the PDP forms alliance with Indian Prime Minister NarendraModi's Hindu nationalist BJP, sending Kashmir into a shock. It is the first time that Hindu nationalists have officially come to power in Kashmir since at least 1947. A Jammu Kashmir Coalition of Civil Society report "Structures of Violence" states: "this report is a part of the continuing work to understand and analyze the role of the Indian State in Jammu and Kashmir, an occupied territory internationally recognized as a disputed territory between India and Pakistan, that has resulted in widespread and systematic violence including the disappearance of 8000+ persons, 70,000+ deaths, 6000+ unknown, unmarked and mass graves, and countless cases of torture and sexual violence." The report also estimates the strength of Indian armed forces in Jammu and Kashmir to be between "656,638 and 750,981" personnel.

2016

On July 8, Indian forces kill Burhan Wani, the 22-year old commander of HM who has become widely popular, partly because of his social media use. Kashmir erupts into stone-pelting protests. Indian forces kill dozens and blind hundreds of young Kashmiris. Half a million people assemble in his hometown of Tral to attend his funeral procession. A months-long curfew is imposed. Wani's death brings the "New-Age Militancy" out of the shadows. South Kashmir becomes the hot-bed of resistance. Media-savvy, charismatic, but without much training, the young New-Age Kashmiri militants become popular. Each Indian siege to kill them is met with entire villages coming out in their defense. Each killing of these young men leads to tens of thousands joining funeral processions.

2017

The Indian counterinsurgency war, known as "Operation All Out," intensifies in South Kashmir. Hundreds are killed, mostly young Kashmiri militants and civilians.

2018

In **June**, the BJP exits the coalition with the PDP and the Indian governor acquires full charge. In **November**, the governor dissolves the Legislative Assembly.

2019

In **February**, a Kashmiri bomber attacks an Indian military convoy in South Kashmir, killing 40 soldiers. India launches air attacks in Pakistan. The next day, Pakistan launches air strikes in Indian-controlled Kashmir, and shoots down an Indian jet, while Indian forces mistakenly shoot down their own helicopter. Pakistan returns a captured Indian air force pilot, but tensions remain high. India bans the JKLF and the JamaatIslami, arresting their leaders, including Yasin Malik. A massive crackdown is launched against APHC activists across Kashmir. Thousands of Kashmiri political and civil society activists are arrested in raids. In late July, tens of thousands of new Indian forces enter Kashmir. On August 5, the Indian government "reads down" Article 370 and revokes Article 35A, removing the last remnants of "autonomy" and "special status" guaranteed under the Instrument of Accession and the Delhi Agreement. The removal of 35A paves the way for Indians citizens to settle in Kashmir, a long standing demand of the RSS. The leaders of NC and PDP are put under detention. Kashmir is under complete curfew and all forms of communication are shut down. On **October 31**, the Indian government splits the historic State of Jammu and Kashmir into two "Union Territories" under the Jammu Kashmir Reorganization Act passed on August 9. One is the "Union Territory of Jammu and Kashmir" which will have a legislative assembly with highly limited powers, and the second is the "Union Territory of Ladakh," which will have no legislative assembly. The Indian government takes full control over determining land use and residency requirements, while its officials speak about instituting "Israeli-style settler colonies" in Kashmir. An intense crackdown and communication blockade in Kashmir ensure Kashmiris are unable to protest. Pakistan and China protest the Indian move. Diasporic Kashmiris in the West become prominent voices of resistance.

2020

The Indian government enacts a new "Domicile Law" for the Jammu and Kashmir Union Territory, allowing certain classes of Indians to become permanent residents of Kashmir. Indian officials in Kashmir start issuing certificates to Indians that would allow them to get state employment in Kashmir and make them eligible to purchase land. In **June**, Chinese and Indian forces clash along the border in Ladakh. 20 Indian soldiers die and the Chinese force India to withdraw several kilometers away from what India claims to be its boundary. In **July**, Geelani leaves his own faction of the APHC, indicating an end to a 70-year-long political career. The Indian government issues new laws to expand military bases and create hundreds of thousands of "new housing units" in the region.

Appendix - 2

Instrument of Accession of Kashmir to India

Whereas the Indian Independence Act, 1947, provides that as from the fifteenth day of August, 1947, there shall be set up an independent Dominion known as INDIA, and that the Government of India Act, 1935, shall, with such omission, additions, adaptations and modifications as the Governor-General may by order specify, be applicable to the Dominion of India,

And whereas the Government of India Act, 1935, as so adapted, by the Governor General provides that an Indian State may accede to the Dominion of India by an Instrument of Accession executed by the Ruler thereof :

Now, therefore, I Shriman Inder Mahander Rajrajeshwar Maharajadhiraj Shri Hari Singhji Jammu and Kashmir Naresh Tatha Tibbet adi Deshadhipathi, Ruler of Jammu and Kashmir State, in the exercise of my Sovereignty in and over my said State do hereby execute this my Instrument of Accession; and

1. I hereby declare that I accede to the Dominion of India with the intent that the Governor-General of India, the Dominion Legislature, the Federal

Court and any other Dominion authority established for the purposes of the Dominion shall, by virtue of this my Instrument of Accession but subject always to the terms thereof, and for the purposes only of the Dominion, exercise in relation to the State of Jammu and Kashmir (hereinafter refrred to as "this State") such functions as may be vested in them by or under the Government of India Act, 1935, as in force in the Dominion of India, on the 15th Day of August 1947, (which Act as so in force is hereafter referred to as "the Act").

2. I hereby assume the obligation of ensuring that due effect is given to provisions of the Act within this State so far as they are applicable therein by virtue of this my Instrument of Accession.

3. I accept the matters specified in the scheduled hereto as the matters with respect to which the Dominion Legislature may make laws for this State.

4. I hereby declare that I accede to the Dominion of India on the assurance that if an agreement is made between the Governor-General and the Ruler of this State whereby any functions in relation to the administration in this State of any law of the Dominion Legislature shall be exercised by the Ruler of this State, then any such agreement shall be deemed to form part of this Instrument and shall be construed and have effect accordingly.

5. The terms of this my Instrument of Accession shall not be varied by any amendment of the Act or the Indian Independence Act, 1947, unless such amendment is accepted by me by Instrument supplementary to this Instrument.

6. Nothing in this Instrument shall empower the Dominion Legislature to make any law for this State authorising the compulsory acquisition of land for any purpose, but I hereby undertake that

should the Dominion for the purpose of a Dominion law which applies in this State deem it necessary to acquire any land, I will at their request acquire the land at their expense, or, if the land belongs to me transfer it to them on such terms as may be agreed or, in default of agreement, determined by an arbitrator to be appointed by the Chief justice of India.

7. Nothing in this Instrument shall be deemed to commit in any way to acceptance of any future constitution of India or to fetter my discretion to enter into arrangement with the Government of India under any such future constitution.

8. Nothing in this Instrument affects the continuance of my Sovereignty in and over this State, or, save as provided by or under this Instrument, the exercise of any powers, authority and rights now enjoyed by me as Ruler of this State or the validity of any law at present in force in this State.

9. I hereby declare that I execute this Instrument on behalf of this State and that any reference in this Instrument to me or to the Ruler of the State is to be construed as including a reference to my heirs and successors.

Given under my hand this 26th day of October, nineteen hundred and forty-seven.

Hari Singh,
Maharajadhiraj of Jammu and Kashmir State.

Acceptance of Accession by the Governor-General of India

I do hereby accept this Instrument of Accession.

Dated this twenty-seventh day of October, nineteen hundred and forty-seven.

Mountbatten of Burma,
Governor-General of India.

Appendix - 3

Tashkent Declaration

The Prime Minister of India and the President of Pakistan having met at Tashkent and having discussed the existing relations between India and Pakistan, hereby declare their firm resolve to restore normal and peaceful relations between their countries and to promote understanding and friendly relations between their peoples. They consider the attainment of these objectives of vital importance for the welfare of the 600 million people of India and Pakistan.

I

The Prime Minister of India and the President of Pakistan agree that both sides will exert all efforts to create good neighbourly relations between India and Pakistan in accordance with the United Nations Charter. They reaffirm their obligation under the Charter not to have recourse to force and to settle their disputes through peaceful means. They considered that the interests of peace in their region and particularly in the Indo-Pakistan Sub-Continent and, indeed, the interests of the peoples of India and Pakistan were not served by the continuance of tension between the two countries. It was against this background that Jammu and Kashmir was discussed, and each of the sides set forth its respective position.

II

The Prime Minister of India and the President of Pakistan have agreed that all armed personnel of the two countries shall be withdrawn not later than 25 February 1966 to the positions they held prior to 5 August 1965, and both sides shall observe the cease-fire terms on the cease-fire line.

III

The Prime Minister of India and the President of Pakistan have agreed that relations between India and Pakistan shall be based on the principle of non-interference in the internal affairs of each other.

IV

The Prime Minister of India and the President of Pakistan have agreed that both sides will discourage any propaganda directed against the other country, and will encourage propaganda which promotes the development of friendly relations between the two countries.

V

The Prime Minister of India and the President of Pakistan have agreed that the High Commissioner of India to Pakistan and the High Commissioner of Pakistan to India will return to their posts and that the normal functioning of diplomatic missions of both countries will be restored. Both Governments shall observe the Vienna Convention of 1961 on Diplomatic Intercourse.

VI

The Prime Minister of India and the President of Pakistan have agreed to consider measures towards the restoration of economic and trade relations, communications, as well as cultural exchanges between India and Pakistan, and to take measures to implement the existing agreements between India and Pakistan.

VII

The Prime Minister of India and the President of Pakistan have agreed that they give instructions to their respective authorities to carry out the repatriation of the prisoners of war.

VIII

The Prime Minister of India and the President of Pakistan have agreed that. the sides will continue the discussion of questions relating to the problems of refugees and evictions/illegal immigrations. They also agreed that both sides will create conditions which will prevent the exodus of people. They further agreed to discuss the return of the, property and assets taken over by either side in connexion with the conflict.

IX

The Prime Minister of India and the President of Pakistan have agreed that the sides, will continue meetings both at the highest and at other levels on matters of direct concern to both countries, Both sides have recognized the need to set up joint Indian-Pakistani bodies which will report to their Governments in order to decide what further steps should be taken,

The Prime Minister of India and the President of Pakistan record their feelings of deep appreciation and gratitude to the leaders of the Soviet Union, the Soviet Government and personally to the Chairman of the 63XiCi.L of Ministers of the USSR for their constructive, friendly and noble part in bringing about the present meeting which has resulted in mutually satisfactory results. They also express to the Government and friendly people of Uzbekistan their sincere thankfulness for their overwhelming reception and generous hospitality.

They invite, the Chairman of the Council of Ministers of the USSR to witness this Declaration.

(Signed) Lal Bahadur (Signed) M.A. KHAN, F.M.

Prime Minister of India President of Pakistan

Tashkent, 10 January 1966,

Appendix - 4

Agreement on Bilateral Relations between the Government of India and the Government of Pakistan

(Shimla Agreement)

Shimla, 2 July 1972

1. The Government of India and the Government of Pakistan are resolved that the two countries put an end to the conflict and confrontation that have hitherto marred their relations and work for the promotion of a friendly and harmonious relationship and the establishment of durable peace in the sub-continent, so that both countries may henceforth devote their resources and energies to the pressing talk of advancing the welfare of their peoples.

In order to achieve this objective, the Government of India and the Government of Pakistan have agreed as follows:-

(i) That the principles and purposes of the Charter of the United Nations shall govern the relations between the two countries;

(ii) That the two countries are resolved to settle their differences by peaceful means through bilateral negotiations or by any other peaceful means mutually agreed upon between them. Pending the final settlement of any of the problems between the two countries, neither side shall unilaterally alter the situation and both shall prevent the organization, assistance or encouragement of any acts detrimental to the maintenance of peaceful and harmonious relations;

(iii) That the pre-requisite for reconciliation, good neighbourliness and durable peace between them is a commitment by both the countries to peaceful co-existence, respect for each other's territorial integrity and sovereignty and non-interference in each other's internal affairs, on the basis of equality and mutual benefit;

(iv) That the basic issues and causes of conflict which have bedevilled the relations between the two countries for the last 25 years shall be resolved by peaceful means;

(v) That they shall always respect each other's national unity, territorial integrity, political independence and sovereign equality;

That in accordance with the Charter of the United Nations they will refrain from the threat or use of force against the territorial integrity or political independence of each other.

2. Both Governments will take all steps within their power to prevent hostile propaganda directed against each other. Both countries will encourage the dissemination of such information as would promote the development of friendly relations between them.

3. In order progressively to restore and normalize

relations between the two countries step by step, it was agreed that;

(i) Steps shall be taken to resume communications, postal, telegraphic, sea, land including border posts, and air links including overflights.

(ii) Appropriate steps shall be taken to promote travel facilities for the nationals of the other country.

(iii) Trade and co-operation in economic and other agreed fields will be resumed as far as possible.

(iv) Exchange in the fields of science and culture will be promoted.

In this connection delegations from the two countires will meet from time to time to work out the necessary details.

4. In order to initiate the process of the establishment of durable peace, both the Governments agree that:

(i) Indian and Pakistani forces shall be withdrawn to their side of the international border.

(ii) In Jammu and Kashmir, the line of control resulting from the cease-fire of December 17, 1971 shall be respected by both sides without prejudice to the recognized position of either side. Neither side shall seek to alter it unilaterally, irrespective of mutual differences and legal interpretations. Both sides further undertake to refrain from the threat or the use of force in violation of this Line.

(iii) The withdrawals shall commence upon entry into force of this Agreement and shall be completed within a period of 30 days thereof.

5. This Agreement will be subject to ratification by both countries in accordance with their respective constitutional procedures, and will come into force with effect from the date on which the Instruments of Ratification are exchanged.

6. Both Governments agree that their respective Heads will meet again at a mutually convenient time in the future and that, in the meanwhile, the representatives of the two sides will meet to discuss further the modalities and arrangements for the establishment of durable peace and normalization of relations, including the questions of repatriation of prisoners of war and civilian internees, a final settlement of Jammu and Kashmir and the resumption of diplomatic relations.

Sd/-

(Indira Gandhi)

Prime Minister Republic of India

Sd/-

(Zulfikar Ali Bhutto)

President Islamic Republic of Pakistan

Source: Indian Ministry of External Affairs (Official Website)

Appendix - 5

The Lahore Declaration

The following is the text of the Lahore Declaration signed by the Prime Minister, Mr. A. B. Vajpayee, and the Pakistan Prime Minister, Mr. Nawaz Sharif, in Lahore on Sunday:

The Prime Ministers of the Republic of India and the Islamic Republic of Pakistan:

Sharing a vision of peace and stability between their countries, and of progress and prosperity for their peoples;

Convinced that durable peace and development of harmonious relations and friendly cooperation will serve the vital interests of the peoples of the two countries, enabling them to devote their energies for a better future;

Recognising that the nuclear dimension of the security environment of the two countries adds to their responsibility for avoidance of conflict between the two countries;

Committed to the principles and purposes of the Charter of the United Nations, and the universally accepted principles of peaceful coexistence;

Reiterating the determination of both countries to

implementing the Simla Agreement in letter and spirit;

Committed to the objective of universal nuclear disarmament and non-proliferation;

Convinced of the importance of mutually agreed confidence building measures for improving the security environment;

Recalling their agreement of 23rd September, 1998, that an environment of peace and security is in the supreme national interest of both sides and that the resolution of all outstanding issues, including Jammu and Kashmir, is essential for this purpose;

Have agreed that their respective Governments:

- shall intensify their efforts to resolve all issues, including the issue of Jammu and Kashmir.
- shall refrain from intervention and interference in each other's internal affairs.
- shall intensify their composite and integrated dialogue process for an early and positive outcome of the agreed bilateral agenda.
- shall take immediate steps for reducing the risk of accidental or unauthorised use of nuclear weapons and discuss concepts and doctrines with a view to elaborating measures for confidence building in the nuclear and conventional fields, aimed at prevention of conflict.
- reaffirm their commitment to the goals and objectives of SAARC and to concert their efforts towards the realisation of the SAARC vision for the year 2000 and beyond with a view to promoting the welfare of the peoples of South Asia and to improve their quality of life through accelerated economic growth, social progress and cultural development.

- reaffirm their condemnation of terrorism in all its forms and manifestations and their determination to combat this menace.
- shall promote and protect all human rights and fundamental freedoms.

Signed at Lahore on the 21st day of February 1999.

Atal Behari Vajpayee - Prime Minister of the Republic of India

Muhammad Nawaz Sharif - Prime Minister of the Islamic Republic of Pakistan

Appendix-6

What Article 370 Means

Under this article, the centre needs the state government's concurrence to apply laws - except in defence, foreign affairs, finance and communications.

It means the state's residents live under a separate set of laws, including those related to citizenship, ownership of property, and fundamental rights, as compared to other Indians. As a result of this provision, Indian citizens from other states cannot purchase land or property in Jammu & Kashmir.

Under Article 370, the Centre has no power to declare financial emergency under Article 360 in the state. It can declare an emergency in the state only in case of war or external aggression.

Scrapping of Article 370 in J&K: Key take aways from Amit Shah's statement in Rajya Sabha

In a major announcement on J&K, Union Home Minister Amit Shah on Monday announced the government's proposal to revoke Article 370 and Article 35A of the Indian Constitution, which provided "special status" to the state. Times Now explains the Key Takeaways from Home Minister Amit Shah's statement on Jammu and Kashmir in Rajya Sabha.

The Article 370 — which comes under Part XXI of the Constitution, which deals with "Temporary, Transitional and Special provisions" — grants J&K a special autonomous status. Constitutional provisions that are applicable to other Indian states are not applicable to J&K.

The provision was drafted in 1947 by Sheikh Abdullah, the then prime minister of J&K appointed by Maharaja Hari Singh and Jawaharlal Nehru. Abdullah had argued that Article 370 should not be placed under temporary provisions; he instead wanted 'iron-clad autonomy' for the state. The centre, however, didn't grant his wish.

What Article 35(A) means

Article 35A allows the state legislature to define the Jammu and Kashmir's permanent residents. The article had been inserted via the Constitution (Application to J&K) Order, 1954. It was issued by the then President Rajendra Prasad under Article 370 on PM Nehru's advice.

The state's Constitution, at the time of its adoption in 1956, defined a permanent resident as someone who was a state subject on May 14, 1954, or who has been a resident for 10 years, and has lawfully acquired immovable property.

What this clause means is that no outsider can now own property in J&K or get a state job.

The article is also known as the Permanent Residents Law. Among other things, it deprives the state's female residents of property rights if/when they marry an 'outsider'.

The provision also extends to children born of any such women.

What will happen to J&K Now?

After Kashmir's special status is gone, people from anywhere in India be able to buy property and permanently settle in the state. This has fuelled fear in the mind of Kashmiris — they think it would lead to the state's demographic transformation from majority Muslim to majority Hindu.

A separate Union Territory will be created for Jammu & Kashmir with legislature, Amit Shah has revealed via a notification. "Keeping in view the prevailing internal security situation, fuelled by cross-border terrorism in the existing state of Jammu & Kashmir, a seperate Union Territory is being created", the notification said.

Under the notificaiton, the Ladakh region is also being given the status of a Union Terrority, without legislature. "The Ladakh division has a large area but is sparsely populated with a very difficult terrain. There has been a long-pending demand of people of Ladakh to give it a Union Territory status to enable them to realise their aspiration", it said.

Following Amit Shah's proposal, President Ram NathKovind promulgated Constitution (Application to Jammu and Kashmir) Order, 2019, stating that the provisions of the Indian Constitution will henceforth be applicable to J&K.

The Constitution (Application to Jammu and Kashmir) Order, 2019 comes into force "at once", and shall "supersede the Constitution (Application to Jammu and Kashmir) Order, 1954".

The presidential promulgation says: "All the provisions of the Constitution shall apply in relation to the state of

Jammu and Kashmir."

For the purpose, a clause 4 has been added to Article 367 which will introduced four changes.

"The references to the person for the time being recognised by the president on the recommendation of the Legislative Assembly of the State as the Sadar-i-Riyasat of Jammu and Kashmir, acting on the advice of the Council of Ministers of the state for the time being in office, shall be construed as references to the Governor of Jammu and Kashmir", said the order.

It added: "References to the Governor of Jammu and Kashmir shall be construed as including references to the Governor of Jammu and Kashmir acting on the advice of his Council of Ministers".

The order further said that in the proviso to clause (3) of Article 370, the expression "Constituent Assembly of the State referred to in clause (2)" shall read "Legislative Assembly of the State".

Bibliography

➢ Primary Sources

A. Government Documents

Annual Report 1998-1999, Ministry of External Affairs, Government of India.

Annual Report 2010-11, Ministry of Defence, Government of India.

Election Commission of India, 2014

India-Pakistan Relations", Ministry of External Affairs, Government of India, April 2014.

Prime Minister Shri Atal Bihari Vajpayee's Independence Day Address, New Delhi, 15 August 2002.

Text of President Musharraf's Address to the Nation", 12 January 2002.

➢ Secondary Sources

A. Books

Ahmed, Asif, "An Analysis of India-Pakistan Relations From Past to Present - Strategic Implications for India", *Suraksha Chintan,* Vol. 3, No. 3, July 2011.

Ahmad, Quazi Shakil, "Pakistan-India Relations: Some

Geostrategic Considerations", *Pakistan Horizon,* Vol. 57, No. 03, July 2004.

Ajith Kumar, M P, *India-Pakistan Relations- The Story of a Fractured Fraternity* (Delhi: Kalpaz Publications, 2006).

Akbar, M.J., *Tinderbox – The Past and Future of Pakistan* (New Delhi: HarperCollins, 2011).

Alam, Mohammed Badrul (ed.), *Contours of India's Foreign Policy: Changes and Challenges* (New Delhi: Reference Press, 2014).

Atwal, Ravjeetsingh, (ed.), *'India's Foreign Policy: Conflict & Cooperation* (New Delhi: White Falcon Publishing, 2016).

Bahl, Arvin, *From Jinnah to Jihad: Pakistan's Kashmir Quest and the Limits of Realism* (Atlantic Publishers New Delhi, 2007.

Behera, Navnita Chadha, *Demystifying Kashmir* (Washington, D.C: Brookings Institution Press, 2006).

Bertsch, Gary K., et. al., (eds.), *Engaging India-U.S. Strategic Relations with the World's Largest Democracy* (New York: Routledge, 1999).

Bhandari, M C Bhandari, *Solving Kashmir* (New Delhi: Lancer Publishers and Distributors, 2006).

Bose, Sumantra, *Kashmir: Roots of Conflict, Paths to Peace* (United States of America, Harvard University Press, 2005).

Bose, Sumantra, *The Challenge in Kashmir: Democracy, Self-determination and a Just Peace* (New Delhi: Sage Publications, 1997).

Chakraborty, Mohor, "India and Pakistan: Chasing the Horizon of Concord and Discord", *World Focus,* Vol. XXXII, No. 5, May 2011.

Chansoria, Monika, "China's Current Kashmir Policy: Steady Crystallisation", *Claws Journal,* Winter 2016.

Chitkara M. G., *Indo-Pak Relations: Challenges before New Millennium* (New Delhi: APH Publishing, 2001).

Chopra, V. D., *Genesis of Indo-Pakistan Conflict on Kashmir* (New Delhi: Patriot Publishers, 1990).

Chopra, V.D. (ed.), *India's Foreign Policy in the 21st Century* (New Delhi: Kalpaz Publications, 2006).

Cohen, Stephen Philip, *Shooting for a Century: Finding Answers to the India–Pakistan Conundrum* (Delhi: Harper Collins Publishers, 2013).

Cohen, Stephen Philip, *The Idea of Pakistan* (New Delhi: Oxford University Press, 2005).

Dalvi, Arun (ed.), *India's Security and Defence - Swatantryaveer Sawarkar Memorial Lectures* (Pune: University of Pune Press, 2006).

Dixit, J.N., *India-Pakistan in War and Peace* (New Delhi: The India Today Group, 2002).

Ganguly, Sumit, *Conflict Unending: India-Pakistan Tensions Since 1947* (New York: Columbia University Press, 2001).

Ganguly, S., *The Crisis in Kashmir: Portents of War, Hopes of Peace* (London, England: Cambridge University Press, 1997).

Gehlot, N.S. and Anu Satsangi, *Indo-Pak Relations: Twists and Turns from Partition to Agra Summit and Beyond* (New Delhi: Deep and Deep Publications Pvt. Ltd., 2004).

Ghosh, Samarjit, "Two Decades of Indo-Pak CBMs: A Critique from India", *IPCS Issue Brief* 132, September 2009.

Godement, Francois (ed.), *What Does India Think* (London: European Council on Foreign Relations, 2015).

Gupta, Sisir, *Kashmir: A Study in India-Pakistan Relations* (New York: Asia Publishing House, 1966).

Habibullah, Wajahat, *My Kashmir: Conflict and the Prospects for Enduring Peace* (Washington, D.C.: United States Institute of Peace Press, 2008).

Ispahani, Mahnaz Z., *Roads and Rivals: The Politics of Access in the Borderlands of Asia* (London: I.B. Tauris & Co. Ltd., 1989).

Jagmohan, *My Frozen Turbulence in Kashmir* (New Delhi: Allied Publishers, 2007).

Javaid, Umbreen, *Peace Building in South Asia: Limitations and Prospects* (Lahore: University of Punjab, 2012).

Kadian, Rajesh, *The Kashmir Tangle: Issues and Options* (San Francisco: Westview Press, 1993).

Karim, Abdul, *Kashmir: The Troubled Frontiers* (London: Oxford University Press, 1996).

Kaw, Mushtaq A., " Border Politics in South Asia: A Case Study of India, Pakistan and Afghanistan", *Eurasia Border Review Part II.*

Khurshid, Salman, *Beyond Terrorism: New Hope for Kashmir* (UBS Publishers, 1994).

Koithara Verghese, *Grafting Peace in Kashmir: Through a Realist Lens* (New Delhi: Sage Publications, 2004).

Korbel, Joseph, *Danger in Kashmir* (New Jersey: Princeton University Press, 1996).

Kothari, Smitu, et al., (eds.), *Bridging Partition: People Initiatives for Peace between India And Pakistan* (New Delhi: Orient Blackswan Private Limited, 2010).

Koithara, Verghese, *Crafting Peace in Kashmir: through a Realist Lens* (New Delhi: Sage Publications, 2004).

Kugelman, Michael and Robert M. Hathaway (eds.), *Pakistan-India Trade: What Needs to be Done? What Does it Matter?* (Washington, D.C.: Woodrow Wilson International Center for Scholars' Asia Program and the Fellowship Fund for Pakistan, 2013)

Kumar, Sanjay and Dhirendra Dwivedi (eds.), *India-China: Conflict or Cooperation* (New Delhi: Pentagon Press, 2015).

Kumar, Sanjay, et al. (eds.), *India-Pakistan Relations: Past, Present and Future* (New Delhi: G B Books Publishers and Distributors, 2018).

Kux, Dennis, *India-Pakistan Negotiations: Is Past Still Prologue?* (US Institute of Peace Press, 2006).

Lange, Klaus, Klara Knapp and J P Panda (eds.), *Revisiting Contemporary South Asia: Politics, Economics and Security* (New Delhi: Pentagon Press, 2012).

Latif, Ahmed Sherwani (ed.), *Foreign Policy of Pakistan* (Karachi, 1964).

Mattoo, Amitabh, et al. (eds.), *India and Pakistan: Pathways Ahead* (New Delhi: KW Publishers Pvt. Ltd., 2007).

Misra, Ashutosh, *India-Pakistan: Coming to Terms* (Palgrave Macmillan, 2010).

Muni, S.D., (ed.), *IDSA Asian Strategic Review 2007* (New Delhi: Academic Foundation, 2008).

Nanda, KK, *Conquering Kashmir - A Pakistani Obsession* (New Delhi, Lancer Publications, 1994.

Nath, Rajendra (ed.), *Musharraf's War* (New Delhi: Lancer's Books, 2003).

Nayar Kuldeep, *Wall at Wagah India-Pakistan Relations* (New Delhi: Gyan Publishing House, 2003).

Pande, Aparna, *Explaining Pakistan's Foreign Policy: Escaping India* (New York: Routledge, 2011).

Paul, T.V. (ed.), *The India-Pakistan Conflict: An Enduring Rivalry* (New York: Cambridge University Press, 2005).

Ralhan, O.P. (ed.), *Agra: India and Pakistan Summit* (New Delhi: Anmol Publications, 2002).

Sattar, Abdul, *Afghanistan: Past, Present and Future, From Jihad to Civil War* (Islamabad: The Institute of Regional Studies, 1997).

Schofield, Victoria, *Kashmir in the Cross Fire* (London: Oxford Books, 1996).

Scott, David (ed.), *Handbook of India's International Relations* (London and New York: Routledge, 2011).

Sen, Gautam (ed.), *National Security - Gen. B. C. Joshi Memorial Lectures* (Pune: University of Pune Press, 2006).

Shafqat, Saeed (ed.), *New Perspectives on Pakistan: Vision for the Future* (Karachi: Oxford University Press, 2007).

Siddiqa, Ayesha, *India-Pakistan Relations: Confrontation to Conciliation* (Islamabad: Centre for Democratic Governance, 2004).

Singh, Jasjit, *Pakistan occupied Kashmir under the Jackboot* (New Delhi, Siddhi Books, 1995).

Singh, N. P. and R. S. Rawat, "Future of Indo-Pakistan Relations", *Suraksha Chintan,* Vol. 3, No. 3, July 2011.

Singh, Swaran (ed.), *China-Pakistan Strategic Cooperation: Indian Perspectives* (New Delhi: Manohar, 2007).

Svensson, Ted, *Production of Postcolonial India and Pakistan: Meanings of Pakistan* (London and New York: Routledge, 2013).

Swami, Praveen, *India, Pakistan and the Secret Jihad: The Covert War in Kashmir, 1947-2004* (London: Routledge, 2007).

Synnott, Hilary, *Transforming Pakistan: Ways Out of Instability* (London: Routledge, 2009).

T., Najmudheen and Farhana Kausar, "Significance of Indo-Pak Cordial Relations in South Asia", *International Journal of South Asian Studies,* Vol. 5, No. 1, Jan-June 2012.

Talbot, I. and G. Singh, (eds.), *Region and Partition: Bengal, Punjab and the Partition of the Subcontinent* (Oxford: Oxford University Press, 1999).

Thomas, Raju G. C. *Perspective on Kashmir: The Roots of Conflict in South Asia* (San Francisco: Westview Press, 1992).

Wolpert, Stanley, *India and Pakistan: Continued Conflict or Cooperation* (California: University of California Press, 2010).

Wirsing, Robert G., *India, Pakistan and the Kashmir Dispute: On Regional Conflict and Its Resolution* (New Deli: Reysa and Company, 1994).

Wolpert Stanley A., India and Pakistan: Continued Conflict or Cooperation, (London: University of California Press, 2010).

B. Articles in Journals

Abhinandan, Netajee, "Turbulence in PoK: The China Factor", *World Focus,* Vol. XXXVIII, No. 7, July 2017.

Adnan, Mubeen and Bushra Fatima, "Peace Process with India: A Challenge for Pakistan", *A Research Journal of South Asian Studies,* Vol. 31, No. 1, Jan-June 2016.

Ahmed, Ishtiaq, "Towards a Kashmiri Settlement Beyond Jihad", *Perceptions, Journal of International Affairs,* Vol. 9, March-May 2004.

Ali, Muhammad, et al., "Pakistan-India Relations: Peace through Bilateral Trade", *Developing Country Studies,* Vol. 5, No. 2, 2015.

Baba, Noor Ahmad, "Resolving Kashmir: Imperatives and Solutions", *Race and Class,* Vol. 56, No. 2, 2014.

Bahadur, Kalim, "Pakistan, India's Neighbour: So Near but So Far", *World Focus,* Vol. XXXII, No.6, June 2011.

Baloch, M. Umar Farooq, "Prospects for Sustained Economic Cooperation between India and Pakistan", *Institute for Strategic Studies, Research and Analysis (ISSRA) Papers,* National Defence University, Islamabad, 2015.

Behuria, A. K., "Pakistan's Approach to Kashmir Since the Lahore Agreement: Is There Any Change?", *Strategic Analysis,* Vol. 33, No. 3, 2009.

Benvenuti, Andrea, *USI Journal,* July-September 95, Vol. CXXV, No. 521.

Bukhari, Syed Waqas Haider and Tahira Parveen, "China's Approach Towards Kashmir Conflict: A Viable Solution", *Journal of Professional Research in Social Sciences,* Vol. 1, No. 1, July 2014.

Chinese Troops Around Kashmir Posing Threat", *Canadian Asian News,* Vol. 15, No. 197, 15-30 April 2011.

Chun-Chuan, Shen, "Peking's Relations with India and Pakistan", *Issues & Studies,* Vol. 25 No. 9, September 1989.

Claws Research Team, "Jammu and Kashmir Realities Revisited", *Scholar Warrior,* autumn 2011.

Dar, Bashir Ahmad, "Major Bilateral Issues between China and India", *Arts and Social Sciences Journal,* Vol. 5, No. 1, 2014.

Dash, Kishore C. and Robert K. McCleery, "The Political Economy of Trade Relations between India-Pakistan", *Journal of Economic and Financial Studies,* Vol. 2, No. 2, April 2014.

Fani, Muhammad Ishaque, "Pakistan-China Security Relations and Mutual Ventures", *JRSP,* vol. 46, No. 2, 2009.

Fayaz, Sadia, "Kashmir Dispute between Pakistan and India: The Way Out", *The Dialogue,* Vol. XI, No. 1.

Ganapathi, M., "Contours of India's Foreign Policy: An Overview", *Indian Foreign Affairs Journal,* Vol. 12, No. 1, Jan-March 2017

Ganguly, Rajat, "India, Pakistan and the Kashmir Dispute", *Asian Studies Institute,* Victoria University of Wellington.

Godbole, Avinash, "India-China Relation: Enhancing Engagement Promises Better Future", *Indian Foreign Affairs Journal,* Vol. 11, No. 1, Jan-Mar 2016.

Hashmi, Rehana Saeed and Aila Sajid, "Kashmir Conflict: The Nationalistic Perspective (A Pre-Partition Phenomenon)", *South Asian Studies,* Vol. 32, No. 1, January-June 2017.

Hilali, A.Z., "Historical Developments of the Kashmir Problem and Pakistan Policy after September 11", *Perceptions, Journal of International Affairs,* Vol. 9, June-August 2004.

Hussain, Mohammad Samir, "India-Pakistan Unending Rivalry: Kashmir as a Factor" *Suraksha Chintan,* Vol. 6, No. 6, January 2013.

Hussain, Safdar and Muhammad Ijaz Latif, "Issues and Challenges in Pakistan-Afghanistan Relations after 9/11", *South Asian Studies,* Vol. 27, No. 1, January-June 2012.

Hussain, Syed Rifaat, "Resolving the Kashmir Dispute: Blending Realism with Justice", *The Pakistan Development Review,* Vol. 48, No. 4, Winter 2009.

Ijaz, Aymen "Pakistan-India Relations under Prime Minister Modi's Government (2014-16)", *Journal of Current Affairs,* Vol. 2, No. 1, 2017.

Iqbal, Khalid, "Pakistan's Relations with India Since 9/11: A Pakistani Perspective", *FPRC Country Specific Studies on Pakistan,* New Delhi, Vol. 2.

Jabeen, Mussarat, "SAARC and Indo-Pakistan Relationship", *Journal of Political Studies,* Vol. 1, No, 2.

Javaid, Umbreen and Marium Kamal, "Security Dilemma in South Asia", *Journal of Political Studies,* Vol. 22, No. 1, 2015.

Jha, Nalinikant Kant, "India and Pakistan: Chasing the Horizons of Discord and Concord", *International Journal of South Asian Studies,* Vol. 4, No. 1, Jan-June 2011.

Kakakhel, Shafqat, "The *Indus Waters Treaty: Negotiation, Implementation, New Challenges,* and *Future Prospects", Criterion Quarterly,* Vol. 9, No. 2, *2014.*

Kalis, Naseer Ahmed and Shaheen Showkat Dar, "Geo-Political significance of Kashmir: An overview of Indo-Pak Relations", *IOSR Journal Of Humanities And Social Science (IOSR-JHSS),* Vol. 9, No. 2, Mar-Apr 2013.

Kamboj, Anil, "Creation of Pakistan Occupied Kashmir and Present Scenario", *World Focus,* Vol. XXXVIII, No. 7, July 2017.

Khalid, Iram, 'Trans-Boundary Water Sharing Issues: A Case of South Asia", *Journal of Political Studies,* Vol. 1, No. 2, 2010.

Khalid, Iram Asia Mukhtar & Zanib Ahmed, "Water Scarcity in South Asia: A Potential Conflict of Future Decades", *Journal of Political Studies,* Vol. 21, No. 1, 2014.

Khan, Amjad Abbas, Sardar Sajid Mehmood and Mehbood Alam, "Kashmir and Global Powers", *South Asian Studies,* Vol. 33, No. 1, Jan-June 2018.

Khan, Zahid Ali, "Post 9/11 Development of Indo-Afghan Ties: Pakistan's Concerns and Policy Options", *Regional Studies* (Islamabad), Vol. XXXI, No. 1, Winter 2012-13.

Khan, Zulfqar, "India-Pakistan: Emerging Trends in Strategic Dynamics", *The Korean Journal of International Studies*, Vol. 13, No. 3, December 2015.

Kiran, Ayesha, "Is International Trade Reduces the External Conflicts? Case Study of Pakistan and India", *International Journal of Economics and Management Sciences*, Vol. 7, No. 1, 2018.

Koithara, Varghese, "Kashmir: Making the Impossible Happen", *Economic and Political Weekly*, Vol. XL, No. 4, 22 January 2005.

Krishan, Kewal, "India, Pakistan and China Border Dispute With Special Reference to Jammu and Kashmir", *Journal of Global Research and Analysis*, Vol. 3, No. 2, December 2014.

Kumar, Rakesh, "Kashmir Issue in Indo-Pak Relations", *Journal of Global Research & Analysis*, Vol. 3, No. 2, December 2014.

Kumar, Sanjeet, "Indo-Pak Relations: New Trends and Challenges", *IOSR Journal of Humanities and Social Science*, Vol. 2, No. 3, Sep-Oct 2012.

Kumar, Sumita, "Trends in Indo-Pakistan Relations", *Strategic Analysis*, Vol. 24, No. 2, May, 2000.

Mahapatra, Chintamani, "US Factor and the Kashmir Issue", *Journal of Peace Studies*, Vol. 8, No. 4, July-August 2001.

Mahesar, Pervaiz Ali, Ali Khan Ghumro, Ghulam Mushtafa Khuskh and Abdul Hamid Mahesar, " *International Journal of Scientific Research and Innovative Technology*, Vol. 3, No. 3, March 2016.

Majid, Abdul and Mahboob Hussain, "KASHMIR: A Conflict between India and Pakistan", *A Research Journal of South Asian Studies*, Vol. 31, No. 1, Jan-June 2016.

Majeed, Gulshan, "South Asian Security Compulsions: A Historical Analysis of India-Pakistan Relations", *Journal of Political Studies* (Lahore), Vol. 20, No. 1, 2013.

Malhotra, Aditi, "The Red Shadow in Pakistan Occupied Kashmir", *Scholar Warrior*, Autumn 2011.

Malik, Mohan, "The China Factor in the India-Pakistan Conflict", *Parameters,* Spring 2003.

Maqbool, Ahmad Bhatty, "China's Emerging Role in the World", *Peace Initiatives,* Vol. V, No. III-VI, May-December 1999.

Mehsud, Muhammad Imran, "Liberalism in India-Pakistan Relations: A Critique of Realism", *Cambridge Journal of China Studies,* Vol. 12, No. 1, 2017.

Minhaj Ul Hassan, Syed, "Pakistan-India Relations in the 21 Century: A Futuristic View", *JHSS,* Vol. XIII, No. 1-2, 2005.

Misra, Ashutosh, "The Problem of Kashmir and the Problem in Kashmir: Divergence Demands Convergence", *Strategic Analysis,* Vol. 29, No. 1, Jan-Mar 2005.

Nair, Neeti, "Indo-Pak Relations: A Window of Opportunity that has Almost Closed", *Economic and Political Weekly,* Vol. 49, Issue No. 51, 20 December 2014.

Naqvi, Zareen F., "Pakistan-India Trade Potential and Issues", *The Lahore Journal of Economics,* September 2009.

Pandey, Savita, "Sino-Pakistan Strategic Relationship: Implications for India", *Scholar Warrior,* Autumn 2015.

Pant, Harsh V., "The Pakistan Thorn in China-India-U.S. Relations", *Washington Quarterly,* Vol. 35, No. 1, Winter 2012.

Paul, T.V, "Chinese-Pakistani Nuclear/Missile Ties and Balance of Power Politics", *The Nonproliferation Review,* Vol. 10, No. 2, Summer 2003.

Saleem, Noshina et al., "Indo-Pakistan Trade Relations: A Critical Discourse Analysis of Daily Dawn", *A Research Journal of South Asian Studies,* Vol. 29, No. 1, Jan-July 2014.

Shafiq, Sumaira, "Pakistan's Policy towards Kashmir Dispute (2001-2014)", *Margalla Papers,* 2015.

Shakoor, Farzana, "The Kargil Crisis: An Analysis", *Pakistan Horizon,* Vol. 52, No. 3, July 1999.

Singh, Jagbir and Barham Prakash, "Kashmir Issue and Article

– 370: A Threat to National Integration", *Journal of Global Research & Analysis*, Vol. 3, No. 2, December 2014.

Sinha, Dilip, "International Dispute Settlement Mechanism and India-Pakistan Disputes", *Indian Foreign Affairs Journal*, Vol. 12, No. 3, July-September 2017.

Swamy, Raju Narayana, "India's Trade Relations with Pakistan: The Effectiveness of SAFTA for Deeper Integration", *International Journal of South Asian Studies*, Vol. 4, No. 1, Jan-June 2011.

T., Najmudheen and Farhana Kausar, "Significance of Indo-Pak Cordial Relations in South Asia", *International Journal of South Asian Studies*, Vol. 5, No. 1, January-June 2012.

Verma, A K, "India's Problems with Pakistan", *South Asia Analysis Group*, Paper No. 185.

Vinod, M J, "Kashmir and India-Pakistan Relations", *Strategic Analysis*, November 1995.

Wojczewski, Thorsten, "The Persistency of the India–Pakistan Conflict: Chances and Obstacles of the Bilateral Composite Dialogue", *Journal of Asian Security and International Affairs*, Vol. 1, No. 3, 2014.

Yaqoob, Asma, "India-Pakistan Confrontation: What Has Changed About Indian - Held Kashmir Since 1947", *Regional Studies*, Vol. XXXIV, No. 2, Spring 2016.

Yuan, Jingdong, "China's Kashmir Policy", *China Brief*, Vol. 5, No. 19, September 2005.

C. Ph. D Thesis

Kumar, Ram, "Indo-Pak Relations in the Post Cold War Era", *Ph. D Thesis Submitted to the Department of Political Science, Himachal Pradesh* University, Shimla, 2012.

Kumar, Sanjeet, "Indo-Pak Relations in the Twenty First Century", *Ph. D Thesis Submitted to the Department of Political Science, Central University of Haryana*, Mahendergarh, Haryana, August 2014.

Manikrao, Sachinkumar, "Areas of Contestation and Debate between India and Pakistan: A Critical Study", *Ph. D Thesis Submitted to the Department of Political Science,* Sahyadri Arts College, Kuvempu University, Karnataka, 2014.

Singh, Ajay Pratap, "Indo-Pak Relations Since 1990", *Ph. D Thesis Submitted to the Department of Defence and Strategic Studies,* T. D. P. G. College, V. B. S Purvanchal University, Jaunpur, 2001.

Singh, Surender, "India-Pakistan Peace Process: Problems and Prospects of Confidence Building Measures (CBMs)", *Ph. D Thesis Submitted to the Department of Political Science,* Kurukshetra University, Kurukshetra, 2015.

Wangwhite, Sherry W., "China's Reactions to the India Deal: Implications for the United States", Thesis Submitted to the Naval Postgraduate School, Monterey, California, December 2007.

D. M.A/M. Phil Dissertation

Taylor, Matthew P., "Pakistan's Kashmir Policy and Strategy Since 1947", *Master Thesis Submitted to the Naval Postgraduate College,* Monterey, California, March 2004.

E. Issue Briefs

Acharya, Loknath and Ashima Marwaha, "Status Paper on India-Pakistan Economic Relations", Prepared by FICCI, February 2012.

Aneja, Urvashi, "Pakistan-China Relations: Recent Developments (Jan-May 2006)", IPCS Special Report 26, June 2006.

Choudhury, Upendra, "The Indo-USA Nuclear Deal and its Impact on India's Ballistic Missile Programme", *South Asian Strategic Studies Institute Research Report* 17, June 2008.

Das, R.N., "China's 'All-Weather Friendship' with Pakistan: Implications for India", *IDSA Comment,* New Delhi, 4 January 2011.

Dumbaugh, Kerry B., "Exploring the China-Pakistan Relationship",

Roundtable Report Prepared by CNA China Studies, June 2010.

Faruqui, Ahmad, "The Complex Dynamics of Pakistan's Relationship with China," Islamabad Policy Research Institute, Summer 2001.

India-Pakistan Bilateral Trade: Past, Present and Future", Study conducted by PHD Research Bureau, PHD Chamber of Commerce and Industry, New- Delhi, February 2013.

Kordon, Isaac B., "China and Pakistan: Emerging Strains in the Entente Cordiale", *Project 2049 Institute*, Arlington, Virginia, 25 March 2011.

Kumar, Sanjeev, "PM Gilani Visit to China: Symbolic or Substantive", *Indian Council of World Affair,* New Delhi, 26 May 2011.

Nandan, Devki, "Sino-Pak Nuclear Nexus and India's Concerns", *Centre for Air Power Studies Issue Brief,* 16 July 2010.

Pakistan-India Relations: Challenges and Prospects", *Foreign Policy Roundtable Series,* No. VI, Centre for Pakistan and Gulf Studies, Islamabad, May 2014.

Pakistan Occupied Kashmir: Changing the Discourse', *IDSA PoK Project Report,* New Delhi, May 2011.

Sarma, Chandrani, "Indo-Pak Trade and Political Balance", *ISAS Insights,* National University of Singapore, No. 271, 21 November 2014.

Wirsing, Robert G., "The Enemy of my Enemy: Pakistan's China Debate", Asia-Pacific Center for Security Studies Special Assessment, December 2003.

Index